Power
Kills

R. J. Rummel

Power Kills

DEMOCRACY AS A METHOD OF NONVIOLENCE

Transaction Publishers

New Brunswick (U.S.A.) and London (U.K.)

Fourth paperback printing 2006
Copyright © 1997 by Transaction Publishers, New Brunswick, New Jersey.

This book is printed on acid-free paper that meets the American National Standard for Permanence of Paper for Printed Library Materials.

Library of Congress Catalog Number: 96-45040
ISBN: 1-56000-297-2 (cloth); 0-7658-0523-5 (paper)
Printed in the United States of America

Library of Congress Cataloging-in-Publication Data

Rummel, R. J. (Rudolph J.), 1932-
    Power kills : democracy as a method of nonviolence / R. J. Rummel.
        p. cm.
    Includes bibliographical references and index.
    ISBN 1-56000-297-2 (cloth : alk. paper); 0-7658-0523-5 (pbk. : alk. paper)
    1. Democracy. 2. Nonviolence. 3. Peace. I. Title.

JC423.R794   1997
321.8—dc21   96-45040
                                                                    CIP

Contents

Figures and Tables

Figures

Tables

Preface

I began research on this book in 1956 as an undergraduate at the University of Hawaii. By then I had selected political science as my major, with an emphasis on international relations. My true interest was in understanding and doing something about the legal killing called war and it was a happy surprise to discover that I could actually focus my studies on the history, conditions, and causes of war. Through undergraduate and graduate term papers, my MA thesis and Ph.D. dissertation in 1963, and the research since, this has been my ultimate concern. This research has taken numerous paths and has expanded to understand violence and conflict generally and their possible explanations, but always down the road and until recent years I hoped to have something specific to recommend about ending war. But in the mid-1980s I was shocked to discover that several times more people were killed in democide (genocide and mass murder) by governments than died in warfare. And with that my aim broadened to help end or at least lessen this killing as well.

This book presents the sum of all this research. And, I believe, I finally can offer what appears a most realistic and practical solution to war, democide, and other collective violence.

1

Introduction

Lust of power is the most flagrant of all the passions.
—Tacitus

Power tends to corrupt, and absolute power tends to corrupt absolutely.
—Lord Acton

It is not power itself, but the legitimation of the lust for power, which corrupts absolutely.
—Richard Howard Stafford Crossman

War has been a scourge of our species, one of the horses of the apocalypse. It has slaughtered many millions of us and left many more permanently scarred in mind and body. In my lifetime alone I have seen my own country, the Unites States, fight in World War II, Korea, Vietnam, and the Persian Gulf, with lesser military actions or interventions in the Dominican Republic, Lebanon, Libya, Panama, Granada, Iraq, and Bosnia. That such killing should come to an end for us all, that we should sometime conquer war, has been a dream.

Peace plans and designs, universal treaties and schemes for multilateral organizations have been put forward to end war. It has been thoroughly studied and researched, its causes and conditions dissected. And solutions have been proposed. Education, cultural exchange, economic development, socialism, internationalism, international sports, free trade, functional organizations, better balancing of power, artful diplomacy, deterrence, crisis management, arms control, world government, peace research, and so on, have their proponents. All to some extent have been tried or been achieved.

Were war and other international violence the only source of mass deaths, it would be enough to demand our greatest effort to eradicate it, but there is also civil violence within states to add to this carnage. Bloody riots, revolutions, guerrilla war, civil war, lethal coups d'états, terrorism, and the like, have also claimed millions of victims. And for this second human plague the solutions have been no less creative and varied. We should eliminate poverty, promote understanding, teach human values, facilitate change, decentralize government, emphasize minority self-determination, institutionalize conflict resolution, and on and on. Yet as of this writing we still have bloody conflicts in Russia, Rwanda, Burundi, Sudan, Somalia, Angola, Afghanistan, Bosnia, Sri Lanka, Myanmar, Iraq, Turkey, and a dozen or more other nations.

And then we have the widespread affliction exemplified by the Holocaust and genocides perpetuated in Bosnia, Rwanda, and Burundi, but whose generality has been ignored or unknown. Mass murder and genocide, or democide in short, has been the worst scourge of all. It has killed in our century not only millions or tens of millions, but possibly hundreds of millions. It has been a revisitation of the Black Death, but now intentionally carried out by human hands. The recognition of this general butchery has been so new that general solutions apart from those for war and civil violence have only recently been proposed.

The extent of mass killing in war, internal collective violence, and democide in our lifetime and throughout history is not only depressing, but makes eliminating it seem hopeless. After all, this killing has been the stuff of history: the Mongol invasions, Thirty Years War, Napoleonic Wars, World Wars I and II; the Mongol massacres, the slaughter of the Crusades, slave deaths in the Middle Passage, the butchery of the Teiping Rebellion. In some cases all we need is a single name to provoke images of mass murder—Genghis Khan, Ivan the Terrible, Stalin, Hitler, Pol Pot. All one needs to do is change the names, places, and dates in Thucydides' *The Peloponnesian War* to those of our century to make it recent history.

How can one even presume, therefore, that there is a solution to war? All alleged solutions must seem only the raving of idealists. To those with an appreciation of history all that seems possible is to moderate and perhaps in some cases to avoid a particular war. And similarly for proposed solutions to civil violence and democide. "Lets be realistic," it is often said, "foreign and domestic violence are in our blood. They have always been with us; they will always be with us." Anyway, some will argue, wars are sometimes necessary when the alternatives are even more horrible, such as having one's country taken over by a foreign state or ideology.

And yet it is the burden of this book to show that these "realists" are wrong. Wrong with regard to war and lesser international violence. Wrong about civil collective violence. Wrong about genocide and mass murder. *There is one solution to each and the solution in each case is the same. It is to foster democratic freedom and to democratize coercive power and force. That is, mass killing and mass murder carried out by government is a result of indiscriminate, irresponsible Power at the center. Or in terms of the title of this book, Power kills.*

This solution has been around for centuries and in one form or another was integrated into the classical liberal view of government: the government that governs least governs best; and freedom promotes peace and welfare. But practitioners and analysts alike were soon persuaded that this was just idealistic thinking, especially because democracies themselves seemed so warlike and under the hammer blows of socialists of all kinds it increasingly seemed that the very core of such thinking, capitalism, was inherently belligerent and the mother of violence.

However, there has been a resurgence of interest in this solution, particularly when put in terms of democracy, and without the ideological baggage that classical liberalism gave to freedom. This renewed interest has been theoretical and empirical. It has been both the result of theoretical work on international relations and democide, and the attempt to disprove empirically that democracies are any more peaceful than other regimes among themselves and in general. This empirical work has been the most intensive and extensive of any in the study of war, civil collective violence, and democide. For war in particular, all recorded wars since the classical Greeks that might involve democracies have been studied in historical detail. All possible historical cases where democracies might have made war on each other have been put under the analytic microscope. All cases of democide in this century have been subject to intensive investigation for the role of power versus democracy. Even wars among tribes within preindustrial societies have been studied to see if the more democratic have lesser violence.

Moreover, other possible factors that might really account for the inverse relationship between democracy and violence, or the lack of wars between democracies, have been checked, such as geographical distance (lack of common borders between democracies might account for this). Perhaps economic development, a common enemy, similarity, and so on, also might explain this, but on careful empirical and comparative investigation such has proved not to be the case.

Of course, because throughout history democracies have been few in number, chance might be the simple explanation for why democracies appear more peaceful. But where data allowed for the calculation of probabilities, often for wars even over two centuries, or other kinds of violence during this century, the findings were consistently very significant. In some studies the odds of finding the inverse relationship between democracy and, for example, wars, ran in some cases to thousands or millions to one. It is important to note also that many of the investigators that looked at this began with great skepticism over such a simple solution. Some thought they would disprove it and ended up convinced of it. Indeed, some were so convinced that this was wrong that in spite of their empirical results to the contrary their conclusions even denied their own evidence.

For the philosopher of science we have here an ideal case of science in action. We have a long dormant hypothesis and first very limited test. We have researchers independently discovering or conceiving of the hypothesis. We have the denial of that which cuts against mainstream beliefs about war and other forms of violence. We have replication after replication that finally create a consensus and forces a more systematic attempt to explain what has been found.[1] That is, we have a multitude of different studies by different researchers using different approaches on different kinds of data with different definitions. All are generally consistent, as will be presented in part I.

What specifically has been uncovered or verified about democracy and violence? First, *well-established democracies do not make war on and rarely commit lesser violence against each other.* The relationship between democracy and international war has been the most thoroughly researched question and all who have investigated this have agreed—democracies do not fight among themselves. Possible exceptions to this, as of the war of 1812 between Great Britain and the United States, or the Spanish-American War, were found not to have been really between democracies or to have been cases in which one or another democracy was either newly established or marginally democratic. Many issues and questions have been raised about these findings and I have tried to answer the most popular ones in the appendix to this chapter.

Second, *the more two nations are democratic, the less likely war or lesser violence between them.* There is a scale of democraticness here, at one end of which are two undoubted democracies with no likelihood of war and virtually zero probability of lesser violence between them, and at the other end are those nations most undemocratic (the totalitarian ones) that have the greatest chance of war and other violence among themselves. This finding shows that democracy is not a simple dichotomy—democracy versus nondemocracy—but a continuum. The implications of this are profound, and will be sketched later.

Third, *the more a nation is democratic, the less severe its overall foreign violence.* This finding in particular is disputed among researchers, but I will show in detail in chapter 4 that on this there should be no disagreement—that the evidence, even in the studies of those who question it, is clear. Most of those investigating this, I will show, have defined war and violence in terms of frequencies and have been therefore misled. They have in effect equated the very small wars with total wars like World Wars I and II; and they have also equated a few dozen deaths in war for one country with that of several million killed for another.

Fourth, in general *the more democratic a nation, the less likely it will have domestic collective violence.* Studies that include the relevant variables and indicators support this empirically. And those studies I have carried out specifically to test this are uniformly positive.

Finally, in general *the more democratic a nation, the less its democide.* Although in the literature democracy has been suggested as a way of reducing genocide and mass murder, data for testing this empirically have been unavailable until recently. Indeed, so far I appear the only one to have explicitly tested this, and have found that democide is highly and inversely related to democracy. This holds up even when controls are introduced for economic development, education, national power, culture, and ethnic/racial and religious diversity. Case studies of the most extensive democides, such as that in the Soviet Union, communist China, Nazi Germany, and Cambodia support this conclusion.

In sum, then, I will show that, overwhelmingly, the evidence supports this general principle: *democracy is a method of nonviolence.* Democracy is a practical solution to war and all other kinds of collective, that is, political regime, violence. It will not end such violence per se. But among all types of regimes, democracy minimizes this violence. And compared to its opposite, totalitarian regimes in which millions may die through democide and rebellions and aggressive wars, democracy virtually eliminates this source of deaths.

How do we explain this? What is the theory? One surface explanation, probably the most persuasive and oldest (going back at least to Immanuel Kant), is that where you have representative government decision makers are restrained from making war by the *public will.* After all, it is argued, the public does not want to bear the awful human cost of war. And in fact this may well account for the inability of democracies to make war, even sometimes to protect other democracies against aggression (as in the extreme reluctance of the United States to overtly help Great Britain during its greatest peril, the Battle of Britain in 1940). But as the history of the Unites States, Britain, and France well show, democratic publics can become jingoistic; they can pressure for or support military action.

A deeper explanation involves basically two factors: *cross-pressures* and *democratic culture.* The first is that democratic structure, the institutions of democratic governance, evolve and create checks and balances on the use of power, and inhibitions due to the political and social diversity that develops. These tie down decision makers and cross-cut and cross-pressure interests such that the strength of purpose required to commit violence cannot easily arise. This is particularly true between two democracies where they have a plethora of common bonds and shared interests.

The democratic culture argument is that democracy requires the arts of conciliation and compromise, an attitude of toleration of differences, and a willingness to lose. The development of this democratic culture is what defines democracy as well established; it infuses and orients domestic and foreign relations. When democrats recognize each other as democrats, they see each other as willing to negotiate and compromise, to resolve conflicts peacefully. Where dictators and totalitarians thrive, however, rule is by coercion and force, command and decrees. This type of system not only selects a particularly aggressive and dominating personality, but puts a premium on deception, force, and especially, winning. When dictator negotiates with dictator, it becomes a struggle to see who can dominate or win.

Beneath institutions and culture, however, is still a deeper and more comprehensive explanation of the democratic peace. This is by social fields and their opposite antifields. A *social field* is a spontaneous society within which individuals interact. Its key is the freedom of people to pursue their own interests, to create among themselves expectations—a social order—in terms of their wants, capabilities, and wills. The primary mode of power is exchange, its political system is democratic, and this democratic government is but one of many groups and pyramids of power in the social field.

Within this field there is a creative diversity of small groups, associations, societies, businesses, and the like, and thereby multiple overlapping, cross-cutting, and cross-pressuring linkages and bonds that isolate and minimize violence. Of necessity such an exchange-based order produces a culture of exchange, that is norms of negotiation, accommodation, concessions, tolerance, and a willingness to accept less than one wants. This field is not isolated to one democratic society. It envelopes all democracies; all are perceived as within the same moral and behavioral universe. The forces of a spontaneous society that thus restrain violence work as well to minimize violence between democratic governments within their social field and particularly to make war between them as unlikely as one between IBM and Apple computer.

The opposite of such an order is the *social antifield*. This is a society that has been turned into a hierarchical, task-oriented organization ruled by command. It divides its members into those who command and those who must obey, thus creating a schism separating all members and dividing all issues, a *latent conflict front* along which violence can break out. Spontaneous behavior can still occur, there is still something of a social field, but it has been isolated in the corners and pockets of the organization where commands do not reach. Many political regimes have created such societies and, indeed, the worst and most repressive of them even have become identified with their creators: Hitler, Stalin, Pol Pot, Mao. They totally restructured their societies to achieve national greatness, racial purity, or the "dictatorship of the proletariat" and eventual communism. Such was the task, the reorganization of society the tool, and the Great Leader at the pinnacle of power provided the unquestionable leadership.

The basis of such antifields, societies turned into organizations, is coercion. The operating framework is repression, controls, spies, concentration camps, torture, executions. The dynamic of obedience is fear. And their most characteristic political regime is totalitarian.

Those totalitarians who rule or officiate within such an antifield are not used to compromise or negotiating with underlings. Their culture is one of command, and unquestioning obedience and their *modus operandi* is naked power. They rule by fear. On big issues, they cannot lose, for that may mean death or imprisonment. In extreme cases, as of Stalin, Mao, or Pol Pot and their henchmen, it could also mean the death of one's whole family and even friends and associates. Such a culture does not favor democratic negotiation with other regimes; it favors disinformation, subterfuge, and aggression.

Moreover, there is little diversity, no meaningful pluralism independent of the regime. All religion, business, unions, education, trade, sports, cultural activities, and so on, for all possible sources of independent power, are controlled at the top. Even, in extreme cases, laughter, holding hands, or honeyed words for a loved one can be dangerous unless explicitly permitted, as in Pol Pot's Cambodia. In such an antifield there can be no cross-cutting, cross-pressuring interests. All is a matter of "them" or "us."

Basic to understanding an antifield is obviously *Power*, the dominance of indiscriminate and irresponsible power at the center. It is this Power that fosters war and lesser international violence. It is this Power that provokes internal rebellion and violent opposition. It is the Power that massacres human beings in the millions, near 61,000,000 in the case of the Soviet Union alone. In other words, this *Power kills.*

At the most fundamental level, then, we have an opposition between Freedom and Power. It is an opposition between the spontaneous society and the society turned into a hierarchical organization. It is an opposition between social field and antifield. This is not to deny the importance of culture and cross-pressures and the influence of public opinion in explaining the democratic peace. It is to say that they are social forces whose presence or absence is best understood in terms of the freedom of a democratic, spontaneous society or the commanding power of one that is tightly organized.

We thus end up with this explanation. Democracy is a method of nonviolence because democratic freedoms create a spontaneous society whose culture promotes negotiation and compromise; and whose social, economic, political, and cultural diversity and cross-cutting bonds inhibit violence. Violence is a product of the appositive of democratic freedom, the massive employment of coercion and force by totalitarian regimes to organize society and mobilize the people to achieve some goal: racial purity, victory in war, national greatness, economic development, or communism. In between are those societies ruled by authoritarian regimes that allow more or less freedom to their people and, accordingly, produce more violence than democracies but less than totalitarian regimes. That is, there is a scale of Power here. The more Power at the center, the more killing. *Power kills; absolute Power kills absolutely.*

The implications of this are obvious. *If democracy is a method of nonviolence, if it is a solution to war, domestic collective violence, and democide, then we should foster democratic freedom.*[2] This does not mean that democracy should be spread by force or imposed on other nations. Nor does it mean that all people will or should accept democratic freedom regardless of their own culture and religion. There is after all the question of social justice, and while nonviolence may be a central principle, some peoples may prefer, for example, an authoritarian government and state religion like Islam to democratic freedom, even if it means more violence.

However, I do not believe this should be a matter for a national elite to determine. I do not accept a governing elite's condemnation of democratic rights as a Western invention unsuitable to their culture. This is a matter for a people to decide and not their unrepresentative elite to determine for them. A plebiscite, a referendum, or a democratic election should be the basis for deciding whether a people will be governed democratically.

There is one question that will bother many who read this: Can we truly predict that a democratic world will be a more peaceful world? While past history does not perfectly predict future history, it is the best basis we have for gauging empirically what ought to be done, leaving aside questions of ethics and values. But it may be true that a wholly democratic world may create new conditions that promote extreme violence. We just do not know the future and cannot deny such a possibility. But the value of having a theory that explains the past is that it also gives good reason for the future being consistent with the past. The explanation in terms of free societies argues strongly that in so far as such free societies exist in the future, violence should be minimal.

Moreover there is the argument from Immanuel Kant. If the hypothesis is more theoretically and empirically reasonable than competing ones, and is most morally desirable, then in our actions and policies we should act as if it is true. As political scientist Bruce Russett writes about the fact that democracies do not make war on each other,

> understanding the sources of democratic peace can have the effect of a self-fulfilling prophecy. Social scientists sometimes create reality as well as analyze it. Insofar as norms do guide behavior, repeating those norms helps to make them effective. Repeating the norms as descriptive principles can help to make them true. Repeating the proposition that democracies should not fight each other helps reinforce the probability that democracies will not fight each other. It is an empirical fact that democracies rarely fight each other. They do not need to fight each other because they can employ alternative methods of conflict resolution, and at less cost than through violent conflict. A norm that democracies should not fight each other thus is prudentially reinforced, and in turn strengthens the empirical fact about infrequent violent conflict.[3]

Our long history of war and revolution and mass murder going back to the most ancient times has come down to this. We now have a solution in our grasp. The question now becomes one of implementation. How do we best protect and promote freedom? How do we control and minimize power?

Notes

1. We also have the final acceptance of the inherent peacefulness of democracies as being obvious. An anonymous reviewer of an early draft of this book claimed it contained "nothing new" and recommended rejection.
2. As to whether the process of democratization will cause greater violence, see footnote 2 of chapter 7.
3. Russett (1993, 136).

Appendix to Chapter 1
Questions and Answers on the Fact that Democracies
Do Not Make War on Each Other

In early 1994, under the title "The Most Important Fact of Our Time," I posted on several internet news groups and e-mail lists the finding that democracies do not make war on each other, and suggested that through democratic freedom we now have a solution to war. This posting stimulated many questions and arguments. I then summarized the most important of these, provided my answers, and posted it on the internet under the title given this appendix. This appendix is a revision of that posting. The research details underlying this appendix are given in chapter 2.

Q: How is democracy defined?
A: By democracy is meant liberal democracy, where those who hold power are elected in competitive elections with a secret ballot and wide franchise (loosely understood as including at least two-thirds of adult males); where there is freedom of speech, religion, and organization; and a constitutional framework of law to which the government is subordinate and that guarantees equal rights.

A list of current *liberal* democracies includes: Andorra, Argentina, Australia, Austria, Bahamas, Barbados, Belgium, Belize, Benin, Bolivia, Botswana, Bulgaria, Canada, Cape Verde, Chile, Costa Rica, Cyprus (Greek), Czech Republic, Denmark, Dominica, Ecuador, Estonia, Finland, France, Germany, Greece, Grenada, Guyana, Hungary, Iceland, Ireland, Israel, Italy, Jamaica, Japan, Kiribati, Korea (South), Latvia, Liechtenstein, Lithuania, Luxembourg, Malawi, Malta, Marshall Islands, Mauritius, Micronesia, Monaco, Mongolia, Namibia, Nauru, Netherlands, New Zealand, Norway, Palau, Panama, Poland, Portugal, St. Kitts and Nevis, St. Lucia, St. Vincent and the Grenadines, San Marino, Sao Tome and Principe, Slovakia, Slovenia, Solomon Islands, Spain, South Africa, Sweden, Switzerland, Trinidad and Tobago, Tuvalu, United Kingdom, United States, Uruguay, Vanuatu, and Western Samoa.

The list would be different, of course, for previous decades. For certain years of the eighteenth century, for example, it would include: the Swiss Cantons, French Republic, and United States; for certain years during 1800 through 1850 it would include: the Swiss Confederation, United States, France, Belgium, Great Britain, Netherlands, Piedmont, and Denmark.

Q: But can you really apply the contemporary definition of democracy to previous centuries?
A: There is a problem and it resides in how far equal rights and the franchise is extended, as before women achieved equal rights, the franchise was limited to property owning males, or slavery existed. For previous centuries the definition of democracy has been loosened by researchers to include at least, as mentioned, two-thirds males having equal rights (as long as the lower classes were not excluded), while maintaining the other characteristics (equal rights, open competitive elections, etc.). For one, democracies so defined in previous centuries, such as the United States in 1800 and democratic classical Athens, saw themselves as democratic, called themselves democratic, and were perceived by other nations as democratic. Second, even with this looser definition, *well-established* democracies so defined still did not make war on each other. Well established means that a regime had been democratic long enough for it to be stable and democratic practices to become established.

The fundamental question about any definition is: Does it work? *Does it define something in reality that predicts systematically to something else?* If we have so defined an x such that it regularly predicts to y, then that is a useful and important definition of x. In the definition I have given above of democracy it predicts to a condition of continuous peace (nonwar) between nations defined as democratic. If one does not agree that these are democracies, fine. Then call them xcracies. We then still can say that xcracies do not make war on each other and by universalizing xcracies we have a solution to war.

Q: Still, is not the historical sample of democracies too small for such a broad generalization?
A: Whether the definition of democracy is broad or narrow, we have statistical means to calculate if the number of democracies is in fact significant (the same kind of statistics medical researchers use to test the significance of drugs or symptoms). That there have been no wars between democracies since, say, 1816, *is statistically significant*. That is, given the historical number of democracies, the probability of the hypothesis that democracies have never made war on each other being

wrong is very low (given the consistency of findings across diverse studies, the odds must be surely millions to one).

Q: But are there not other factors really accounting for the lack of war between democracies, such as geographic distance?
A: A number of studies of whether democracies made war on each other have tried to determine if there is a hidden factor accounting for this, such as economic development, industrialization, geographic distance, trade, alliances, and so on. Always, democracy comes out as the best explanation.

Best is meant in a statistically significant sense. That is, the probability that democracy would not be a determinant when these other factors are considered is very low (odds also of tens of thousands to one). This has been gauged through analysis of variance and various kinds of regression analysis.

Q: Cannot statistics be used to prove anything?
A: True, statistics can be misused and have been, but this is true of any scientific method. Virtually all the medical drugs one takes today are based on statistical tests, not unlike those used to test whether democracies do not make war on each other is a chance occurrence. If one is going to be cynical about statistics, then one should also be very wary of taking any modern drugs for an illness or disease. This issue is really not statistics but how well they have been applied and whether the data meet the assumptions of the statistical model used.

Now, some statistics. If one defines an international war as any military engagements in which 1,000 or more were killed, then there were 33 wars, 353 pairs of nations (e.g., Germany versus USSR) engaged in such wars between 1816 and 1991. None were between two democracies, 155 pairs involved a democracy and a nondemocracy, and 198 involved two nondemocracies fighting each other. The average length of war between states was 35 months, and the average battle deaths was 15,069.

A good way of calculating the statistical significance of democracies not making war on each other is through the binomial theorem. For both one requires several statistics: the number of nondemocratic pairs and democratic pairs of states in the world for the period during which the wars between these types of pairs occurred, and the number of wars between each type. The problem has not been in determining the number of democratic pairs, but how many nondemocratic pairs there are for some period of time. This has been confronted in the literature, and for those periods in which this number could be defined the zero wars between democracies has been very significant (usually much less than a probability of .01 that this zero was by chance). Just one example follows.

For the years 1946 to 1986, when there were the most democracies and thus the hardest test of the proposition that democracies do not make war on each other, there were over this period 45 states that had a democratic regime; 109 that did not. There were thus 6,876 state dyads (e.g., Bolivia-Chile), of which 990 were democratic-democratic dyads, none of which fought each other. Thirty-two nondemocratic dyads engaged in war. Thus the probability of any dyad engaging in war from 1946 to 1986 was $32/6876 = .0047$; of not engaging in war is .9953. Now, what is the probability of the 990 dyads not engaging in war during this period? Using the binomial theorem, it is .9953 to the 990th power $= .0099$, or rounded off .01. This is highly significant. The odds of this lack of war between democracies being by chance is virtually 100 to 1.

One should not take this result in isolation, since the lack of war has been tested in different ways for other periods, definitions of democracy, and ways of defining war, and in each case has been significant. Thus, the overall significance is really a multiple (or function, if some of these studies are not independent) of these different significant probabilities, which would make the overall probability (subjectively estimated) of the results being by chance alone surely at least a million to one.

Q: But your statistics are for the cold war period. Was not the lack of war between democracies really due to the threat of the Soviet Union?
A: My above test for the years 1946 through 1986 is not the only one. As mentioned, other tests have been done for different years, including 1816 to 1960. Now it may be true that the cold war accounted for the particular lack of war between democracies, but what about other periods. Also, ignore the statistics and consider Europe, the historical cauldron of war, and what has happened since the end of the cold war. Unity has continued to grow, rather then hostility. And, incredible, those old enemies, France and Germany, have even considered forming a common army. Moreover, once many of those former enemies

became democratic, they have tried to join NATO and are being integrated into a larger Europe.

Q: But can you meet the assumptions of the statistical model, particularly that of randomness?
A: All statistical tests on humans suffer from the inability to truly meet the assumption of randomness (equal likelihood of each case, event, sample point) basic to the model. In medical tests, whether double-blind or not, the sample is usually constrained to Americans, students, doctors, and the like, and thus may introduce unknown masking factors. Even ignoring this, any statistical test is only giving results in terms of probabilities, and for that one test the improbable may in fact have occurred. This is why no researcher should accept any one or two tests as definitive. Only if a range of tests are consistent over many kinds of data, researchers, and methods can one have confidence in the results. This is true for vitamin E supplements reducing the risk of cancer; it is true for the proposition that democracies do not make war on each other.

Q: But such is raw empiricism. You must have theory. Where is your theory for democracies not making war on each other?
A: The first theory for this goes back to Immanuel Kant's *Perpetual Peace,* published in 1795, way before any related empirical research. Kant's theory (which is presented in chapter 10) has been elaborated and absorbed into the modern explanation, which is that:

(1) democratic leaders are restrained by the resistance of their people to bearing the costs and deaths of war;
(2) the diversity of institutions and relations within and between democracies creates checks and balances and cross-pressures inhibiting belligerence among them;
(3) a democratic culture of negotiation and conciliation means that in their interaction with other democracies, democratic leaders are basically dovish;
(4) democracies see each other of the same kind, sharing the same values, and thus are more willing to negotiated than fight.

Q: But what about the American Civil War, War of 1812, Spanish-American War, democratically appointed Hitler and WWII, Finland versus the Allies in World War II, the recent wars in former Yugoslavia, and so forth? Did not these constitute wars among and between democracies?

A: Those who have investigated these and many other exceptions [and especially Ray (1995) and Weart (1995)] have concluded that these do not constitute meaningful exceptions. The United Kingdom versus Finland is perhaps the most often mentioned, next to the war of 1812, as a possible exception. Although the United Kingdom did bomb German-run mining operations in Finland, there was no actual fighting between Finnish forces and those of the democratic allies. Regarding the war of 1812, the United Kingdom was not a democracy by any definition until later in the century. Regarding Hitler, once he was given the power to rule by decree in 1933 and suppressed opposition, his government was no longer democratic. Freedom of speech and religion, along with other rights, was eliminated; regular competitive elections were no longer held; and the Nazis acted above the law.

Regarding the American Civil War, an often-mentioned exception, the South was not a sovereign democracy at that time. For one, it was not recognized by any major power, which means that it was not recognized as an independent state. But aside from this, the franchise was limited to free males (which constituted about 35 to 40 percent of all males in the Confederacy), President Jefferson Davis was not elected, but appointed by representatives themselves selected by the confederate states. There was an election in 1861, but it was not competitive.

As with many facts by which we guide our lives, we need not be hung up on such possible exceptions. All alleged exceptions are at the margins of what we call liberal democracies. Although none have been accepted as exceptions to the rule by those who have done research on them, let us suppose that they are in fact exceptions. This still would not weaken the proposition that well-established democracies do not make war on each other. This is because in no case have *undoubted* democracies (such as Sweden, Norway, Belgium, France, United States, and Canada) made war on each other and none are mentioned as exceptions.

Q: What are undoubted or well-established democracies?
A: A well-established democracy is one for which enough time has passed since its inception for peace-sufficient democratic procedures to become accepted and democratic culture to settle in. Around three years seems to be enough for this.

Then what is an undoubted democracy? It is what all who write on liberal democracy would recognize as clearly a democratic country; it is what all published definitions of democracy would include as a democracy; it is what all scales of democracy based on operational definitions measure as a democracy. These would currently include such nations as: Denmark, Sweden, Canada, the United States, France, Great Britain, and the like. They all have in common several characteristics: their citizens regardless of class have equal rights; policies and leaders are determined through open and competitive elections and voting; and there is freedom of speech. One can be precise about these characteristics and related ones, scale them, weigh and sum them some way, and thus measure an array nations on a scale of democracy. This has been done by a number of researchers, including those who have tested whether democracies make war on each other.

Q: Okay, okay, what about democracies, particularly the United States, carrying on covert action against other countries, some of which were democracies?
A: Yes, but this was during the cold war and was part of the largely successful policy to contain communism, particularly Soviet power. Mistakes were made, actions were taken which in hindsight embarrass many democrats. Even then, there was no military action between democracies.

This having been said, there is also a deeper explanation. Democratic regimes are not monolithic; they are divided into many agencies, some of which operate in secrecy and are really totalitarian subsystems connected only at the top to democratic processes. The military, especially in wartime, and the secret services, such as the CIA, are examples. These *near isolated islands of power* operate as democratic theory would assume. Outside of the democratic sunshine and processes, they do things that were they subject to democratic scrutiny would be forbidden. The answer to this problem is more democratic control. And with the spread of democracy around the world, armies and secret services would be less and less needed. Indeed, *with near universal democratization, they could be eliminated altogether.*

Q: Even if that democracies do not make war on each other is true, how can you generalize to the future? Because something never happened in the past you cannot say it will not in the future.
A: That democracies do not make war on each other, that they create a zone of peace among themselves, is now the most firmly established

proposition in international relations—and the most important. Given this, we have a solid base for forecasting that there never will be a war between democracies and that universalizing democracy will end international wars.

All public policies are based on perceptions of historical patterns. Indeed, all scientific predictions are based on established theoretical/empirical patterns. No prediction of the future is thus certain; all are based on the past. The question is how good the established patterns are that underlie the predictions. Are they reliable, well verified, theoretically understood? The historical pattern that there is no war between democracies meets all these requirements. Even those who have been very skeptical when starting their research on this have become convinced. One has said that this is now the best established law of international relations.

Given all this and the absolute importance of eliminating war, should we not implement the best empirical/theoretical solution now in our hands? That is, as practical and desired by the people involved, to universalize democracy?

Q: Yes, yes, but how can you *be so sure?*
A: No one can be certain. There is always the possibility that one can be wrong in fact and theory. But I am confident enough that democracies do not make war on each other to believe that it is the best solution to war. I started research on war and peace in 1956 and have spent a professional research career in political science on it since. The whole character of this lifetime of research supports the proposition. But others have done their own research and come to the same conclusion. And like others I have gone from unbelieving (its too simple and simplistic) to a maybe/but, to full acceptance as the number of positive research studies and theoretical elaborations have accumulated.

Q: Since everyone is in favor of democracy anyway, why make a big thing of this?
A: Because it will take the investment of much resources by the United States and other democracies to help nations democratize. Russian alone needs tens of billions in aid to further democratization. Such aid will be more forthcoming and more broadly supported if there is a wider understanding among the democracies that by providing human

and financial resources toward democratization we are not only promoting the freedom and prosperity of other countries but also peace and nonviolence. Such aid is cheap compared to the likely human and material cost of future wars.

There is also the struggle for human rights in many countries. It helps the struggle to not only justify human rights for their own sake, but to point out their importance for global and domestic peace and security.

Q: You keep mentioning research. What research on this has been published?

A: See the citations in chapter 2.

Part I

The Most Important Fact of Our Time

To sum up, it appears that absolutist states with geographically and functionally central- ized governments under autocratic leadership are likely to be most belligerent, while consti- tutional states with geographically and func- tionally federalized governments under demo- cratic leadership are likely to be most peace- ful.

—Quincy Wright, *A Study of War*

Recognition of the democratic-peace result is probably one of the most significant nontrivial products of the scientific study of world poli- tics. It may also be the basis of far more im- portant insights into the workings of the inter- national political world in modern times. . . .
—Zeev Maoz and Bruce Russett, "Normative and Structural Causes of Democratic Peace, 1946–1986"

This absence of war between democracies comes as close as anything we have to an em- pirical law in international relations.
—Jack Levy, "Domestic Politics and War"

Introduction to Part I

One important fact is that liberal democracies[1] do not make war on each other. Another important fact is that the more two nations are democratic, the less violence between them. Yet another is that the more democracy, the less collective domestic violence, such as riots, rebellions, guerrilla warfare, and the like. A fourth important fact is that the more democracy, the less democide (genocide and mass murder). Finally, a more disputed fact but one that I show is well supported by the evidence, when properly interpreted, is that the more democracy, the less foreign violence. Putting all this together, *the most important fact of our time is that democracy is a method of nonviolence.*

That is, by creating democracies we create zones of peace.[2] These are zones within which there is no war, virtually no military action, the very least internal political violence, and almost no genocide and mass murder. As more nations become democratic and these zones of peace are thus enlarged, the zone of violence and war should thereby decrease. If ever all nations were to become democratic we have the promise of eliminating war and sharply reducing the amount of political violence.

There are several questions immediately provoked by these claims. For one, what is my proof that all this is true? Second, if this be true, how is it that this has only recently been discovered, especially since through the centuries philosophers, historians, diplomats, and others have been searching for a solution to war and violence? Finally, and most important, what is the explanation for why democracy is a method of nonviolence? Empirical correlation is not causation, as professors

23

always tell their college students. To accept the proposition that democracies minimize violence demands that we understand why this linkage exists.

The following chapters will sketch the empirical research supporting this fact. And the final chapter in this part will try to answer whether this connection between democracy and violence has only recently been discovered. Then the rest of the book will explain why democracy is a method of nonviolence.

Notes

1.   In early professional work I have termed *libertarian* those nations that assure civil liberties and political rights, rather than democratic. For one, the latter term has become blurred by its use in the battle for people's minds, as in "democratic centralism" or "people's democracy," and thus sometimes has stood for what used to be its opposite—dictatorship. Moreover, technically democracy (of which liberal democracy is a particular kind) does not stand for civil rights and political liberties, but for majority rule, and such a majority within the historical meaning of democracy could eliminate minority rights and liberties. While there is not a one-to-one relationship between democracy on the one side and rights and liberties on the other, therefore, there is this identity for libertarian systems. A majority denying minority rights and liberties can still be democratic; it cannot be libertarian. And it is these very rights and liberties that create the conditions reducing the likelihood of collective violence, as I will later argue. However, in spite of this I now use the term *democratic* in this book. For one, within the context of this book the differences between democratic and libertarian systems are academic. Moreover, democracy is the settled term for those doing research on the relationship between political systems and violence and practitioners who have argued that freedom promotes peace, the major subject matter here, and for me to use the term libertarian may promote more ambiguity and confusion than light.
2.   For an excellent development and application of this idea to contemporary international relations, see Max Singer and Aaron Wildavsky (1993).

2

No War between Democracies

The Interdemocratic Peace Proposition: Democracies Do Not Make War On and Rarely Commit Lesser Violence Against Each Other.

Since the early years of our century one scholar or statesman or another has pointed out that democracies are more peaceful than other types of regimes. This was certainly the view of President Woodrow Wilson in proposing his Fourteen Points for a stable post-World War I peace, for example, or in his war message of April, 1917, in which he proclaimed:

> Our object now, as then, is to vindicate the principles of peace and justice in the life of the world as against selfish and autocratic power and to set up amongst the really free and self-governed peoples of the world such concert of purpose and of action as will henceforth ensure the observance of those principles.[1]

And note the epigraph to this part of the book by Quincy Wright, the premier student of war whose two-volume *A Study of War* was published in 1942. Moreover, through the 1960s and 1970s some social scientists included in their research on international violence variables measuring certain aspects of political regimes and have found, among other things, that the more democratic or less repressive or more open regimes have had less violence overall or between them. With the exception of the few studies to be discussed below, however, none of this work specifically tested or statistically analyzed the proposition that democracies do not make war on each other or are inherently pacific.[2]

The first statistical test of this idea was published in 1964 in *The Wisconsin Sociologist* by Dean Babst, a criminologist then working with the Wisconsin State Department of Public Works.[3] Without citations to any literature, without any abstract theory, Babst put his case simply.

> In 1961 Congress created the United States Arms Control and Disarmament Agency. One of the goals assigned to it was to carry out research toward achieving a "better understanding of how the basic structure of a lasting peace may be established." One approach to this problem is to inquire whether there are certain type of governments which do not make war against each other.
>
> Purely impressionistically the hypothesis was formulated that these would be freely elected governments of independent countries the borders of which are firmly established. This is based on the assumption that the general public does not want war, if it can choose. However, the possibility of choice requires independence and the existence of an elective government. The tendencies of such governments to work out international differences by means other than war would be most obvious in their dealings with other such governments.

He then defined democracy in terms of national independence, some freedom of speech and the press, regular and competitive elections by secret ballot to a legislature that controls national finances, and an elected executive that has administrative control over the government.

Then consulting the premier work on war, Wright's *A Study of War*,[4] he found that for 116 major wars of 438 countries from 1789 to 1941, not one war involved democracies on opposite sides. Only two cases came close, that of the war of 1812 between the United States and Great Britain and the American Civil War. In the former case, he argued, Great Britain was not yet a democracy, and in the latter case the South was not independent and was fighting to be so. Babst was correct in rejecting these cases, as recent work would show, particularly that by James Lee Ray discussed below.[5]

However, Babst recognized that there were few elected governments prior to the twentieth century, so he focused particularly on participants in World War I and II. Of the thirty-three independent nations involved in World War I, ten were democracies and none fought against each other. And of the fifty-two independent nations participating in World War II, fourteen democracies were on the same side and one, Finland, fought with Germany against the Soviet Union (but there was no military action between Finland and the other democracies).

If Dean Babst had stopped here and presented just his tabulation, it would still have been a breakthrough in the study of war. However, he went one step further and analyzed these results probabalistically. He asked whether they could be by chance. A myriad of political and economic factors might underlie who fought whom and who were allies, such that democracy really had nothing to do with it. To check this possibility Babst statistically tested for the likelihood that democracy was irrelevant. He found that the odds against democracies all being on the same side in these wars by chance was over 100 to 1. One should thus reject the notion of chance. There is probably something about democracies per se that prevents them from fighting each other.

Babst also looked further at wars after 1945 and saw *none* involving democracies, even though many more democracies existed.

He then concluded this pioneering six-page contribution modestly:

> This study suggests that the existence of independent nations with elective governments greatly increases the chances for the maintenance of peace. What is important is the form of government, not national character. Many nations, such as England and France, fought wars against each other before they acquired freely elected governments, but have not done so since. The rapid increase in the number of elective governments since World War II is an encouraging sign. Diplomatic efforts at war prevention might well be directed toward further accelerating this growth.[6]

J. David Singer, principle investigator of one of the largest and influential quantitative projects on war, the Correlates of War Project,[7] and his colleague and historian Melvin Small took note of Babst's findings and the arguments of Quincy Wright that democracies tended to be less warlike,[8] and devoted a whole article to the war proneness of democratic regimes.[9] Drawing on their project's data on war,[10] they listed all fifty interstate wars among sovereign states between 1816 and 1965 for which there were at least 1,000 total battle dead. They then defined which of those states were democratic in terms of a "rather crude dichotomy:" having or not a strong legislature with representatives competitively elected in regularly scheduled elections by a "fair faction" of the population.[11]

With these criteria they then tabulated for all fifty interstate wars the opposing pairs of nations (henceforth called *dyads*) and whether or not they were democratic. They went far beyond Babst, who did such a tabulation for only the two World Wars. Given the great importance of the Babst finding, it is remarkable that Small and Singer spent less than one page on whether their results supported Babst or not. Indeed, virtually the whole article addresses whether democracies are more warlike or not, an entirely different question that I will deal with in chapter 4. This lack of attention to Babst's key point is even more surprising, *since their results support Babst.*

For all fifty interstate wars during a century-and-a-half they found *no* wars between democracies, except for only two "marginal exceptions," which are "an ephemeral republican France attacking an ephemeral republican Rome in 1849 and a rightward-drifting Finnish democracy joining Germany to attack Russia (and thus technically putting it at war with the Allied Nations) in 1941."[12] Although their tabulation is a startling confirmation of Babst's results, they proceeded to argue them away as a result of the lack of common borders between democracies, pointing out incorrectly that 76 percent of the wars occurred between contiguous states. In fact of all opposing states involved in these wars only 26 percent, not 76 percent, were contiguous.[13]

In a conclusion running over a page, they virtually ignore these results in favor of discussing the less important statistical findings that allegedly show that democracies are just as warlike as other states (which in chapter 4 I will also see show to be in error). At most they can only say that "we cannot agree with optimistic conclusions about either the relationship between bourgeois democracies and war or the continuing democratization of the world. It may be true that freely elected governments rarely fought against one another; but they did become involved in quite a few wars, and not always as defenseless victims of a dictator's aggression."[14] In their last words on this they go even further to deny their own results on wars between democracies and perhaps hint at their underlying fear about favoring one side or another in the cold war:

> Yet, such a finding should not be cause for despair. Perhaps the recognition that all governments, democracies and autocracies alike, are prone to war will turn our attention away from rival domestic systems to the conflict-generating properties of the system in which we all must live.[15]

And this was hardly a tentative denial of Babst's and his own findings. Singer really had discarded the idea. Years later when he published an overview of the results of quantitative research on war, he not only ignored Babst's findings but even his own results mentioned above that showed no wars between democracies between 1816 and 1965 (except for the two possible aforementioned marginal exceptions).[16] To J. David Singer it made no difference whether regimes were democratic or not as far as their wars were concerned. Period.

When Small and Singer's article was published I was working on volume 2 of my five-volume *Understanding Conflict and War.* I started these volumes in 1973, after having found among many other things that the type of political system is statistically uncorrelated with domestic or foreign conflict and violence, results as a matter of fact that appear to provide support for Singer and Small.[17] But once engaging the theory, redoing many empirical analyses, and overviewing all the accumulated empirical findings in the literature, by 1979 I concluded in volume 4 (*War, Power, Peace*) that "violence does not occur between free societies," one of twenty-three final theoretical-empirical propositions.[18] This was not only supported by the work described previously and other research in the literature,[19] but by the field theory developed in these volumes and the other propositions finding empirical support by my analyses and those of others. In other words, by then *the whole theoretical and empirical character of my understanding of conflict and war upheld this proposition.*

Through work on volume 5, *The Just Peace,* I increasingly saw the freedom proposition as the culmination of all this research. These were the words of the final volume.

In total, some violence is inevitable; extreme violence and war are not. To eliminate war, to restrain violence, to nurture universal peace and justice, is to foster freedom.[20]

Scientifically, I was confident of this conclusion. But by stating as it does that we have a solution to war and other extreme violence, it surely was a most bold and revolutionary assertion with the utmost importance for domestic and international policy. I thought I had better go much further, therefore, than even the extra mile. I decided to do even more analyses, especially very tight statistical studies with the aim of trying to disprove my conclusions, and a systematic reevaluation of all relevant quantitative studies.[21]

Now, to test whether any violence occurs between democratic regimes, I classified regimes as free, partially free, or nonfree from the ratings given by Freedom House.[22] As for data on conflict and violence, these I had collected from the daily press, including the *New York Times* and *Washington Post,* and major news magazines. At the time I was collecting these data I had no idea that they would be used for the tests eventually applied to them.

From this event data I developed an intensity scale of conflict and violence such that states were coded on their highest level of conflict or violence reached between them for the five years from 1976 to 1980. During this period there were ten international wars and fourteen other cases of international violence. Regardless, *no* violence was found to have occurred between regimes that were both free. Moreover, given that there were 3,530 of such dyads out of 62,040 total dyads, this was a statistically significant result.[23]

Now, Small and Singer had argued away Babst's results as probably the result of democracies having few common borders. For the period 1976 to 1980 there were 1,164 contiguous dyads, 104 of them involving two free states. For just contiguous states it was still statistically significant that none of these 104 had violence.[24]

I also turned to the data compiled by Wayne Ferris on thirty-three cases of the threat and use of force, from 1945 through 1965.[25] These data give a much longer period over which to test the significance of the results and were collected for different purposes by someone not interested in these results. Moreover, I also used a scale of democracy this time, one calculated by Ivo and Rosalind Feierabend.[26] The result was that for these twenty-one years and 3,403 cases of the threat of or use of force between regimes, including 276 cases of such behavior by democracies, not one involved two democracies against each other. And there was little probability that this was by chance.[27] Moreover, even when this is calculated only for the 125 contiguous regimes that made threats or used force against each other, that *none* involved two democracies is still significant.[28]

If we just rely on war data we can extend the test over even more years. Richard Pride had defined[29] democratic regimes for the period 1920 to 1965 and the list of wars for this period was available from Small and Singer.[30] There were 1,540 pairs of independent regimes during this period,[31] 192 of which made war on each other that cost at least 1,000 combat related deaths, and ninety-one involved democracy on one side. In *no* case, however, did democracies fight against each other. Given the number of wars this could hardly be by chance.[32] Nor is it likely that lack of common borders among democracies accounted for this.[33]

Recall that the purposes of these analyses in 1983 were to rigorously test further the 1981 published conclusion of my extensive theoretical and empirical work—that democratic regimes do not commit violence against each other—and redo my comprehensive survey of the quantitative literature. The 1983 results unambiguously supported this. Not only did democratic regimes not make war on or commit violence against each other, but this was highly unlikely to be a chance result. Moreover, it is very unlikely that these results were due to the lack of common borders between democratic regimes.

There was yet a fourth strand of relevant research at this time. Independently of the work of Babst, Small, and Singer, and myself, Michael Doyle published his own analysis of Immanuel Kant's idea that creating republics is a road to peace, and of the classical liberal view that democracies are naturally pacific. In doing so he tabulated a list of forty-nine liberal democratic regimes in existence during the eighteenth century and after. He also tabulated from Small and Singer a "partial list" of international wars, between 1816 and 1980, in which there were at least 1,000 combat dead.[34] With these tabulations as evidence he pointed out that

> *even though liberal states have become involved in numerous wars with nonliberal states, constitutionally secure liberal states have yet to engage in war with one another.* No one should argue that such wars are impossible; but preliminary evidence does appear to indicate that there exists a significant predisposition against warfare between liberal states. Indeed, threats of war also have been regarded as illegitimate. A liberal zone of peace, a pacific union, has been maintained and has expanded despite numerous particular conflicts of economic and strategic interest.[35]

That was the last of the published research on this critical finding about war for *six years.* To understand this gap one must appreciate the political and social scientific context within which these works were published. This was during the cold war and the administration of President Reagan. Many social scientists looked upon any statements of the value of democracy, particularly that democracies were more peaceful, as right-wing, anti-communist propaganda. To espouse freedom appeared a flag waved by cold warriors. Moreover, there was the fear that emphasizing the peacefulness of democracies (or some other democratic virtue) could be an excuse for violence against nondemocratic regimes and would heighten the possibility of war between the United States and Soviet Union. As Small and Singer put it,

The concluding paragraph of Babst's article could, paradoxically enough, turn out to be a major stimulus *to* war. That is, after suggesting that elective governments were a force for peace, he urges that we discover how such governments came into being so that the "foreign policies of free nations can be formulated more effectively to assist the gradual conversion of the rest of the world."[36]

Jack Vincent put this fear even more directly:

This finding, if valid, has important foreign policy implications. It might suggest, for example, that American covert and overt interventions for the purpose of democratizing a society would help promote peace in the world system. On the other hand, if Rummel's finding is suspect, supporters of such interventions would have to look elsewhere for possible justification. This caution may be of particular importance in an epoch characterized by an increasing tendency to declare "holy wars" on dissimilar systems. That is, some, not necessarily Rummel, might *ironically* (given Rummel's basic hypothesis) see his findings as a good basis for aggressive interventions against nondemocratic or non-American type systems. If nondemocratic systems are the major cause of conflict in the world, why not exert every effort to democratize the world, even if a temporary period of forceful change is required? His findings, then, might have the curious effect of justifying possible temporary violence to eliminate nonfreedom in the world by "free states," i.e., by the very states which should be least violent according to the theory.[37]

As a consequence of the perceived ideological nature of the findings, the fear that their propagation might encourage war rather than discourage it, and also perhaps because they were stated too boldly for the social scientific culture of the time,[38] these results on democracies not making violence on each other tended at first to be disregarded by many social scientists.

Indeed, it was not until the Soviet Union was breaking up and, thus, the likelihood of a Soviet-American nuclear war was disappearing completely, that a new confirmation was published. In 1989 Zeev Maoz and Nasrin Abolali published a test of, among other hypotheses, that "democracies do not wage wars against each other." For their war data they used data on 960 militarized international disputes (1816–1976) that coded which regimes had issued threats of force, displayed force, used force short of war, or fought a war against which others.[39]

Their measurement of regime type was based on the work of Ted Robert Gurr. In what has become known as Polity I data, Gurr scaled the different regimes existing since 1816 on a variety of political characteristics, which when aggregated provided a rating of how democratic or autocratic a regime was.[40] A change of regime occurred within a state when there was a significant change in political characteristics. Thus Germany's Weimar republic and the following Nazi period would be two different German regimes. Using these data Maoz and Abolali were able to define the type of regimes involved for 1,625 pairs of regimes that might be involved in war.

Maoz and Abolali then cross-tabulated these data in various ways and tested the significance of the results. They showed that out of 920 cases in which force short of war was used, fifty-two were by democracies against democracies; for 332 cases of war, *none* involved opposing democracies.[41] These results thus support the no war between democracies proposition.

Second, even though there were fewer cases of force than one would expect by chance (which would be about eighty-three versus the actual fifty-two),[42] there was still the use of force between democracies, which by theory and my 1983 empirical results should be zero. This may however be due to the way Gurr's Polity I data were aggregated, perhaps defining as democracies regimes that only marginally or near democratic. Maoz and Abdolali do not provide sufficient information to fully evaluate this, nor what cases of force these were.[43] Their results on this lack of violence between democracies short of war should be considered a small negative until more information is available.

In any case, they ignore this aspect of their results and find *no* war between democracies and on this their results must be added to those of Babst, Small and Singer (their protests not withstanding), Doyle, and myself. In the words of Maoz and Abdolali,

> The dyadic analyses generally provide clear support to the joint freedom proposition [now renamed the Interdemocratic Peace Proposition]. This proposition receives relative clear support both when the analyses were performed on the population of dispute dyads alone and when we analyzed the dispute dyad population relative to the entire population of states in the system. The support for this proposition is robust; it holds across various substantive and historical breakdowns of the population of disputes.[44]

The next year Timothy Michael Cole presented to the annual meeting of the American Political Science Association a paper on "Politics and Meaning: Explaining the Democratic Peace," in essence a revision of his Ph.D. dissertation done at the University of Washington.[45] He tabulated liberal states and their wars for the years 1600 to the present, relying on Small and Singer's list of wars after 1815.[46] After analyzing these tabulations, he concludes that it can be stated rather unequivocally . . . democratic states do not resort to arms against one another. In studying interstate war in which democratic states were involved, from the War of the Armada (involving the United Provinces of the Netherlands, 1585–1604) to the Yom Kippur war (involving Israel, 1973), I have noted only six exceptions to this rule: i) the brief naval war between the United Provinces and England from December, 1780 to September, 1783; ii) the American effort to gain independence; iii) the coalition that battled France during the period of the French Revolutionary wars (which pits England against a France that is intermittently democratic in this period); iv) the desultory war of 1812; v) the Spanish-American war; and vi) Finland's situation in WWII (where, in a sense, it finds itself opposed to the "democratic" camp, as do France and Italy prior to their liberation).[47]

We will find later that these exceptions can be dismissed.

This analysis by Cole was done on sovereign nation-states. But the question about democracies making war on each other is a more general one. Is there something about democracies that restrains any democratic-social system from fighting another. In a notable paper by Russett and Antholis[48] completed in 1991 (later to be revised for a chapter in Russett's *Grasping the Democratic Peace*[49]), Russett and Antholis tried to answer this question by looking at wars among Greek city-states.

With due qualifications about the difficulty of classifying Greek city-states of the Peloponnesian War period as democratic or not, and the severe lack of historical information, Russett and Antholis did find that democracies sometimes fought each other, but reluctantly, and "neighboring democracies rarely fought each other; the Athens-Megara skirmish was the sole exception among clear democracies."[50]

Of course, given our lack of knowledge about this ancient period others may come up with much different results, as did the historian Spencer Weart. Investigating the historical possibility of wars between democracies he believes that when the character of the Greek regimes and the context of their wars is taken into account, in fact *no* wars occurred between democracies.[51] It is noteworthy that this difference in historical analysis between Russett and Weart ranges in conclusion from "rarely" to none at all among "well established democracies."

In 1992 there was a burst of published quantitative studies on democracies not making war on each other. They comprised a momentous shift in emphasis, for now these works turned largely from the question of whether or not democracies made war or violence on each other to that of developing and testing theory of why this should be so. *That democracies do not make war on each other had become ac-*

cepted. And by doing so these studies helped solidify the consensus on this proposition that is now extant among many if not most quantitative students of war and, indeed, has now been boldly stated even by politicians, including President Clinton during his election campaign.[52]

Without trying to indicate which study came first in 1992 and 1993, I will simply outline the relevant articles and then the books.

1. T. Clifton Morgan and Valerie L. Schwebach (1992) did a contingency analysis of the Gochman and Maoz (1984) militarized dispute data on 707 dyads, with democracy ratings based on Gurr's Polity I (1978) data; although they found *no* wars between democracies, their systematic analysis of the constraints operating on a democratic or nondemocratic regime lead them to say that

> the strongest conclusion that we can reach with confidence addresses the hypothesis that democracies do not fight each other—*we cannot, on the basis of these analyses, reject the null hypothesis* (i.e., the evidence can be explained quite well by theoretical arguments that predict democratic dyads will occasionally escalate a dispute to war).[53]

2. Randall Schweller (1992) did a cross-tabulation of twenty Great Power wars and regime types, from 1665 to 1990, particularly focused on the transition in power from one world leader to another, and found that

> *democratic states have not gone to war against one another,* though they have experienced power shifts. Conversely, declining authoritarian regimes have often exercised the preventive (war) option regardless of the regime type of the rising challenger.[54]

3. Erich Weede (1992) did a contingency analysis for the Gochman and Maoz militarized dispute data (1984), wars from Small and Singer (1982), and regime types for 3,321 dyads for 1962 to 1980, and found that

> it is possible to demonstrate that the "peace among democracies" proposition receives *significant* support in the technical sense. . . . [And] replacing my earlier "peace by subordination (under some superpower)" proposition by a *"peace among democracies" proposition* (italics added) consistently improves the fit between theoretical expectations and observations.[55]

4. Zeev Maoz and Bruce Russett (1992) did a contingency analysis for the Gochman and Maoz militarized dispute data (1984), and regime types, using Ted Robert Gurr's (1990) updated Polity II codings,

for 264,819 dyad years, 1946 to 1986. After controlling for geographic distance, wealth, economic growth, alliances, and political stability, they concluded that

> we find no reason to reject the proposition that the political systems of democratic regimes inherently cause them to *refrain fighting one another, and even from frequent militarized disputes.*[56]

5. Stuart A. Bremer (1993) did poisson and negative binomial regressions of the Gochman and Maoz militarized dispute data (1984) and wars from Small and Singer (1982) on type of regime data from Steve Chan (1984) for 202,778 dyad years, 1816 to 1965. They controlled for geographic proximity, relative power, alliance, power status, development, militarization, and the presence of a hegemon, and concluded that

> even after controlling for a large number of factors (more than in any other study of which the author is aware) democracy's conflict-reducing effect remains strong. When we compare its estimated effect on militarized interstate disputes to its estimated effect on interstate wars, it appears to be somewhere around ten times more potent in reducing wars than in reducing disputes. This confirms some speculation that the principal war-reducing character of democracy is attributable not so much to the propensity of democracies to avoid conflict but rather to the *propensity of democracies to keep conflict at lower levels of intensity.*[57]

The first book since my volume 4 of *Understanding Conflict and War* (1979) to explicitly test whether democracies don't make war on each other was *War and Reason* (1992) by Bruce Bueno de Mesquita and David Lalman. Their primary concern was to apply to international war a game-theoretic perspective on foreign policy: that decision makers make choices about war and peace in terms of the perceived utility of the alternatives. Within this context they deal with the "democratic puzzle" as to "why war is absent between democracies."[58] Note that for them also the question is no longer whether democracies make war on each other, but why they do not. For 238 randomly selected European dyads, the Gochman and Maoz militarized dispute data, from 1816 to 1970 (1984), and defining liberal democracies as given by Michael Doyle (1986), they find through binomial regression that

> clearly, as we move up the violence ladder, the observed likelihood that the relevant dyad is made up of two democracies becomes smaller and smaller, eventu-

ally reaching zero. *It appears that democracies do abhor even low levels of violence toward one another.*[59]

And with regard to the statement that no war has occurred between democracies, they say,

> Indeed, *no war (with at least 1,000 battle dead) . . . has occurred between liberal democracies, at least during modern times.* There have, however, been nine instances of reciprocated violence between democracies and an additional thirteen instances in which one or the other member of a liberal democratic dyad used force to get what it wanted from another democratic state. These are still rather small numbers, and the events themselves were small in terms of loss of life or duration.[60]

The first book, however, to wholly deal with this question is Bruce Russett's *Grasping the Democratic Peace* (1993). In it he presents a series of studies the basic purpose of which is to test whether in fact the lack of war between democracies holds up when other variables are held constant, and to test for and between two explanations of why this should be so: democratic norms and democratic structure. In the beginning he defines international war in terms of at least 1,000 battle fatalities, allowing for exceptions that are close to this such as the Falklands Islands War between Great Britain and Argentina. He defines democracy by a variety of standard criteria, but excluding civil rights and political liberties so as to be less exclusive when considering possible wars between democracies. Even then, however, he must conclude that

> it is impossible to identify unambiguously any wars between democratic states in the period since 1815. A few close calls exist, in which some relaxation of the criteria could produce such a case. But to have no clearcut cases, out of approximately 71 interstate wars involving a total of nearly 270 participants, is impressive. Even these numbers are deceptively low as representing total possibilities. For example, as listed by Small and Singer (1982), 21 states count as participating on the Allied side in World War ll, with 8 on the Axis side. Thus in that war alone there were 168 pairs of warring states. Allowing for other multilateral wars, approximately 500 pairs of states went to war against each other in the period. Of these, *fewer than a handful can with any plausibility at all be considered candidates for exceptions to a generalization that democracies do not fight each other.*[61]

As possible exceptions he considered the War of 1812 between the United States and Great Britain, Roman Republic (Papal States) versus France (1849), American Civil War, Ecuador-Colombia (1863), Franco-Prussian War (1870), Boer War (1899), Spanish-American War

(1898), Second Philippine War (1899), Imperial Germany versus western democracies in World War I, Finland versus western democracies in World War II, and Lebanon versus Israel (1948 and 1967).[62] He ends up discarding these exceptions, noting that several are close calls, almost all in the nineteenth century when the number of democracies were small.

He also makes use of the Gochman and Maoz militarized dispute data (1984) that has been relied on by several studies already mentioned, and shows that for 29,081 dyad years from 1946 to 1986 there were *no* wars between democracies and eight cases of the use of force. The odds during this period of two democratic states having a militarized dispute—one in which there is the threat, display, use of force, or war—in any year "were only 1 in 276. By contrast if one or both states in the pair was not a democracy, the odds were as short as 1 in 36—eight times greater. Surely this is a very dramatic difference in behavior."[63] Among all researchers mentioned above who have found cases of force between democracies in the militarized dispute data, Russett is the only one to mention some of the comparatively few cases involved:

> The actual use of military force involved trivial occasions like the "Cod War"; very minor fire by Israel against Britain during the 1956 Suez intervention, in which the British and Israelis were in fact accomplices; brief conflict between British and Turkish forces during a 1963 peacekeeping operation on Cyprus; and Turkish sinking of a Greek boat in 1978.

Russett's book also contains a variety of other analyses, some more relevant to the propositions to be discussed later. Relevant here, Russett (with Maoz) included in a chapter a logistic regression based on a new measure, one that indexes both (1) whether two regimes are democratic; and (2) also the political distance between regimes. Let REG_i be an index of democraticness for regime i and REG_j be a similar index for regime j, where the highest scores are the most democratic. The measure he used is then $(REG_i + REG_j)/(REG_i - REG_j + 1)$, where i is always the regime with the highest score.[64] However, the results of using this are uninterpretable, since it confounds the difference and similarity of two regimes with the degree to which the regimes are democratic, and thus I will ignore the favorable results based on it.

Bruce Russett also includes in his book a revision of the studies he did with William Antholis mentioned above,[65] and one with Carol and

Melvin Ember[66] to be discussed with regard to the Democratic/Dyadic Violence Proposition.

Overall, Russett establishes the following:

> First, democratically organized political systems in general operate under restraints that make them more peaceful in their relations with other democracies. . . . Second, in the modern international system, democracies are less likely to use lethal violence toward other democracies than toward autocratically governed states or than autocratically governed states are toward each other. Furthermore, *there are no clearcut cases of sovereign stable democracies waging war with each other in the modern international system.*[67]

Another book, *Democracy and International Conflict: An Evaluation of the Democratic Peace Proposition,* is by James Lee Ray.[68] Like so many of those who have turned to investigate the idea of a democratic peace, he at first thought, reasonably enough, that the finding about democracies not making war on each other was spurious in some way. But his own research convinced him otherwise. He begins his book with a critical review of the literature on the "democratic peace proposition," including the empirical works that I have summarized above, and concludes that his review

> of the philosophical and historical roots of the proposition that democratic states will not fight wars against each other, of the empirical evidence relevant to it, and of its theoretical base, support, I believe, the conclusion that the proposition is worthy of continued serious consideration.[69]

After then considering the general trends of democratization in the world, he focuses on the question of whether democratic regimes have never or rarely fought wars against each other. He does this by case studies of each alleged war between democracies. In addition to those mentioned by Russett, above, Ray lists Athens versus Syracuse (415–413 B.C.), United Provinces versus England (1780–1783), England versus France (1782–1802), Belgium versus Holland (1830), Swiss Civil War (1847), Nazi Germany in World War II,[70] India versus Pakistan (1948), Turkey versus Cyprus (1974), Peru versus Ecuador (1981), and various cases of post-cold war violence, such as Serbia versus Croatia and Serbia versus Bosnia-Hercegovina.[71]

Of course, in considering this list (and Russett's) all critically depends on how democracy and war are defined. In a discussion of the definition of democracy Ray presents a case for selecting one such that without exception these "democracies" don't make war on each other. In a justification of his approach that is remarkable for its honesty and sensitivity to the nature of science, Ray points out that this is in part a question of

> "public relations." People in general, undergraduate students, graduate students, policymakers, as well as scholars will be impressed to a rather strictly limited extent by assertions to the effect that democracies are, say, 80% less likely to get involved in wars against each other than other kinds of states. All those categories of people will be much more interested in a claim that democratic states never fight wars against each other.

What we are engaged in here (as is everybody engaged in research in social sciences) is a battle for the attention of the general public, students, policymakers, as well as other researchers.[72]

Then, noting that "democracy" is on a continuum, he specifies theoretical importance (that about democracy which prevents democracies from making war on each other should help define the threshold) and simplicity as criteria for demarcating the threshold between democracy and nondemocracies. After searching through the empirical definitions of democracy and discarding one or another, he settles for "democracy" as the regime in which "the leaders of the executive branch and the members of the national legislatures are determined in fair, competitive elections."[73] He stipulates that for elections to be fair and competitive two formally independent political parties should provide candidates, the franchise extends to at least half of the adult population, and the true competitiveness of the regime has been shown by government leaders having in fact lost an election and being replaced. In his emphasis on the peaceful and constitutional transfer of power according to the expressed wishes of a majority he well expresses a fundamental meaning of democracy.

As to interstate wars, Ray accepts Small and Singer's definition of what is an independent state (e.g., having after World War I over 500,000 people, membership in the League of Nations or United Nations, or receiving two or more diplomatic missions from any two or more major powers); and of war (at least 1,000 battle dead).

With the definitional job done, Ray investigates in detail whether any of the alleged exceptions, each having prompted consistent or prominent mention in the literature, indeed constitutes a war between democracies. He says, as a result:

My conclusion is that none of those cases is accurately categorized as an international war between democratic states. The proposition that democratic states never fight international wars against other (democracies), based on definitions of "democracy" and "war" that are simple, operational, and (I hope) intuitively appealing, as well as theoretically grounded, can be defended. *Within the last 200 to 250 years, at least, there do not appear to be any exceptions to the rule that democratic states do not fight international wars against each other.*[74]

The most recent book on the democratic peace is in the process of being written by the historian and physicist Spencer Weart.[75] Like Ray and Russett and Antholis, he is trying to assess all possible cases of wars between democracies as far back in history as possible, including those between the classical Greek city-states. I have read preliminary drafts of his book and his conclusions have been published elsewhere.[76] They are consistent with those reviewed above. He finds throughout written history *"no undoubted case of wars between well-established democracies."*[77] It was not unusual to find that two city-states or nations would often fight each other when one or both were nondemocratic. But when both became clearly and well settled democracies, democracy worked its magic and there was peace between them. And this magic disappeared and fighting reoccurred when one or the other again became nondemocratic. If there was any doubt before about the interdemocratic peace, Spencer Weart's historical study is the final and conclusive evidence that there is such a fact as the interdemocratic peace.

This is not all, however, that Spencer Weart has contributed. He discovered something entirely new and unexpected. This is that *"well established oligarchic republics have hardly ever made war on one another. Very nearly as completely as democracies, oligarchic republics have kept peace with their own kind,"*[78] even though they have been far more frequent in history than democracies. Such a republic is one in which rule is by an oligarchic minority that have equal and democratic rights among themselves, but deny this to at least two-thirds of the population. South Africa under apartheid is a modern example, where the country was governed by a regime competitively elected only by Whites while the greater majority of Blacks had no votes, no representation. While such oligarchic republics rarely made war on each other, surprisingly, *they fought frequent wars with democracies.* This fact must be accommodated within any explanation of the interdemocratic peace.

Finally, the most recent relevant research and exchange on whether democracies make war on each other has appeared in the journal *International Security*. In one article John M. Owen (1994) argued that a "liberal democracy will only avoid war with a state that *it believes to be liberal*."[79] He "derived" this by testing propositions about the democratic peace against a dozen war-threatening crises involving the United States, between 1790 and 1917.[80] Through tracing the decision and event processes in each crises he found that it is the ideology of liberalism that is the force for peace between liberal democracies and not democratic structure or norms themselves.

In a second article Christopher Layne (1994) uses the same process-tracing method to study four cases in which there was a war-crises between democratic states, but they did not fight: the Anglo-American Crisis of 1861 (the Trent Affair), the Anglo-American Crisis of 1895–1896 (Venezuela), the 1898 Anglo-French Struggle for control of the Nile (Fashoda), and the Franco-German Crisis of 1923 (the Ruhr). Contrary to Owen, Layne argues that in each case a democracy was ready to go to war against another democracy, but pulled back, not because the other was democratic, but because of realist factors. Such he believes were the lack of military capability to fight a successful war or concern that other countries would exploit the war.

This is not a negative result for the proposition, however, since in fact these democracies, if one accepts that the countries engaged in each crises were democracies, *did not fight*. Why they did not for each case, whether for those of Owen or Layne, becomes a matter of factual, event, institutional, and normative exegesis, always subject not only to the perception and inclinations of the researcher, but also to the biases of the historians consulted.[81] Moreover, to my knowledge, no historian writing of these crises had in mind that the democratic character of the parties accounted for their avoiding war. This is where quantitative *comparative* research makes a contribution. For if different researchers with different definitions of democracy and war consistently find that regardless of time, countries, and their attributes, democracies do not make war on each other, then *the very fact of democracy must be the fundamental explanation*.[82] And this fact then becomes the unavoidable context for historical process tracing. For by definition such begins with democracy and thus incorporates at the very beginning the factor responsible for peace, regardless of what the process tracing itself uncovers.

The third article in *International Security* by David Spiro (1994) then deals with the question of quantitative significance, and thus strikes at the heart of the Interdemocratic Proposition. He tries to show that the lack of wars between democracies from 1816 to 1980 is a random phenomena—it is not statistically significant. His conclusions are primarily based on year-by-year assessments of the probability that for a particular year democracies would not make war on each other (he also did the same analysis for longer periods, but at the expense of his sample size, which for the whole period was reduced to twelve countries). He finds that for few years is the lack of war significant. However, this study is deeply flawed, as Russett (1995) pointed out in a critique.[83] Not only is what are considered participants in war raise serious questions, as with his interpretation of Finland's joining Germany in its war on the Soviet Union as war with the allied democracies, but his statistical approach is problematical.

Consider this problem. A college administrator wants to determine if there is a gender bias in the grade of A given to three classes taught by a particular professor. He finds that in one class only three men are given As, with a probability of this happening by chance of .22—nonsignificant. In a second class he finds again that only men are given As, two in this case and with a probability .25—but also insignificant. Finally, in the third class one women and two men get As, with this distribution being nonsignificant at .11. Therefore, the administrator might conclude, as Spiro did about democracies, that there is no bias in favor of boys, since in each case the distribution of As was nonsignificant. But the error should be plain: the hypothesis really extends over all classes, and given the classes are independent (an assumption that Spiro makes for each year), the probabilities should be multiplied together. Thus $.22 \times .25 \times .11 = .006$, very significant. The A grades are very likely biased, as intuition would tell us. And that for each year between 1816 and 1980 there was no war between democracies is also intuitively and significantly meaningful. If one multiplies all of Spiro's annual probabilities together, as in the above example, the product would be 2×10^{-21}, surely statistically significant.

A good approach for determining the significance that democracies did not make war on each other is to do the test for the longest possible period and on the number of democratic and nondemocratic dyads with or without wars.[84] An example of this approach is shown in the appendix to chapter 1 and in Russett (1994). In his critique of Spiro, Russett reanalyzed the data presented in his book (1993). He found that over the period 1946–1986 democracies did not make war on each other, significant at .004. He also found that democratic dyads were less involved in the use of force short of war with even a greater significance, a probability of 1×10^{-7}.

As a result of this review of research on the democratic peace, it is clear that:

(1) *Democracies do not make war on each other*. And there is a consensus on this. Moreover, in those few cases were researchers and scholars believe that there are a few exceptions to this claim, specifically those listed above by Ray and Russett, the analyses of each alleged exception showed that by reasonable and significant criteria as to what is a democracy, an independent state, and interstate war, these can be dismissed. This is further confirmed by the historical research of Weart. The only truly negative statistical results are those by Spiro. And it is not that he finds democracies have made war on each other, which with few arguable exceptions he does not. It is that he does not find this statistically significant. But his methodology is questionable and his results contradict all other statistical analyses on this proposition.

(2) *There are a few minor cases of violence short of war between democracies,* but these are much fewer than one would expect were democracy irrelevant. For theoretical reasons yet to be given, I would expect no violence between democracies at all. In those cases where violence has occurred it appeared under extraordinary circumstance, as some gunfire by Israel against Great Britain while they were allied in the Suez War, or the countries involved were marginally democratic, as when Turkey sunk a Greek boat in 1978.[85] The few minor cases of such violence can be treated as rare exceptions to the rule that democracies do not make violence on each other.

The findings on the Interdemocratic Peace Proposition are robust, they are solid, they no longer can be denied. On this I must agree with Nils Peter Gleditsch, the editor of the *Peace Research Journal,* when in an article summarizing this research on democracy and war he concludes that,

> as far as third variables are concerned, *the perfect or near-perfect correlation between democracy and nonwar in dyads* should soon begin to have a very different effect: all research on the causes of war in modern times will be regarded as

suspect if it is not first corrected for this factor. In fact, I would argue that most behavioral research on conditions for war and peace in the modern world can now be thrown on the scrap-heap of history, and researchers can start all over again on a new basis.[86]

Notes

1. Quoted in Doyle (1983, p. 216).
2. Chapter 7 suggests some answers to why there had been so little systematic research on the relationship between democracy and war.
3. Babst (1964); see also (1972).
4. Wright (1942); see also (1965).
5. Ray (1993, 1995) does a case-study of both the war of 1812 and the Civil War. He also concludes that Great Britain was not then a democracy, and for different reasons than given by Babst, argues also that the Civil War was not a war between democracies. The head of government was not then chosen in a national election and the franchise was anyway limited to less than 50 percent of adults.
6. Babst (1964, p. 14).
7. For a contemporary description and critique of this project, see Hoole and Zinnes (1976, part II).
8. See Wright (1942, 839–48).
9. Small and Singer (1976).
10. Singer and Small (1972). They later updated this data to 1980 (Small and Singer, 1982).
11. Small and Singer (1976, p. 54).
12. Ibid., p. 67.
13. In 1980 I tabulated the number of contiguous states using Small and Singer's list and came up with a much different figure. I wrote to Singer about this and after recalculating their results, his assistant Scott G. Gates replied in a personal communication that "they indicate that for all wars, 25.8% of the dyads showed common borders. When the two world wars are excluded, 41.3% of the dyads were directly contiguous. Finally, when the World Wars, the Korean War, and the Austro-Prussian War (major alliance wars) are excluded, 58.5% of the dyads shared common boundaries." For a most recent and thorough examination of whether common borders or geographic distances account for the lack of wars between democracies, see Gleditsch (1995).
14. Small and Singer (1976, p. 68).
15. Ibid.
16. Singer (1981).
17. These correlations were for all nations and were exploratory, not the test of the subsequent theory. Once the theory was clear, then it followed that these correlations were an improper test of the relationship between democracy and violence. The reason is that democracy, in a probabilistic sense, is necessary but not sufficient for nonviolence. This means that both democracies *and nondemocracies* may have no violence, but when violence occurs, it is less intense for democracies than it is for nondemocracies. Let the x-axis in a plot be a measure of, from left to right, decreasing democracy; and the y-axis be, from low to high, increasingly severe violence. Then the plot of nations in this space should fall within a triangle, with the hypotenuse rising from left to right, and the opposite side lying along the x-axis. (For an example of such an empirical plot, see Rummel, 1983, figure 2.)

This is theoretical, and indeed, as will be made clear, this *is what is found empirically*. However, this is not the type of data suitable to a product moment correlation coefficient, which should lie along an upward or downward slanted line. Consequently, one should expect low correlations on such data, which is in fact what I found. This correlation only means that their is no meaningful necessary *and* sufficient linear relationship between democracy and violence (Rummel, 1968).

18. Rummel (1979, p. 374).
19. See Rummel (1979, table 16C.3 for proposition 11) and the discussion (pp. 277–79).
20. Rummel (1981, p. 283).
21. I did this reevaluation of the literature in Rummel (1985).
22. See the Freedom House *Freedom at Issue* numbers for January–February for each of the years 1977 to 1981.
23. Rummel (1983, p. 41). This was significant at p<.005, chi-square test (one-tailed); .001 for the binomial test. Also regimes were classified as to whether they had both a free market and political freedom, with similar results.
    This is the first reference to my statistical tests of significance and there will be many to follow in this book. A number of these will be on populations or on samples that hardly can be considered randomly chosen. How then can one use the formal and heavy apparatus of statistical tests to appraise them, since an often reported assumption is that one have a random sample so that inferences to a population can be made? But statistical tests also can be used also to gauge the mathematical probability of getting a particular combination of results, given the original data. For example, if one has a product moment correlation between two variables X and Y for all nations, one hardly has a sample. But for all the combinations of the data for 100 nations on X and Y, one can ask about the probability of getting a particular combination of data that would give a specific correlation. It is as though one had two hats, X and Y, with 100 numbers in each. Then if one randomly selects a pair of numbers, one from X and one from Y, records each number and hat and then replaces them, does this 100 times, and then correlates the 100 numbers from X and Y, one then can ask as to the probability that one will get a particular correlation, that is, a particular combination of numbers. The significance test estimates this probability. Thus a correlation of .25 significant at .05 for a random sample would be interpreted as the probability being one out of twenty or smaller that in the population there is zero correlation between the two variables. If the sample is in fact the population or for some reason nonrandom, then the significance test may be interpreted as the probability being one out of twenty or greater of getting the specific correlation by chance out of the universe of correlations for all the possible combinations of the given data.
    There is, however, the requirement that the numbers be considered independent of each other, as though drawn randomly. This requirement is usually met by the studies considered here, since from one time period to the next it is possible for a nation to go from total war to peace and vice versa, and the involvement in war or peace, or other kinds of violence from one nation to the next can also be considered statistically independent in general. True, alliances and historical bonds between nations may draw them into war together or against each other, but this is still a matter of independent decisions among the leaders, and not a necessary contingency.
24. Ibid., pp. 42–43. These results were significant at p<.005 for the chi-square test (one-tailed) and p<.0003 for the binomial test.
25. Ferris (1973).

26. From Feierabend and Feierabend (1973, table 12). Democratic nations are defined by their combined scores on suffrage, internal press censorship, party opposition, general civil rights, and executive permissiveness for each of the years between 1945 and 1966. The total scores range from 1.0 to 6.0 (the least democratic overall). I made the cut between democratic and nondemocratic nations at 2.00, for this was where a gap appeared in the scores, and it gave approximately the same percentage (thirty-three) of democratic nations as in the Freedom House data. A second list of Feierabend and Feierabend (1972, table 11) was consulted for six additional regimes (China, Greece, Guatemala, Iran, Malaya, and Yugoslavia). This list was based apparently on similar criteria and covered the years 1948 through 1960; I used the same 2.0 cutoff between democratic and nondemocratic regimes. Six regimes (Burma, North Korea, South Korea, Mongolia, North Vietnam, and South Vietnam) were not on either list and were judged nondemocratic over the time period. The total sample was eighty-three regimes and excluded those not independent for at least half the period covered by the Ferris (1973) list of threats and use of force.
27. Rummel (1983, table 8); Significant at p<.004, one-tailed chi-square.
28. Ibid., significant at p<.027, one-tailed chi-square.
29. Pride (1970: figure 3). His list includes fourteen stable, unstable, and quasi-democracies during the twentieth century. These are: stable = Australia, Canada, Denmark, Great Britain, Netherlands, New Zealand, Norway, Switzerland, United States; unstable = France; quasi-democracies = Belgium, Chile, Mexico, Sweden. Those regimes not among Pride's list of democracies were assumed nondemocratic over this period.
30. Small and Singer (1976).
31. This was the number of dyadic combinations among all the states independent since 1920, based on the three lists of Ferris (1973: table A-l). Germany and Korea were considered as one after 1945, and the loss of independence among regimes during World War II was ignored.
32. Rummel (1983, table 7), significant at p<.0002, chi-square (one-tailed).
33. Ibid. For those dyads with common borders, the result is still significant at p<.07 chi-square, one-tailed (if corrected for continuity, p<.027 one-tailed if uncorrected); p<.034 binomial (one-tailed).
34. Doyle (1983, tables 1-2); Small and Singer (1982).
35. Doyle (1983, pp. 213, 215, italics in the original). He also published the list of wars and an updated list of liberal regimes in Doyle (1986). His conclusions were the same.
36. Small and Singer (1976, p. 51.n3).
37. Vincent (1987, p. 104).
38. Why was I not more cautious in expressing the nature of my work and the conclusions? Because I am philosophically opposed to highly qualified conclusions when the work and results warrant a straight or categorical expression of them. By this time, as mentioned, the whole nature and sense for my research had led me to conclude that freedom promotes nonviolence. To say otherwise in order to be politically correct would not only have been dishonest, but more important, to highly qualify the conclusion would have made it difficult to disprove. And this is my philosophy of science: empirical statements should be such that they can be falsified if the science of conflict and violence is to be furthered. One can hardly falsify an "it seems" or "may be."
39. The data are described in Gochman and Maoz (1984).
40. See Gurr (1974).

41. Maoz and Abdolali (1989, table 3).
42. Ibid., table 4.
43. Among other things, Gurr rates regimes on three different scales: democracy, autocracy, and an in-between mixed type he calls anocracy. The correlation between these three is a warning about too much reliance on these scales for the analysis of these political types and violence. The Tau b correlation between democracy and anocracy is -.04, between democracy and autocracy is -.32, and between anocracy and autocracy is -.24. See Maoz and Abdolali (1989, p. 12). These correlations mean that the scales do not distinguish between democracy and anocracy, and only poorly between democracy and autocracy, even though the are presumably at the extremes of the scales. Ideally, the correlation between democracy and autocracy should approach -1.00.
44. Maoz and Abdolali (1989, pp. 30–31).
45. Cole (1987).
46. Small and Singer (1982).
47. Cole (1990, p. 19).
48. Russett and Antholis (1991). This has been published in the *Journal of Peace Research* (1992) and revised by Russett for his book (Russett with Antholis, 1993, chapter 3).
49. Russett with Antholis (1993).
50. Ibid., p. 62.
51. Personal communication. See Weart (1994, 1995). I thank Dr. Weart for making available to me a preliminary draft of his forthcoming book.
52. He is quoted as saying that "Democratic countries do not go to war with one another. They don't sponsor terrorism or threaten one another with weapons of mass destruction." *U.S. News & World Report* (December 28, 1992): 70.
53. Morgan and Schwebach (1992, p. 218, italics added).
54. Schweller (1992, pp. 268, italics added).
55. Weede (1992, p. 382).
56. Maoz and Russett (1992, p. 263, italics added). They did find, however, that for 17,876 democratic-democratic dyads, there were nine cases of the use of force less than war out of 711 cases for all dyads. The chi-square expected value for the democratic dyads is near fifty. Not enough information was given to know what these nine cases were.
57. Bremer (1993, p. 246, italics added). See also Bremer (1992).
58. Bueno de Mesquita and Lalman (1992, pp. 155–58).
59. Ibid., p. 152, italics added.
60. Ibid., p. 157, italics added.
61. Russett (1993, p. 16, italics added).
62. Ibid., p. 17.
63. Ibid., p. 21.
64. Russett with Maoz (1993, p. 77).
65. Russett and Antholis (1992).
66. Ember, Ember, and Russett (1992).
67. Russett (1993, p. 11, italics added).
68. Ray (1995). The conclusions of his book was published in Ray (1993).
69. Ray (1995, chapter 1 conclusion). This quote is from a preliminary draft and may be changed slightly in the final publication. I thank Professor Ray for making this available to me.
70. Since Hitler became head of government through democratic procedures in 1933, and the legislature gave him the right to rule by decree, and a national referendum

approved his rule, even though throughout intimidation and violence was used, some argue that Germany under Hitler was democratic.
71. Ray (1995, chapter 3, table 3.1).
72. Ibid. chapter 3. This quote is from a preliminary draft and may be changed slightly in the final publication. I wish to thank James Lee Ray for making this draft available to me.
73. Ibid., chapter 3, p. 21, italics added.
74. Ray (1993, pp. 269-270). I have quoted this conclusion from his summary article on these possible exceptions to the proposition, since it is more specifically stated there.
75. Weart (1995).
76. See Weart (1994).
77. Personal communication, italics added. By well established he means one that has existed for at least three-years.
78. Weart (1994).
79. Owen (1994, p. 102).
80. In Owen (1993) these crises are presented in detail through "process tracing."
81. For a critique of Layne's article, see Russett (1995). For comments, see Doyle (1995).
82. Of course, the question then becomes: "What is it about democracies that makes for this peace?" This is the question I hope to answer in the theoretical part II of this book.
83. For a response to Russett's critique, see Spiro (1995).
84. Spiro did this also, but required (1994, p. 74–75) that his countries be in existence, and that democracies be so, for the whole extended period, thus seriously reducing his sample size.
85. Freedom House rated Greece and Turkey barely free for 1978. See *Freedom at Issue* (January-February 1979): 4–5.
86. Gleditsch (1992, p. 372, italics added).

3

Democracy Limits Bilateral Violence

The Democracy/Dyadic Violence Proposition: The More Democratic Two Regimes, the Less Severe Their Violence Against Each Other.

If democracies do not, or rarely, fight each other, does this mean that there is an either-or boundary around the zone of democracies such that inside this zone there are no wars and rare foreign violence short of war, while outside of this zone violence occurs unaffected by the type of regimes involved? Or is this a continuum? That is, do we have no war among democracies and increasingly severe violence between regimes as they become less democratic, with the most severe violence among the least democratic regimes?

The Democratic/Dyadic Violence Proposition gives a positive answer to the last question. It implies that we can place pairs of nations along a continuum according to their types of political regimes. For example, assume that there are basically three types of regimes: democratic, authoritarian, and totalitarian. Then the idea of a continuum assumes that we can place these types of regimes along a scale of increasingly severe violence, where democracy-democracy pairs have no severe violence between them, democracy-authoritarian pairs tend to have some severe violence, and upwards through authoritarian-authoritarian, democracy-totalitarian, and authoritarian-totalitarian pairs to the totalitarian-totalitarian ones that should have the most severe violence.

This proposition is hardly as exciting as the joint democracy one.

51

But it is nonetheless interesting and important. If it is true, then it is not only by democratizing nations—a most difficult matter in many parts of the world, such as the Middle East—that we reduce violence. *Just reforming regimes in the direction of greater civil rights and political liberties will promote less violence.*

When I first proposed that there was such a continuum in 1983,[1] which I then called the Freedom/Dyadic Violence Proposition,[2] it was a new idea. Neither Dean Babst, Melvin Small and J. David Singer, and Michael Doyle had considered it. Nor was it clearly a view of democracy within classical liberalism or an aspect of Kant's *Perpetual Peace.* And it has tended to be confused with that of democracies not making war on each other. It changes the focus from some dichotomous aspect of regimes that prevents or reduces violence—democracy—to some characteristics that when enlarged or reduced accordingly decreases or increases the severity of foreign violence. This characteristic is the degree to which a people are free—have civil and political rights.

In order to test this proposition in 1983, I used Freedom House's seven-point scale ratings on civil liberties and political rights for each nation, for 1976 through 1980. I added these two ratings together for each nation and then for the pair of nations in a dyad for a year. Thus for 1976, one nation with civil liberties and political rights ratings of 1 and 2 (this would give the nation an overall rating of 3, or "free") and another nation with ratings of 7 and 6 (or overall a 13, which means "nonfree"), would together total 16, or midrange on a scale running from 4 to 28. When these scale values for all dyads are cross-tabulated with the severity of their violence, there is a clear tendency for the violence to increase as the degree of democracy within the dyad decreases.[3] These results were very unlikely to be accidental—the probability of getting the tabulated relationship between the severity of violence between two nations and the degree to which they were jointly democratic was less than one out of 10 million[4]; for six points along this scale and the associated severity of violence, the correlation of .94 was also significant.[5] To see if these results were due to common borders, they were recalculated for those pairs of nations that were contiguous, with similar results.

Of course, these tests were only for 1976 to 1980. But there is one apparently relevant quantitative analysis by Zeev Maoz and Nasrin Abdolali for a much longer period of time that bears on this.[6] They used the Gochman and Maoz militarized dispute data (1984) and Gurr's (1978) Polity I measurements of type of political system (democratic, autocratic, and an in-between anocratic) to analyze the type of regime and their disputes from 1816 to 1976. Among other analyses, they cross-tabulated the expected and observed number of 1,625 dyads involved in such disputes, their use of force, and their wars. For all disputes and each level (nonviolence, force, war) they found a significant tendency for the frequency of nonviolent militarized disputes, force, and war to differ with the degree of democracy in the dyad, ranging from democracy-democracy, democracy-anocratic, democracy-autocratic to anocratic-anocratic, anocratic-autocratic, and autocratic-autocratic[7]; and there appears a slight tendency for these disputes to increase from democratic-democratic to autocratic-autocratic dyads. But these are *frequencies* and, as I now will show, can be very misleading for this and, especially, the Democratic/Foreign Violence Proposition considered in the next chapter.

When considering whether democracies use force against each other, it does not matter whether one evaluates this by looking at the frequency of force or its severity, since there should be no force. Of course if there are exceptions, as we found may be the case at the lowest level of force, then one should evaluate these exceptions in terms of their severity. Whether one person was killed in official violence between democracies is one thing; but 900 is another.

But for the Democracy/Dyadic Violence and remaining propositions to be discussed later, it is the severity of violence that is most affected by the degree to which a regime is democratic. Consider this. The most often used data in testing these propositions, as should be obvious by now, has been that on war published by Small and Singer (1982), and the related Gochman and Maoz militarized dispute data (1984). In both cases there must be at least 1,000 battle-dead for a war to be defined as such. But, first, to be a participant,

the nation must be a qualified member of the interstate system. Second, it must have had regular, uniformed, national military personnel in sustained combat. Third, no matter how brief or lengthy that combat, these forces must have either numbered at least 1,000 or sustained at least 100 battle-connected deaths. Forth, a nation need not have been, either formally or physically, at war with *all* of the nations on the opposing side in order to be classed as an active participant.[8]

This means that a regime that is coded as having a war can have virtually no one killed in the war as long as it had over a thousand troops involved; or that a state suffering 800 killed in a violent confrontation in which the overall toll is 950 would not be counted as having fought a war. For example, in the Boxer Rebellion, classified as a war by Small and Singer since there were over 3,000 battle dead, Great Britain lost 34 killed, the United States 21, and France 24.[9] *Yet this was classified as a war for each of these nations.* Then consider the Falklands War of 1982 between Great Britain and Argentina. Figures vary on the number killed, but somewhat less than 1,000 seems a good number, with about 650 to 700 of those being Argentineans. But by virtue of the Small-Singer criterion that to be a war a 1,000 battle dead threshold has to be reached, the Falklands War should not be a war they would include, and thus in spite of her high number killed compared to Great Britain, the United States, and France in the Boxer rebellion, *this should not be counted as a war for Argentina.*[10]

This problem with this simple count of wars for a regime can be seen in another way. Counting wars or military actions equate conflicts that are vastly different. For example, according to Small and Singer the Philippines lost 90 killed in the Korean War,[11] and this is counted as a war for the Philippines because it had over 1,000 troops involved. But in the Small and Singer tables,[12] the Soviet Union lost 7,500,000 battle dead in World War II, and this is also counted as one war. Thus, in comparing the democraticness of regimes and their use of force, if we measure force by a frequency count of wars, then Great Britain in the Boxer Rebellion, the Philippines in the Korean War, and the USSR in World War II, are treated as *equally* using force, *since each gets a count of one for war,* although Great Britain lost only thirty-four in combat, the Philippines ninety, and the Soviet Union over seven million. *Yet, such frequency counts of wars or the use of force have been the main way the propositions on democracy and violence have been tested.*

Consider also that whatever we theorize to be the underlying conditions inhibiting or preventing democracies and near democracies from violence, no one would argue that democracies are equally inhibited from using force in a conflict in which the expectation is of losing a dozen or so soldiers versus engaging in a total war in which one may suffer the loss of millions. But this is the theoretical implication of the use of a simple count of wars.

To avoid this problem I try to make clear that the type of regime affects the choice of conflict behavior by the political leadership in terms of four basic considerations: (1) what is the issue and the nature of the opposing regime; (2) is the use of military violence against it an option, and if so (3) how much force would be required and (4) what would be the expected gains versus losses, particularly the number of one's own casualties.[13] The argument of the Democratic/Dyadic Violence Proposition is that as two regimes are more democratic, the costs of violence, especially the expected human toll, increasingly inhibits their mutual violence. Even if one party is willing to use violence, the more democratic it is for a given level of anticipated cost, the less likely it will so act.

Returning now to the Maoz and Abdolali (1989) study, because of their utilization of frequencies, the relevance of their results to the Democratic/Dyadic Violence Proposition is questionable. There is only one way of making good use of their results. They give a cross classification of dyadic regimes at the level of force short of war, and then at the level of war. Because of the examples given above we cannot conclude in all cases that war will be more severe in total deaths for a regime than for those cases of force short of war. But if we assume that this is true on the average, then we find that the relationship between the democraticness of two regimes and their force short of war is less significant than it is for that involving war.[14] However, this is a best an indirect test and should be looked at as only suggestive.

Bruce Russett with Zeev Maoz includes a cross-tabulation similar to that of Maoz and Abdolali for the Gochman and Maoz militarized disputes since World War II (1984) and Gurr's (1990) Polity II regime scores.[15] The difference between the expected and the actual frequencies of force short of war and war are similar to those for Maoz and Abdolali (1989) in that they are in the correct direction—the more democratic two regimes, the lower the frequency of violence tends to be. But when Maoz and Russett include a similar table, now with a statistic measuring the level of significance, that for force short of war is more significant than that for war,[16] the reverse of the finding of Maoz and Abdolali for the 1816–1976 period. Regardless, these are frequency data and at best indirectly relevant. Still we might note their conclusion that, "The less democratic a democracy's adversary is, the greater the likelihood of a high-level militarized dispute."[17]

There is one more study to be mentioned. Bruce Russett with Carol and Melvin Ember (1993) did an analysis of wars among nonindustrial societies. They first coded these societies on political characteristics that reflect their degree of democracy, such as the checks on power and extent of participation in policy. They then counted the dyadic wars between tribes within each of these societies. They found as a result that the degree of democracy, as best they could measure it for thirty-seven preindustrial societies, predicts very well to the number of wars between independent units within these societies, controlling for population, distance, the localization of polities, multilocalness, and outliers.[18] Although their measurements were for societies, the analysis was dyadic (between preindustrial units within societies) and seems to strongly support the Democratic/Dyadic Violence Proposition. However, because they relied on the frequency of war, their results also are not directly relevant to the proposition.

There are other studies that might be mentioned, but because of methodological faults in addition to relying on frequencies of violence or war they may be ignored.[19]

Most of the studies of the Interdemocratic Peace Proposition have relied directly or indirectly on the Small and Singer data (1982) on wars between 1816 and 1980, or the Gochman and Maoz (1984) militarized international dispute data set. I will do so also to again test the Democratic/Dyadic Violence Proposition. I first will limit the wars to all interstate wars in this century, from 1900 to 1980, for which we have a good sample of democracies. Second, I will limit the dyads to those that actually fought each other. Thus I exclude, for example, Japan versus Bulgaria in World War I; Bulgaria and Rumania in World War II (1944–1945); or China versus Italy in World War II. Then I classified each warring regime as to whether it was democratic (= 0), authoritarian (= 1), or totalitarian (= 2). I largely relied on the Small and Singer (1976) classification of democracies and Gurr's Polity II classification (1990) to make these distinctions. I rated a regime as totalitarian based on how absolute was a regime's power and the degree to which it commanded virtually every aspect of society, as did the Soviet and communist Chinese regimes. All communist regimes were classified as totalitarian. The underlying theoretical variable is the freedom of a people to govern their own lives, that is, their civil liberties and political rights. In democracies people ordinarily have the most freedom, under totalitarian regimes the least.

As to the criteria for wars, since I am relying on the Small-Singer data I am limited to any war in which there was at least 1,000 battle dead, and to any regime that suffered at least 100 battle-dead or had 1,000 or more troops involved in these wars.

I then created two operational variables. One is the democraticness of the pair of regimes in a dyad, which is the sum of the rating of each. Thus, the dyad Nazi Germany (rated totalitarian = 2) and Great Britain (rated democratic = 0) had a democraticness score of $0 + 2 = 2$; the Soviet Union-Nazi Germany dyad had a score of 4.

The second operational variable was the sum of the number killed in battle in the war for each member of the dyad. Thus, for example, in the 1906 Central American War of Guatemala versus El Salvador and Honduras, Honduras lost 300 battle dead and Guatemala 400. Therefore, for the Honduras-Guatemala dyad the total dead was 700, my measure of the dyadic severity of their violence.

The hypothesis is that the higher the actual or potential severity, and the more democratic the two regimes, the less likely they have or will fight each other. When both are democratic, then the Interdemocratic Peace Proposition kicks in and there is no war. At the other extreme when both regime are totalitarian there should be the most extreme violence—the number of killed should be the highest.[20]

Applying these measurements to wars 1900 to 1980 I found a perfect step function for the distribution of means for each level of democraticness for pairs of regimes. This is shown in table 3.1. There was no war between democracies, so their mean of zero battle dead between them is also shown in the table. Figure 3.1 plots these scores.

Of course there is the question whether these mean battle dead at each level of democraticness could have happened by chance. Notice first that they all are in line with what we should expect by the Democratic/Dyadic Violence Proposition. Such a close fit between expectations and data is very unlikely by chance. An analysis of variance of the democraticness of two regimes to their battle dead in wars they fought against each other ties this down. With this positive relationship between the lack of democracy of two nations and the severity of their wars against each other, the odds of it in fact being an accident— that there is really no relationship or one in the opposite direction—is more than 5,000 to 1 against.[21]

Are the differences among the means significant, ignoring that for democratic-democratic dyads? Table 3.2 presents the probabilities of the difference in means. Looking at the table, the probability (Bonferroni adjusted)[22] that the mean battle dead should be larger and as large as it

TABLE 3.1
The More Democratic Two Regimes, the Less Intensely
They Fight Each Other, 1900–1980

Dyadic Democraticness	Dyadic Dead[a]	Number of Regimes
democracy-democracy	0	[b]
democracy-authoritarian	567,108	66
democracy-totalitarian authoritarian-authoritarian	940,796	107
authoritarian-totatalitarian	1,664,220	40
totalitarian-totalitarian	2,560,202	11

a. This is the mean of the sums of battle dead for regimes of the given
   regime type that fought each other in wars.
b. There was no war between any democracies

FIGURE 3.1
The Less Democratic Two Regimes, the More Severe Their Wars, 1900–1980

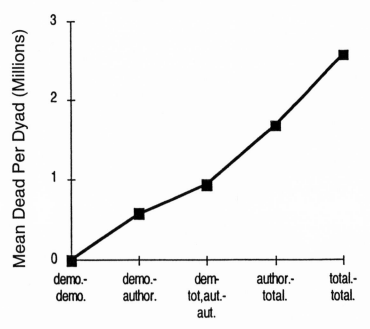

TABLE 3.2
It is No Accident that the More Democratic Two Regimes, the Less Deadly Their Wars, 1900–1980

	DEMOCRATICNESS IN THE DYAD [a]		
	demo.-author.	dem.-tot.,auth.-auth.	author.-total.
author.-author.	.436 (.230)		
demo-total, author.-total.	.003 (.002)	.053 (.034)	
total.-total.	.0005 (.0005)	.006 (.004)	.326 (.186)

Analysis of variance: F-Ratio = 7.093; p < .000

a. Bonferroni adjusted pairwise comparison
   probabilities. Those in parentheses are the
   Tukey probabilities. All one-tail.

is for democratic-totalitarian and authoritarian-authoritarian dyads compared to democratic-authoritarian ones is .44. That is, the probability is .44 that in fact there may be no difference or one in the opposite direction. This is hardly significant. Neither is the difference between the means for the authoritarian-totalitarian and totalitarian-totalitarian dyads significant. The remaining four differences are significant at least at a probability of .05, which can be seen from table 3.2. That the differences among two out of the six comparisons of means are not significant should not distract us from the strong positive results. That they are all in the right direction, that overall this is highly significant (by analysis of variance, as shown in the table), and that they tend to curve upward (ignoring the artificial mean for the democratic-democratic dyad—see figure 3.1) are all signs of something truly substantial in this relationship.

These results in conjunction with the others mentioned above well support the Democratic/Dyadic Violence Proposition. Moreover, keep in mind that the democratic-democratic end of this proposition is in fact the Interdemocratic Peace Proposition, and by itself has been established as a fact of international relations.

Notes

1. Rummel (1983).
2. Rummel (1985, pp. 442–43). I have changed the label to better connect with the emphasis on democracy by the public and in the literature.
3. Rummel (1983, tables 12 and 13).
4. Chi-square distribution, p<.2 X 10^{-8} (two-tailed). See Ibid., table 14.
5. Significant at p<.025 (one-tailed).
6. Maoz and Abdolali (1989).

7. Ibid., table 4. Overall and for each level (dispute dyads, wars dyads, and use of force dyads), the chi-square was p<.001 (two-tailed). The appropriate test here would be one-tailed, and thus p<.0005.
8. Small and Singer (1982, p. 67). See also Ibid., p. 55.
9. Ibid., p. 87.
10. I say *should* rather than *would*, since in Singer's more recent compilation, the Falklands Islands War is included.
11. Ibid., p. 92.
12. Ibid., p. 91.
13. This is not to imply that all regimes are concerned about casualties for reasons of humanity. Depending on the regime and personalities involved, the number of anticipated casualties may effect the decision for violence because of how these losses sap national capability, how they may be viewed by other potentially hostile regime, how they may weaken the regime internally, how they may effect the next election, or how sensitive the leaders are to the deaths involved.
14. Maoz and Abdolali (1989, table 4). The chi-square for force is 23.46 and that for war is 43.38, or nearly twice as high.
15. Russett with Maoz (1992, table 4.1).
16. Maoz and Russett (1993, tables 2 and 3).
17. Russett with Maoz (1993, p. 78, italics omitted).
18. The multiple correlation coefficients squared range from .60 to .87, all highly significant from p<.0005 (interpreting the p=.000 given in the table) to <.08 (Russett with Ember and Ember, 1993, table 5.1).
19. These are Vincent (1987), Wang, Chang, and Ray (1992), and Russett with Maoz (1993, the regression analyses results shown in tables 4.2–4.5). Except for the Vincent study, the problem is the joint measure (JOINREG) of democraticness of two regimes and their political distance, which confounds the results. The problem with Vincent's study is both the use of frequency data, and its inappropriately weighting by his source. See Rummel (1987b). For Vincent's response to my criticisms, see Vincent (1987b).
20. It should be clear that the number killed for the dyad is that suffered for each member in the war of which they were both a part and in which they actually fought each other. This is only a approximate measure. More desirable would be a count of the number of killed they each suffered from fighting the other, but such figures for multilateral wars, like World War II are not available.
    In a personal communication James Lee Ray suggests that according to my logic about the relationship between democracy and severity, the number of killed inflicted on the other nation in the dyad would be a more pertinent measure of severity. I do not see the logic of this. If anything, it seems to me, democratic decision makers should be and have been restrained in allowing too many of their own military casualties while using maximum strategic and tactical firepower to inflict casualties on the other side. Witness, for example, the massive use of firepower in World War II and the Korean, Vietnam, and Gulf Wars by American forces in order to soften up the enemy and minimize American casualties. On the other side, totalitarian regimes were quite willing to squander the lives of their forces, as in the Chinese communist human wave attacks, and put their civilians at risk, as did the Japanese military in trying to counter the American Pacific Island campaign during World War II.
21. This is one-tailed.
22. This adjusts the probability for a particular mean difference to take into account

the significance of the other mean differences. For twenty mean differences one should expect by chance that one of them would be significant at a $p<.05$. One should therefore adjust for this when considering the probability of one mean difference among others. The Tukey probabilities shown in table 3.2, however, are simply the probabilities for particular mean differences. I calculated these through the Macintosh SYSTAT statistical program.

4

Democracies are Least Warlike

The Democratic/Foreign Violence Proposition: The More Democratic a Regime, the Less its Foreign Violence.

While a consensus has grown that democracies don't make war on each other, as described in chapter 2, a second consensus has developed in parallel that democracies are neither more nor less likely to make war or commit violence than other types of regimes. Just note the following quotes, which exemplify this agreement.

Statistics can hardly be invoked to show that democracies have been less often involved in war than autocracies. (Quincy Wright)[1]

Liberal states are as aggressive and war prone as any other form of government or society in their relations with nonliberal states. (Michael Doyle)[2]

And Kant was clearly wrong in his presumption that democracies are inherently peaceful. (William Dixon)[3]

[R]esearch on this question has been near unanimous in finding that democracies are as war prone as nondemocratic states. Only Rummel has dissented from this result. (Harvey Starr)[4]

[T]he results of most studies indicate that democracies are no less war-prone than other forms of government. (T. Clifton Morgan and Sally Howard Campbell)[5]

As the empirical evidence grew that democracies are just as warlike as other states, even if in a somewhat perplexing way, the idea arose that, nevertheless, there may be characteristics associated with democracies that tend to discourage war. An early attempt to identify such a characteristic was Rummel's (1983) argument that the political freedom of individuals promotes peace. But Rummel's empirical results were subsequently shown to lack generality. (D. Marc Kilgour)[6]

. . . democracies fight about as much as nondemocracies. (Nehemia Geva, Karl DeRouen, and Alex Mintz)[7]

. . . how are we to explain the fact that [democracies] wage war with other types of states with as much frequency and vigor as do nondemocratic regimes. (Bruce Bueno de Mesquita and D. Lalman)[8]

In my reading of the evidence . . . there is little difference in the war involvement of democracies and other regimes. (Erich Weede)[9]

The thesis that the democratization of systems of rule eliminates the most important cause of war collides with many empirical findings . . . there is a long chain of articles denying a relationship between democracy and non-violence. Rummel's is the significant exception. (Ernst-Otto Czempiel)[10]

In spite of this consensus, it does not well reflect the evidence. As I will try to show here, a careful reading of the studies underlying this consensus and at my own 1983 piece that is assumed to be the only exception (actually there are many more, which I will cite below) will show that democracies are in fact the most pacific of regimes. Moreover, an analysis of the methodology of the core research studies that underlie this consensus will further support this conclusion.

To begin with the "exceptional findings" in my *War, Power, Peace,* I offered the proposition that "the more libertarian a state, the less it tends to be involved in violence."[11]

A prior question has to do with the kind of violence limited by libertarian [democratic] systems. Libertarian systems are the natural enemies of authoritarian and totalitarian states. By their example and the products of freedom they are naturally subversive of authoritarian or totalitarian systems; and these freedoms seem to make libertarian states defenseless against unilateral changes in the status quo. Thus, libertarian states are often involved in reactive and defensive violence against the initiatives of nonlibertarian states. Therefore in general, *I do not expect that there will be a correlation between libertarianism and the frequency [note: the frequency] of involvement in war or violence.* Nor should there be for the conflict behavior variables. The predicted correlations for these variables are therefore random. . . .

However, once a libertarian state is involved, domestic forces will usually begin to coalesce against increased violence and for a settlement of some sort. The growth in anti-Vietnam war sentiment and its impact on the American leadership's war policies and decisions are a paradigm case of [this proposition]. It follows that the *intensity of violence variable* (which measures the scope, occurrence, and degree of violence) and the conflict scale (which has intense violence at the extreme) should be negatively correlated with libertarianism [democracy].[12]

There are two things to note about this. One is that it emphasizes the severity of violence as the crucial variable; and second it discards the frequency of war involvements or other violence as a relevant variable, predicting that the correlation between democracy and the frequency of violence should be random. Ironically, this near zero correlation that I predicted is in fact what allegedly has been found by the subsequent studies underlying the consensus that democracies are no less or more violent than other types of regimes, to which my positive findings on severity are supposed to be an exception. Indeed, I also had found through factor analyses and correlation studies that there was little correlation between a dimension of foreign conflict and violence and a dimension of democratic versus authoritarian and totalitarian regimes.[13]

In *War, Power, Peace* I then looked at all quantitative studies I could find, published and unpublished, to see if in fact this proposition held up against findings in the literature on the severity of foreign violence and democracy. I found twenty-three directly relevant analyses and after considering their methods, scope, and assumptions, I concluded that on balance they supported the proposition.[14]

But I was not entirely satisfied with so relying on the literature. Moreover, there were a number of negative studies that, although in the minority or of relatively minor scope, concerned me. Also, none of these studies had really focused on the relationship between democracy and the severity of its wars; they had relevant findings arrived at in the process of researching other questions.

So for this, and also for the reasons mentioned above for the Interdemocratic Peace Proposition, I decided to do an intensive research study in 1983, the now well-cited "exception" to the consensus. The data were that which I had collected on all foreign conflict for all nations, 1976 to 1980. The democracy scale (free, partially free, nonfree) was from the Freedom House ratings of all nations on civil and political rights and liberties. With these data and an appropriate scaling of conflict by its level of violence, I found that the highest levels of violence significantly increased as the level of freedom decreased.[15] This was strong confirmation of the proposition.

After completion of this work, and another on democracy and domestic violence,[16] I then tried to reevaluate all the empirical studies relevant to this proposition that I had surveyed in *War, Power, Peace,* and those that had subsequently come to my attention.[17] This included those by Small and Singer (1976), Erich Weede (1984), and Steve Chan (1984), which had specifically directed their research at this proposition. Again I evaluated the importance, methodology, and relevance of the studies, quantitatively weighed them in terms of these considerations, and concluded that on balance the results supported the proposition, although not robustly.[18]

I will deal in detail with the Small and Singer, Chan, and Weede studies and show that their results are not as advertised. But first I will again empirically test this proposition that the more democratic a regime, the less its foreign violence. To do this and show that my results are not due to the peculiarities of my own data set, I first used the most commonly employed data on war in this area—that of Small and Singer.[19] As previously noted, they define war as any military action in which there are 1,000 or more battle dead and provide figures on battle dead for each participant in a war. It is these battle dead data that I employed to operationalize foreign violence, since as should be clear from the above, it is severity and not frequency of war that the theory predicts (the more democratic a regime and the more deadly a potential war, the more domestic and psychological restraint a leader will have to go to war[20]).

The sample consisted of all state regimes participating in the Small-Singer wars from 1900 to 1980. Each was classified as to whether democratic (= 0), authoritarian (= 1), or totalitarian (= 2). For this I again largely relied on the Small and Singer (1976) classification of democracies and Gurr's Polity II classification (1990) to make these distinctions. I rated a regime as totalitarian based on how absolute a regime's power and the degree to which it commanded virtually every aspect of society, as did the Soviet and communist Chinese regimes. All communist regimes were classified as totalitarian, as was Hitler's Germany. The underlying theoretical variable was the freedom of a people to govern their own lives as reflected in their civil liberties and political rights. In democracies people ordinarily have the most freedom, under totalitarian regimes the least.

Table 4.1 gives the comparison of means, 1900–1980, for the three different regime types included in the dyadic analysis of the previous chapter.[21] There is here also a clear step function—the less democratic the regime, the higher their mean battle dead.

TABLE 4.1
The More Democratic a Regime, the Less Intense Its Foreign Violence,
1900–1980

Democraticness	Mean Battle Dead[a]	Mean Battle-Dead as % of Population [b]	N
democratic	66,130	0.235	66
authoritarian	92,111	0.345	111
totalitarian	393,776	0.564	37

Analysis of Variance:
Rows 1 vs. 2: F-Ratio = 4.033 p < .009 (one-tailed).
Rows 1 vs. 3: F-Ratio = 1.462 p < .1 (one-tailed).
a. This is the mean of the battle dead for the given
type of regime.
b. This is the mean of the percent of the population killed
in battle for the given type of regime.

The table also presents the comparison of means for battle dead as a percent of the regime's population. This is a less important (not unimportant) measure than that of battle dead itself. For democratic people and interest groups, as well as the governing elite, that a war may cost thousands of dead, or is in fact causing hundreds of deaths per week, seems the salient factor—not that a certain percent of the population is being killed. Indeed, whether in the American pre-Pearl Harbor debate about coming actively to the aid of Great Britain, whose defeat appeared imminent, or the great domestic debate about ending the Korean or Vietnam Wars, or launching military action against Iraq after its invasion of Kuwait, no one, at least according to my resources, phrased concern about casualties in terms of the number of Americans as a percent of the population. Nonetheless, the political effect of the number of killed may be quite different for very small countries than it is for very large ones, and is included in table 4.1 for that reason. Figure 4.1 plots the means listed in the table.

As can be seen from the figure, there is a clear increase in means as we move from democratic through authoritarian to totalitarian regimes. While the means for the battle dead are too close for democratic and

FIGURE 4.1
The Less a Regime is Democratic, the More Severe Its Foreign Violence,
1900–1980

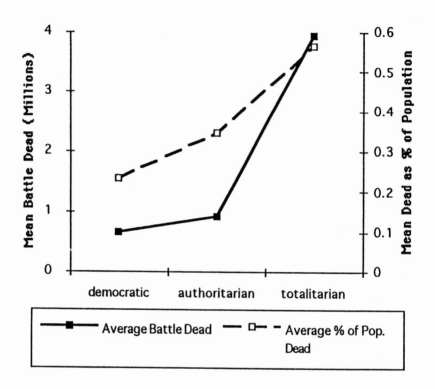

authoritarian regimes to be significant, those for both regimes differ very significantly from the totalitarian ones.[22] Moreover, the analysis of variance for the differences among the battle dead means overall is significant as well.[23] For the percent of population means, however, none of the comparisons among the means are significant and the analysis of variance is barely significant, if at all.[24] Still, the means increase as expected and this along with the highly significant and more pertinent results for battle dead give clear empirical support for the Democratic/Foreign Violence Proposition.

I also tested the proposition using a second set of data I collected in the process of doing research on democide.[25] For all 141 regimes committing any kind of democide in this century I surveyed I wide variety of estimates of their war dead in international violence and determined a total that best accorded with the quality and central tendency of the estimates. Among these 141 demociders, seventy-seven were involved in some sort of violent international conflict.

Then I selected seventy-three additional regimes that did not commit democide, that reflected major regional and cultural patterns, and that involved large differences in type of regime from previous or succeeding ones. For the foreign violence dead of these nondemociders, I relied on the Singer and Small data (keep in mind that regimes with very low battle dead are included as long as the war they joined accounted for at least 1,000 dead), supplemented by my own data for the years 1981 through 1987. This therefore gives us a sample of 214 regimes, 129 of which have been involved in some sort of foreign violence (that the sample of 214 in this case equals that tested above for the Small and Singer war data is entirely accidental). The sample is about half of all regimes existing during the years 1900 through 1987.[26]

Table 4.2 and figure 4.2 give the results. Those for the most relevant means between the types of regimes show the proper direction and are about as significant as was the case for the Small and Singer war data.[27] Results for the means of percent population killed are, however, less favorable, showing no difference between the means for democratic and authoritarian regimes, although both differ in the proper direction from totalitarian ones. This notwithstanding, the means of those killed in international violence are as they should be and provides more support for the Democratic/Foreign Violence Proposition.

There may be some underlying factor that is responsible for this relationship between democracy and violence, such as wealth. To check this I divided states into three different levels of wealth (economic development) according to their energy consumption per capita: those below the global mean, those between the mean and one standard deviation above, and those above one standard deviation.[28] Although the 214 regimes in my sample exist for different periods throughout our century, the data on wealth for all regimes was for 1981.[29] I choose to do it this way to make the data regimes comparable. If I compared the different regimes on their mid-period development, this would mean that although a country like Kaiser's Germany was among the wealthiest in 1914, it would be among the bottom third in comparison to present regimes. Indeed, all the major powers that fought wars in the early part of the century would, taking their contemporary data, be considered only mean or even poor today. To therefore compare

TABLE 4.2
The Less Democratic a Regime, the More Intense Its Foreign Violence:
Selected Sample, 1900–1987*

Democraticness	Mean Violence Dead[a]	Mean Violence Dead as % of Population [b]	N
democratic	55,000	0.49	42
authoritarian	145,000	0.49	139
totalitarian	1,001,000	0.84	33

Analysis of Variance:
    Rows 1 vs. 2: F-Ratio = 4.797 p < .0045 (one-tailed).
    Rows 1 vs. 3: F-Ratio = 1.275 p < .1 (one-tailed).

* Sample of regimes with and without violence.
a. This is the mean of the battle dead for the given
   type of regime.
b. This is the mean of the percent of the population killed
   in battle for the given type of regime.

regimes in the context of their relative wealth at the time I have fixed the measure of wealth at one point in time.[30]

With this understood, for the selected sample of 214 regimes with or without foreign violence table 4.3 subclassifies regime types by level of wealth or economic development, mean battle dead, and the mean of battle dead as a percent of the population. Figure 4.3 shows the plot of these regime means at each level of wealth. One can see immediately that the relationship between regime type and the severity of its foreign violence—the central theoretical indicator here—is independent of its wealth, as it should be. Moreover, also in the proper direction are six of nine differences within each level of wealth for the mean of battle dead as a percent of the population, with wealthy nations most departing from the proposition. This does not question the

FIGURE 4.2
The Less Democratic a Regime, the More Severe Its Foreign Violence:
Selected Sample, 1900–1987

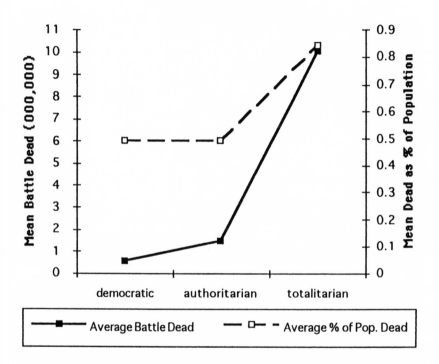

proposition, however, since the theoretical expectation is that the absolute number, not proportion, of one's potential battle dead most restrain democracies from a war. And this is shown in the perfect consistency with this theory of the table's mean differences for battle dead across levels of wealth.

Among national attributes, more are highly correlated with a nation's wealth than with any other dimension among nations. As shown by factor analyses (a method for determining the independent patterns of intercorrelation among, in this case, national attributes) whether a nation is poor or wealthy (measured by national income per capita or energy consumption per capita) accounts for their differences in educational levels, economic modernization, transportation web, health statistics, urbanization, science and technology, international transac-

TABLE 4.3
Regardless of Wealth, the Less Democratic a Regime,
the More Intense Its Foreign Violence:
Selected Sample, 1900–1987*

Wealth[a]	Democraticness	Mean Battle Dead[b]	Mean Battle Dead as % of Population [c]	N
low	democratic	733	.0002	15
low	authoritarian	127,953	.0040	107
low	totalitarian	451,737	.0090	19
mid	democratic	2,000	.0090	11
mid	authoritarian	15,467	.0070	15
mid	totalitarian	744,167	.0140	6
high	democratic	142,062	.0070	16
high	authoritarian	365,824	.0110	17
high	totalitarian	2,498,000	.0030	8

* Sample of regimes with and without violence.
a. Low = less than the mean energy consumption p.c. for 1981;
   mid = between the mean and the + 1 standard deviation;
   high = greater than the mean + 1 standard deviation.
b. This is the mean of war dead for the given
   type of regime.
c. This is the mean of the percent of the population killed
   in battle for the given type of regime.

tions, diplomatic involvement abroad, membership in international organizations, and of course trade.[31] *That the wealth available to its regime is therefore independent of the relationship of its democraticness to foreign violence is a critical test.*

There is another factor that many would consider even more important, and that is of physical power, or what I will call here *capability* (to avoid confusion with my upcoming theoretical use of the term *power* for a regime in chapter 9). For describing a nation per se, for the number and quality of attributes correlated with the dimension, its capability to exercise power is the second most important dimension. This dimension reflects such national attributes as a nation's population, geographic size, gross national product, defense expenditures, military personnel, energy resources and consumption, number of treaties, density of international communications, and sheer exports.[32] Even in considering the role of capability in the behavior of nations, it is primarily their level of wealth that accounts for the greatest variety of behavior, while that of capability is most related to their conflict.[33]

Based on the findings of factor analysis, I measured capability by

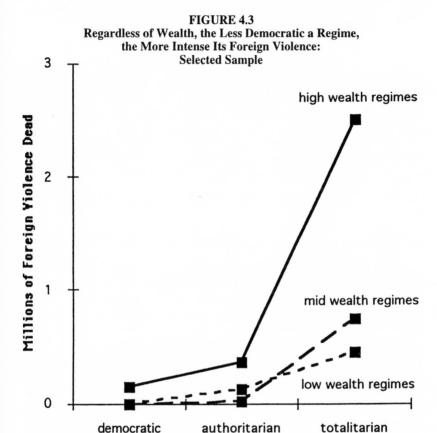

FIGURE 4.3
Regardless of Wealth, the Less Democratic a Regime,
the More Intense Its Foreign Violence:
Selected Sample

the total amount of energy consumption in a nation, and for this used 1980 data.[34] The argument for using current data here is the same as that given for wealth, perhaps even with greater force. I divided nations into low, mid, and high capability as I did on the wealth indicator: below the mean, between the mean and the mean plus one, and above this. The resulting classification of regime type by their level of capability is listed in table 4.4 and figure 4.4 shows the associated plots. The results are all as they should be for mean battle dead: regardless of their capability (or power, GNP, size), *democracies have the least foreign violence.*

As with wealth, in table 4.4 six of the nine differences in mean dead as percent of the population are in the right direction, with the most capable nations departing from the proposition. Considering also the

TABLE 4.4
Regardless of Capability, the Less Democratic a Regime,
the More Intense Its Foreign Violence:
Selected Sample, 1900–1987*

Capability[a]	Democraticness	Mean Battle Dead[b]	Mean Battle Dead as % of Population [c]	N
low	democratic	0	.0000	9
low	Authoritarian	817	.0030	71
low	Totalitarian	29,067	.0100	15
mid	democratic	6,000	.0060	22
mid	Authoritarian	111,397	.0070	58
mid	Totalitarian	366,417	.0100	12
high	democratic	197,636	.0060	11
high	Authoritarian	1,362,300	.0040	10
high	Totalitarian	4,699,833	.0020	6

* Sample of regimes with and without violence.
a. Low = less than the mean energy consumption for 1980;
   mid = between the mean and the + 1 standard deviation;
   high = greater than the mean + 1 standard deviation.
b. This is the mean of war dead for the given
   type of regime.
c. This is the mean of the percent of the population killed

results for wealth in table 4.3, it is among the Big Powers that the correlation between democracy and the proportion of their population killed breaks down. This simply shows that for the Big Powers, *realpolitik* dominates over proportional human costs. However, when it comes to the absolute costs of violence, as shown by the mean battle dead differences in tables 4.3 and 4.4, even for Big Powers, realpolitik for democracies is secondary.

I have tried to establish so far two things in this chapter. First is that the consensus in the literature is that while democracies do not (or rarely) make war on each other, they proportionally make as much war as do nondemocracies. Second, that when the Democratic/Foreign Violence Proposition is defined in terms of the severity of violence, instead of frequencies, we get a perfect negative relationship between the degree of democracy and the number of people for a regime killed in international wars or violence.

With this as background, let us look at the studies that are most often cited as showing that democracies are as warlike as other regimes. Among these is certainly the aforementioned article by Melvin

FIGURE 4.4
Regardless of Capability, the Less Democratic a Regime,
the More Intense Its Foreign Violence:
Selected Sample, 1900–1987

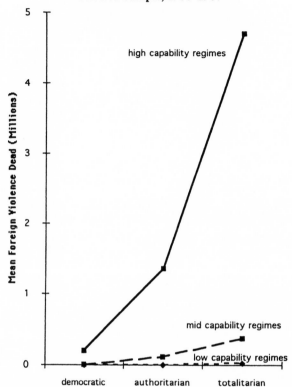

Small and J. David Singer (1976) that followed up the Dean Babst finding of no war between democracies. Although Babst's findings were dyadic and Small and Singer do present a list of wars, participants, and whether they were democratic or not, virtually all their statistical analyses are directed at the wars by, not between, democracies. In one table they show that wars involving democracies are not significantly shorter or longer than those fought by nondemocracies. But this is an uninteresting finding, since I know of no theory that would argue that wars involving democracies should be shorter.

Small and Singer do, however, have a table of battle deaths for democratic and nondemocratic participants from 1816 through 1965. This does test the proposition properly in terms of severity. They find the mean battle deaths for all interstate wars to be 91,937 for democracies and 167,270 for nondemocracies,[35] or near 82 percent higher. This difference of means is comparable to what I found above for severity. However, they then apply a significance test (t-test) to this, which gives virtually even odds of there being a real difference but which is incorrectly calculated—the corrected test gives odds of near 7 to 1 or greater of this result being by chance. They also give the mean battle dead excluding the two world wars, which is 5,059 killed for democracies versus 38,436 for nondemocracies. Here also their significance test is wrong; the correct one would make this highly significant—odds of 500 to 1 or more of being a chance result.[36] On balance these results support the Democratic/Foreign Violence Proposition, but have been almost universally cited in line with Small and Singer's mistaken conclusion, as showing that democracies are no more or less warlike as nondemocracies.[37]

A second frequently cited study on this proposition is that by Steve Chan (1984). Using the Small and Singer war data, Chan did three analyses to determine the relationship between democracy and war. The first was on all wars (interstate, colonial, and others) from 1816 through 1980, measured by the number of war years. This is a count of the years during which democratic or nondemocratic (he coded all regimes himself as free or unfree) regimes had war. For these measures he found significant positive relationships between democracy and the number of their years of war for the entire period from 1816 through 1980 and the subperiods 1816 to 1945 and 1946 to 1972; however, for interstate war years there was only a significant relationship for 1946 to 1976. But for all war years or only interstate ones, there was a significant negative relationship between democracy and war years for 1973 through 1980.[38] But the results for all wars should be ignored, since they include mainly colonial wars and count only the independent states as fighting. Presumably those uncounted nonstate groups fighting on the other side were generally unfree and by their omission Chan skews the results against democracies. Thus I only will consider interstate wars where all sides were counted. And for the interstate war-years there is one significant positive (for 1973 to 1980) and one negative result (for 1946 to 1972), both equally significant. Thus, of one accepts these war year counts, the result is mixed.

However, his analysis suffers from the severe problem with war frequencies mentioned above, since he is in fact counting the number of wars a regime is engaged in *for each year*. He justifies this, in part, by quoting from my 1983 study, where I apparently did the same.[39] But I was then measuring the severity of violence reached for each year, not counting the frequency of violence.[40]

Finally, he used the Small and Singer (1982) war data, defined by at least 1,000 battle dead for a war. As discussed in the last chapter, this includes some nations with few killed while possibly excluding those with several hundred, and in any case equates those with only dozens of battle dead to those with millions.

Chan's second analysis tried to determine if democracies initiated fewer wars, and limited itself this time to the frequency of interstate wars (not war years) for which democracies or nondemocracies were on the initiator or defender's side. While the direction of the frequencies favored the proposition, they were nonsignificant.[41] But these were frequencies again, and moreover although many including Chan favor the idea that democracies should initiate wars less often than do nondemocracies, this is irrelevant to the proposition: nothing is stated about whether democracies tend to be or to side with the violent aggressor or not. After all, a democracy may find a hostile state clearly preparing to attack it, and the only recourse for its own survival is a preemptive strike (as was the case for Israel in its attack on Egypt in 1967, launching the Six Day War).

Chan's third analysis was a cross-tabulation of a regime's change in internal freedom with its wars.[42] He found that for thirty-two states, eight had more wars than expected during their freer years; twenty-four had less. Moreover, leaving out two cases significantly opposing the proposition that Chan discounts, there were seven cases "strongly" and significantly favoring the proposition (only 1.6 significant cases would be expected by chance). That is, as a regime changes from democratic to nondemocratic or vice versa its frequency of wars tends to change as one would expect by the proposition. Still, here also frequencies were used and thus this favorable result also must be ignored.

In sum, out of Chan's three analyses, the result of the first is ambiguous (though strongly positive for the post-World War II years), the second is irrelevant, and the third is supportive. This means that *on balance, Chan should be cited as tending to favor the proposition,* if one accepts the use of frequencies as relevant.[43] Uniformly, however, he has been cited without qualification as showing that democracies are as warlike as nondemocracies, surely a misreading of his work. In any case, because of his use of frequencies and for the reasons previously explained I cannot accept his results as truly relevant to the proposition.

The final study often cited as negative on the proposition is that by Eric Weede (1984). He collected data on all interstate wars from 1960 to 1980 using data from Small and Singer (1982), Butterworth (1976), and Kende (1979). He measured democracy according the Bollen's scales (1980), the Freedom House ratings,[44] and other sources. Then for each collection of data he calculated the correlation (product moment) of the frequency of wars with democracy for the years 1960 through 1980, 1960 through 1974, and 1975 through 1980. He found for Butterworth wars (1960–1974) a significant negative correlation (one-tailed); he found for Small and Singer interstate wars an almost or barely significant negative correlation for 1960 through 1980, a highly significant negative correlation for 1975 through 1980, and a nonsignificant positive correlation for 1960 through 1974[45]; and for Kende's wars he found a nonsignificant negative correlation for 1960 to 1980, a nonsignificant positive correlation for 1960 to 1974, and a significant negative correlation for 1975 to 1980.[46] That is, seven correlations out of ten were in the proper direction, among which *five* were significant and one was almost or barely (at p < .09) significant, depending on how much random error one assumes in the data. And three were in the opposite direction, *none* significant and all for the subperiod 1960 to 1974. On balance, therefore, *these results tend to favor the proposition,* taking Weede's way of evaluating significance. Actually, they very strongly favor the proposition. This, even though Weede concludes that

> democratic states were about as frequently involved in war as other states were in the sixties and seventies. This is the most important finding of this analysis . . . [which] contradicts Rummel's . . . [1983] findings.[47]

Weede carried out one more study. To compensate for difficulties in his democracy scale, he dichotomized the scale into democracies and nondemocracies, and war frequencies into presence of at least one war or no war for the regime. The result for the different data sets on war and the three different periods is that *all* the cross-tabulations are in the proper direction, although only one specific cross-tabulation is significant by itself.[48] But here also the results are questionable. Although frequencies are dichotomized into the presence or absence of war, they still do not avoid the problem of equating regimes with a few killed in war with those losing millions.

Over all, then, were we to accept frequencies as an adequate test of the proposition, we should conclude that *Weede's results are on balance favorable for the proposition.* Nonetheless, he also has been cited as finding that democracies are no more nor less warlike than other types of regimes.[49]

Thus for the three most cited studies, those of Small and Singer, Chan, and Weede, that are at the core of the consensus in the field that the proposition is false, Small and Singer's results tend to support the proposition, and if only one accepts their measurement of violence Chan and Weede also support the proposition. In the case of Small and Singer, they used an appropriate measure of severity (battle dead) and their results are relevant to the proposition. But the Chan and Weede studies are inappropriate, since they measure violence by the number of years at war, by the frequency of wars, or by the existence of war, none of which measure the severity of violence central to the proposition.

There are five other studies following on these that do analyses bearing on the proposition. But they all use the Small and Singer (1982) war or the Gochman and Maoz (1984) militarized dispute data and cross-tabulate or correlate violence or war frequencies with some measure of democracy. Were their use of frequencies relevant to the proposition, one study would be positive (Morgan and Schwebach, 1992),[50] two studies would tend to be ambiguous (Domke, 1988; Maoz and Abdolali, 1989), and three studies negative (Cole, 1990; Morgan and Campbell, 1991; and Mansfield and Snyder, 1995), none strongly so.

I should also mention the study of *Crises in the Twentieth Century* by Jonathan Wilkenfeld, Michael Brecher, and Sheila Moser. Among other things they cross-tabulate 627 actors involved in 278 crises, from 1929 to 1979, according to whether they were democratic, authoritarian, or military dictatorships. They found that

> the more authoritarian a regime the greater was the probability of violent crisis triggers [provoking crisis by the use of violence] (democratic—37%, civil authoritarian—49%, military—56%). . . . As expected, there was a higher frequency of violence responses by military regimes (50%) than by democratic (30%) and civil authoritarian regimes (33%). Non-violent military responses were most often employed by democratic regimes (32%), compared to 20% for the other two types. . . .

In short, the effect of type of regime on an actor's responsive behavior was evident for violent response—the more authoritarian a regime the more likely its response to a crisis would be violent.

The data on crisis management technique reveal an even sharper escalation of violence [democratic (37 percent), civil authoritarian (49 percent) and military regime (63 percent), with a considerable higher tendency toward full-scale war as well (18 percent and 21 percent for civil authoritarian and democratic, 39 percent for military regimes]. Conversely, democratic regimes that were most likely to perceive non-violent acts as triggers to their crises tended to choose pacific (crisis management techniques), with negotiation the most frequent among them: it was highest among democratic regimes (32 percent), and dropped to 11 percent for military regimes,[51] and are relevant to and supportive of the proposition and positive.

In sum, then, we find that when the proposition is properly tested in terms of the severity of violence, all correlations or cross-tabulations of democracy and violence are in the proper direction. That is, democracy is less warlike (severity) than other regimes. This is contrary to the prevailing wisdom among students of war, but upon careful inspection the results underlying their consensus have been shown: (1) to be based on frequency measures of violence or war and therefore theoretically to imply (since the consensus also accepts that democracies do not or rarely make war on each other) that as democracies increase in number the number of wars between nondemocracies will tend to zero; (2) to equate for a nation wars involving a few dozen killed with wars killing millions; and (3) to even then tend to support the proposition, not negate it.

Regardless, one does not need to rely on the nuances of these studies or their logic. As empirically shown in my 1983 study, by other work in the field that used relevant and appropriate variables, and by the analyses I did here, when properly measured democracies are less violent than nondemocracies.

Notes

1. Wright, (1942, p. 841).
2. Doyle (1983, p. 225).
3. Dixon (1994, p. 1).
4. Starr (1992c, p. 43).
5. Morgan and Campbell (1991, p. 188).

6. Kilgour (1991, p. 267)
7. Geva, DeRouen, and Mintz (1993, p. 217).
8. Bueno de Mesquita and Lalman (1992, p. 146).
9. Weede (1992, p. 377).
10. Czempiel (1992, p. 264).
11. Rummel (1979, pp. 292-293).
12. Ibid., italics added.
13. Rummel (1968, 1972, 1979b).
14. Rummel (1979, p. 293).
15. This significance was for two different ways of calculating the highest violence in the sample, which were significant at chi-squares, $p < .006$ and $p < .5 \times 10^{-10}$, one-tailed. Also the correlation between regime type and severity was significant at $p. < .05$, one tailed.
16. Rummel (1984b).
17. Rummel (1985).
18. I leave to the sociologist of social science why I am continually cited as the exception to the alleged findings that democracies are no less warlike than other regimes, when in my 1979 book and 1985 article I list over a dozen studies whose empirical results also support the proposition.
19. Small and Singer (1982).
20. See chapters 10 and 12.
21. The average battle dead for the given type of regime is the sum of all those killed in battle of all the regimes of that type (such as Americans killed in battle for the United States plus Canadians for Canada plus Australians for Australia, etc., for democracies) divided by the number of regimes of that type.
22. For both Bonferroni adjusted pairwise comparisons and Tukey, $p < .015$ (one-tail).
23. F-ratio of 4.03, $p < .008$ (one-tail).
24. The significance for the analysis of variance is $p < .1$ (one-tailed), and that for the paired comparisons among the averages are nonsignificant.
25. Rummel (1994, 1995).
26. How many regimes have existed depends on how different regimes have been defined. For the Gurr (1990) Polity II data there are 427 regimes, from 1900 to 1987. And I largely have relied on Polity II characterizations of regimes, but adjusting the count where I thought Polity II was mistaken. For example, Polity II gives three Chinese regimes from the years 1949 to 1987; I count only one. Polity II gives three regimes for the Soviet Union, from 1918 to 1987; I count only one here as well.
27. The Bonferroni adjustment and Tukey pairwise comparisons were significant at $p < .01$ (one-tailed).
28. I should also point out that energy consumption per capita has been found by factor analysis to be among the best indicators of the wealth of nations (Rummel, 1972, 1979b).
29. Data were from Global Data Manager (1990).
30. A way around this problem is to use the standard score of a nation's wealth at the beginning of its war (or the average standard scores if it has more than one war). This requires in effect that the year-by-year wealth of all nations, from 1900 to 1987, be determined in order to calculate these standard scores. This was beyond my resources.
   Upon reading this footnote in draft, James Lee Ray kindly made available to me an IBM disk of Correlates of War attribute data. I use a Macintosh and with

considerable frustration must confess that, even trying a roundabout way through the University of Hawaii UNIX system and trying to download through a modem, I was not able to convert the data into a file usable through my Macintosh statistical programs.

31. Wealth is a distinct dimension from one with which political characteristics are correlated.

32. The capability dimension is also distinct from that with which political characteristics are correlated.

33. This statement is based on a simultaneous factor analysis (called super-p factor analysis) of behavior and attributes for 1950, 1955, 1960, and 1963; and a canonical analysis of dyadic behavior regressed on the distances between nations, such as along wealth and capability dimensions, among others. See Rummel (1979b).

34. Data are from Global Data Manager (1990).

35. Small and Singer (1976, table 6).

36. The t-test should be 2.84, p < .0023 (one-tailed), not the 1.45 Small and Singer give. In a personal communication of 10 September 1980, I informed Singer of the errors in this and the previously mentioned t-test. Scott G. Gates, an assistant on Singer's Correlates of War Project (COW), subsequently responded "on behalf of the COW project" that they had verified my calculations. In a note written on Gate's response Singer confirmed his acceptance of this.

37. They do have another table giving the number of democracies and nondemocracies participating in wars (table 3). The number of democracies is always a small percentage of the total number of nations involved, but nothing can be made of this without knowing the total number of democratic regimes in the international system.

38. Chan (1984, table 2). The significance tests were by chi-square.

39. Rummel (1983, p. 53).

40. Admittedly, my phrasing of this led Chan to conclude I was using frequencies. However, my previous discussion of the methodology and proposition should have warned him away from this interpretation. I should also say that when I wrote the 1983 article I did not realize that virtually without exception subsequent research would use frequencies.

In any case, Chan (1993, p. 207) now also recognizes the problem in frequency counts equating vastly different kinds of wars. He writes that "research on the democracy/war proneness question has focused on war involvement as a dichotomous dependent variable. At the very least, *this approach assumes that the analyst has a homogeneous set of war involvements.* Thus, World War II and the Western power's participation in China's Boxer Rebellion are given the same weight." Moreover, he sees the value of using a severity measure like "casualties," and points out that "to focus on an undifferentiated categorical variable of war involvement [frequencies] when more sensitive scalar data on the destructiveness of war efforts are available does not seem to be helpful to our analytic interests. I suspect that *depending on the particular measure of war or conflict used, one can arrive at very different conclusions about the relative pacifism of democracies.*" Indeed.

41. Ibid., table 3.

42. Ibid., table 4.

43. Chan has come around to the view that democracies may be more peaceful (but still in terms of frequencies). In his latest piece (1993, p. 206) he wrote: " To the extent that due to their limited capabilities many nondemocracies have had less opportunities to get into wars with one another (such as between Nepal and

Senegal, or between Ethiopia and El Salvador), and to the extent that due to their greater capabilities democracies have had more such opportunities among themselves and vis-à-vis many more nondemocracies, the historical data of war involvement would appear to lend greater support to the hypothesis that democracies are more pacific than nondemocracies."

44. These are given in the January-February numbers for each year.

45. I will ignore the results for extrasystemic wars, since only independent states are counted.

46. Weede (1984, table 2). All significance levels were one-tailed.

47. Ibid., p. 637.

48. Ibid., table 3. The direction of the relationship is given by Yule's Q; significance by chi-square (one-tailed). If we assume that there is no relationship between democracy and having fought wars, then the probability of getting ten cross tabulations out of ten in the hypothesized direction by chance is 0.001. But these ten cross-tabulations were not all independent. The different data sets overlap, as do the subperiods with the full periods, and this is enough to vitiate the probability. Nonetheless, it is possible for these ten cross-tabulations to be either positive and negative and therefore that they were all in the proper direction should be considered substantively important, if one accepts the underlying measurements.

    Note also that it is incorrect to test separately the significance of coefficients arrayed in a table as Weede does here. For 100 such coefficients, five should be significant at p < .05 entirely by chance.

49. Weede ignored the Interdemocratic Peace Proposition and as he later wrote, did not accept it at this time. He now does. In his latest article (1992) he wrote on it, "I did not accept the "peace among democracies" proposition then [in his previous three articles]. . . . Now, the weight of the evidence makes me accept this proposition" (p. 378).

50. When a revised version of this chapter was under consideration for publication in the *European Journal of International Relations,* two reviewers, one strongly, argued that Bremer (1992) should also be included as positive, since "he found that democratic-nondemocratic dyads are significantly less likely to become engaged in war than nondemocraticnondemocatic-nondemocratic dyads." But these results are dyadic, not monadic, and thus irrelevant to whether democracies are more or less warlike. However, these results do bear positively on the different proposition that the more democratic two regimes, the less likely there will be violence between them.

    Russett (1993) does not present results relevant to the monadic proposition, but in a personal communication he reported reanalyzing his data on democracy, wars, and disputes. He found that the data, from 1946 to 1986, clearly supported the proposition.

51. Wilkenfeld, Brecher, and Moser (1988, p. 197).

5

Democracies are Most Internally Peaceful

The Democracy/Internal Collective Violence Proposition: The More Democratic a Regime, the Less Severe Its Internal Collective Violence.

The previous propositions concern foreign violence and, as we have seen, democracy works to reduce or, between democracies, eliminate interstate violence. All the recent quantitative work of which I am aware has focused on this relationship between democracy and foreign violence. But because of the lives lost, there is another, *even more important fact* about democracy and violence—it sharply reduces the severity of domestic collective violence, genocide, and mass murder by governments. The Democracy/Domestic Violence Proposition concerns the first part of this. It says that democracy is inversely related to the intensity of collective internal violence, such as revolutions, bloody coups d'états, political assassinations, antigovernment terrorist bombings, guerrilla warfare, insurgencies, civil wars, mutinies, and rebellions.

There are a large number of quantitative studies that have in the process of pursuing other questions correlated or cross-tabulated measures of democracy, among others, with domestic violence. I found thirty-one such studies (excluding my own, to be discussed below), of which in methodology and measurement eighteen were directly relevant to the proposition. Of these the empirical results of five studies strongly supported it, twelve were positive, and only one was negative, but not strongly so. These are listed in table 5.1.[1]

TABLE 5.1
Empirical Studies Overwhelmingly Find that
Democracies Have the Least Internal Violence

Studies [a]	Results
Alcock and Eckhardt (1974)	strongly positive
Feierabend and Feierabend (1971, 1972)	strongly positive
Feierabend and Feierabend (1973)	strongly positive
Nesvold (1971)	strongly positive
Yough (1981)	strongly positive
Alcock (1974, 1975)	positive
Banks (1972)	positive
Bwy (1972)	positive
Feierabend, Feierabend, and Nesvold (1969)	positive
Flanigan and Fogelman (1970)	positive
Gurr (1969)	positive
Gurr (1979a, 1979b)	positive
Gurr and Lichbach (1979)	positive
Orbell and Rutherford (1973)	positive
Phillips and Hall (1970)	positive
Tilly, Tilly, and Tilly (1975)	positive
Zinnes and Wilkenfeld (1971)	positive
Gregg and Banks (1965)	negative

a. These are studies directly relevant to the proposition. For fourteen
additional studies the were indirectly relevant or while relevant
could not be used because of the data procedures or techniques,
and for notes and qualifications on all the studies, see
Rummel (1984b, table 8).

To further satisfy myself that the proposition was empirically sound,
in the early 1980s I did an intensive statistical analysis of it. I collected all incidents of internal conflict and violence for all nations on
thirteen indicators of violence from the daily press, 1976 to 1980. I
then scaled the resulting data from low to high violence. And for the
democracy scale I used the Freedom House ratings of nations in their
civil liberties and political rights.[2] The sample constituted all nations
for each of the five years.

I first did a cross tabulation of whether nations were free, partially
free, or unfree, with increasing levels of internal collective violence.
The results for all regimes were strongly positive and highly significant.[3] By implication of the proposition, we should also find that the

TABLE 5.2
The Less Democratic a Regime,
the More Severe Its Internal Political Violence:
Selected Sample, 1900–1987*

Democraticness	Mean Internal Violence Dead[a]	Mean Internal Violence Dead as % of Population [b]	N
democratic	11,500	0.14	42
authoritarian	33,660	0.59	139
totalitarian	181,606	1.48	33

Analysis of Variance:
  Rows 1 vs. 2: F-Ratio = 5.36 p < .005 (one-tailed).
  Rows 1 vs. 3: F-Ratio = 6.15 p < .003 (one-tailed).

* Sample of regimes with and without violence.
a. This is the mean of the battle dead for the given
   type of regime.
b. This is the mean of the percent of the population killed
   in internal violence for the given type of regime.

peak level of violence reached in each nation should decline, the more democratic its regime. That is, there should be an upper bound on internal political violence that decreases with greater democraticness. This is in fact what I also found, and with great statistical significance.[4]

Since these results have been so robust and noncontroversial, I have not kept track of such studies since the early 1980s. One, however, that did come to my attention recently is that by A. J. Jongman. He has a chart that ranks countries according to their human rights and number of casualties from internal wars. He shows that those nations with the highest killed domestically have the worst human rights problems.[5]

I can also report on a new statistical analysis here. Recall that for the analysis of foreign violence I used a selected sample of 214 regimes, where 141 of them were nations with some form of democide. In the process of collecting these democide data I also collected information on the extent of their internal political violence and the number

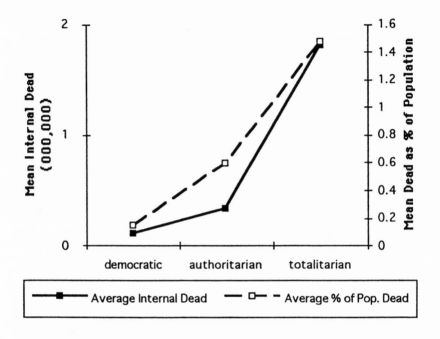

FIGURE 5.1
The Less Democratic a Regime,
the More Severe Its Internal Political Violence:
Selected Sample, 1900–1987

killed. Then I added to these 141 regimes seventy-three others without democide, for which I took data on the number killed in internal violence killed from Small and Singer.[6] Then on all the data I did the cross-tabulation by democraticness shown in table 5.2 and plotted the results in figure 5.1. Analysis of variance shows the overall differences among the means to be significant, as given at the bottom of the table.

Overall, then, on the basis of all my results described above and those published by others, I conclude that the Democracy/Internal Violence Proposition states a well-supported fact about nations.

Notes

1. As noted in the table, the results of these studies are qualified in Rummel (1984b, table 8). Many also are extensively discussed by Rummel (1976, chapter 35) in the context of various related theoretical propositions about conflict, such as that change produces conflict.

2. I also scaled nations according to their economic freedom. Including this did not change the positive nature of the results and will be ignored here.
3. See Rummel (1984b, table 5). The main result for the full sample was significant (chi-square) at $p < .5 \times 10^{-10}$ (one-tailed).
4. Ibid., p. 458. The correlation squared was .85, significant at $p < .000004$ (one-tailed).
5. Jongman (1990).
6. Small and Singer (1982, table 13.2).

6

Democracies Don't Murder Their Citizens

Democracy/Democide Proposition: The More
Democratic a Regime, the Less its Democide.

This is a new proposition. It asserts that the more democracy the less democide (genocide and mass murder by a regime). It is a counterpart to the internal violence proposition that focuses on collective violence—that between a political regime and some opposing group. Both sides have arms and people are killed in armed combat or clashes. For democide, however, the killing is wholly one-sided. Only the regime is armed and those it kills are in its control or otherwise helpless.

As everyone knows, Nazi Germany murdered near some 6,000,000 Jews. That was genocide, a type of democide. What is much less known is that this regime also killed millions of non-Jewish Poles, Ukrainians, and Russians, and tens or hundreds of thousands of others, such as Yugoslavs, Balts, Czechs, and Frenchmen. In total Nazi Germany murdered around 21,000,000 people.[1] But this incredible toll is overshadowed by the genocide and mass murder (democide) of the Soviet Union, which from 1917 to 1987 murdered some 61,000,000 people, near 55,000,000 of them its own citizens (among the foreigners killed were Romanians, Bulgarians, Hungarians, Poles, Germans, Czechs, Koreans, Japanese, and others that fell under Soviet rule). Stalin alone is responsible for almost 43,000,000 of these deaths.[2] Even those killed by Communist China, especially under Mao Tsetung, slightly over 35,000,000, exceed the Nazi toll.[3]

But then there are the lesser murderers, such as Nationalist China under Chiang Kai-shek (about 10,000,000 killed), Japan in World War

91

II (almost 6,000,000), and Cambodia under the Khmer Rouge (some 2,000,000). Indeed, for our century there are also about a dozen other regimes that have murdered in the millions. Some of these are well-known for their killing; some have been forgotten; some never did reach public consciousness. Table 6.1 lists their total democide, domestic democide, and more specifically, their genocide. It also shows their annual rate of democide, the percent of their population they murdered each year. Figure 6.1 graphs the democide of the megamurderers and their annual rates.[4]

For over eight years I combed through thousands of general works, specialized studies, human rights reports, journal articles, and news sources to do the full accounting of democide shown in the table. I collected and consolidated almost 8,200 estimates of genocide, politicide, massacres, terrorism, extrajudicial executions, and other types of intentional cold-blooded government killing. This covered all state regimes, quasi-state regimes (e.g., the communist soviet enclaves in Nationalist China or the White army territories in Russia during the civil war in 1920), and autonomous groups (such as the Palestine Liberation Organization). The total, a conservative figure that well may be too low, is also given in the table.

As shown, over 169,000,000 people probably have been murdered by one regime or another. If very high estimates for specific regimes are taken into account, this total could even reach near 341,000,000 killed.

The listed fifteen megamurderers alone have murdered over 151,000,000 people, *almost four times the almost 38,500,000 war dead for all this century's international and civil wars up to 1987.*[5] The most totalitarian regimes, that is the communist USSR, China, and preceding Mao guerrillas, Khmer Rouge Cambodia, Vietnam, North Korea, and Yugoslavia, as well Nazi Germany, account for nearly 128,000,000 of them, or 84 percent (this alone is strong support for the Democracy/Democide Proposition). In addition to this democide by these megamurderers, 203 lesser murdering regimes have killed near 17,700,000 more people.

Moreover, as listed in the table genocide accounted for almost 38,600,000 of those murdered overall, or near 23 percent of this toll. *This alone is virtually the same in number as those war dead in all this century's international and civil wars.*

What are the causes and conditions underlying this democide, and genocide in particular? Based on case studies of each of the fifteen megamurderers[6] and multivariate statistical analysis of all 141 state regimes committing democide and for comparison severity-seven regimes without democide (the same selected sample of 214 regimes that I used to test the previous propositions), I can say the following.[7]

The more totalitarian and less democratic a regime, the more its democide. A political regime's domestic democide in general and its genocide in particular can be predicted to the degree that Power is indiscriminate and irresponsible. Power is the means through which a regime can accomplish its goals or whims. When a regime's power is magnified through its forceful intervention in all aspects of society, including its control over religion, the economy, and even the family, then when conjoined with an absolutist ideology or religion, mass killing may appear to its rulers a practical and justified means of achieving their ends. Thus we have the megamurders shown in the table, such as the totalitarian USSR, communist China, Nazi Germany, and Cambodia under the Khmer Rouge. And thus, when the rulers of such regimes find for whatever reason that the continued existence of a social group is incompatible with their beliefs or goals, totalitarian power enables them to destroy that group. Genocide follows. On the other hand, democratic elites generally lack the power to, and democratic culture anyway opposes, the outright extermination of people or social groups for whatever reason.

Pictures speak louder than words and figure 6.2 well displays this relationship. The vertical dimension in the figure is domestic democide, which in this relationship also includes genocide. The two other dimensions define the two scales, one for totalitarian power and other for democratic power, which together predict democide (and genocide). The figure also shows that as a regime has greater totalitarian power its overall domestic democide in general and genocide in particular are likely to increase exponentially.

The likelihood of genocide by a regime increases significantly the greater the characteristic number of its people killed in war and rebellion. Independent of a regime's power, the more a regime has or will suffer dead from involvement in war or rebellion, the greater its foreign democide and genocide. Clearly, war or rebellion provide an excuse and cover for a regime to eliminate those social groups it finds objectionable. But also, analysis shows that over the life of a regime the more disposed it is to be involved in deadly foreign and domestic

TABLE 6.1
Governments Have Murdered Nearly
170,000,000 People in Our Century*

| REGIMES | YEARS | DEMOCIDE (000)[a] | | | ANNUAL |
		TOTAL	DOMESTIC	GENOCIDE	RATE %[b]
MEGAMURDERERS	1900-87	151,491	116,380	33,476	.92 [d]
U.S.S.R.	1917-87	61,911	54,769	10,000	.42
China (PRC)	1949-87	35,236	35,236	375	.12
Germany	1933-45	20,946	762	16,315	.09
China (KMT)	1928-49	10,075	10,075	Nil	.07 [e]
Japan	1936-45	5,964	Nil	Nil	Nil
China (Mao Soviets) [c]	1923-49	3,466	3,466	Nil	.05 [e]
Cambodia	1975-79	2,035	2,000	541	8.16
Turkey	1909-18	1,883	1,752	1,883	.96
Vietnam	1945-87	1,670	944	Nil	.10
North Korea [f]	1948-87	1,663	1,293	Nil	.25
Poland	1945-48	1,585	1,585	1,585	1.99
Pakistan	1958-87	1,503	1,503	1,500	.06
Mexico [f]	1900-20	1,417	1,417	100	.45
Yugoslavia (Tito)	1944-87	1,072	987	675	.12
Russia [f]	1900-17	1,066	591	502	.02
LESSER MURDERERS	1900-87	17,707	13,529	5,090	.26
WORLD TOTAL	1900-87	169,198	129,909	38,566	.09 [g]

* From R.J. Rummel (1994).
a. Includes genocide, politicide, and mass murder; excludes war-dead. Genocide totals are a subset of the domestic totals. All figures are a most probable mid-estimates in low to high ranges.
b. The percent of a population killed in democide per year of the regime
c. Guerilla period.
d. Average.
e. The rate is the average of that for three successive periods.
f. Suspected megamurderer: data insufficient for a final judgment.
g. The world annual rate is calculated for the mid-century 1944 global population.

FIGURE 6.1
The Distribution of Megamurderers and
Their Annual Rate

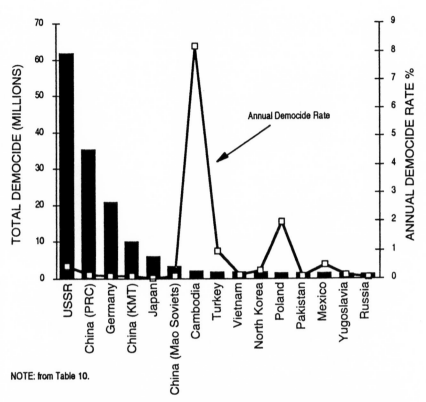

NOTE: from Table 10.

wars, the more likely it will commit democide, whether or not carried out during these wars. This is because totalitarian power not only underlies democide and genocide, but also because this power underlies as well the occurrence and intensity of war.

The social diversity of a nation is not correlated with nor does it predict its regime's overall domestic or foreign democide or the regime's genocide in particular. This is the most difficult to accept, especially in the light of the present (1993–1994) genocide in Bosnia-Hercegovina, Rwanda, and Burundi, but cases studies and quantitative analyses are consistent. A nation's ethnic, religious, racial, linguistic, or national divisions, the relative size of such minorities, or the nation's overall social diversity are uncorrelated with its domestic or foreign democide or its genocide. This is true even when various controls are

FIGURE 6.2
The Less Democratic and More Totalitarian a Regime,
the More It Tends to Murder Its Own Citizens

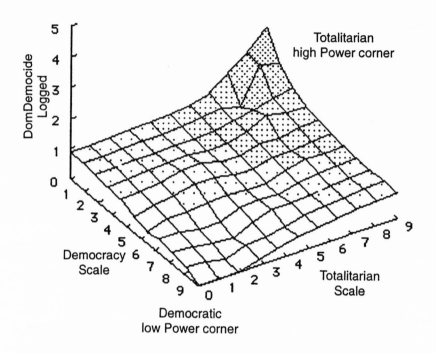

introduced for the level of power, involvement in war or rebellion, education and level of economic development, or the nature of the culture. In other words, some regimes whose societies are riven with social diversity will commit little genocide and some regimes with little diversity will commit much genocide; and some with much diversity will also commit much genocide and those with little diversity will have little genocide. Substantial diversity is neither necessary nor sufficient for genocide to occur.

And this lack of correlation is apparently not caused by any intervening or masking conditions. For domestic genocide to occur, of course, there must be some social diversity and such usually will exist even in apparently homogenous nations. For example, Japan is looked at as highly homogenous, yet its premilitarist regime allowed 2,600 to

11,000 Korean residents in Japan to be massacred after the 1923 Yokohama earthquake (Koreans as a group were accused of poisoning public water, hoarding food, and starting fires). It is not diversity that predicts to genocide, but a regime's power. Even large numbers of a small minority have been massacred by authoritarian or totalitarian regimes, as in Khmer Roug Cambodia, while in democracies very large minorities usually are secure in their lives, as in Switzerland.

The nature of a nation's culture is uncorrelated with and does not predict to its regime's overall foreign or domestic democide or its genocide. This is almost as hard to accept as the lack of correlation of diversity, but the analyses are consistent for this also. The variation among regimes in the degree to which they are Christian or Moslem, or influenced by English culture, or antiwomen, or even whether they are located in Africa, Europe, Asia, and so forth does not generally explain a regime's overall domestic or foreign democide or its genocide. As with diversity this is generally true for genocide even if one introduces various socioeconomic controls.

The level of education or economic development of a nation is uncorrelated with and does not predict to the foreign or domestic democide or the genocide of its regime. This finding may be no surprise to those who realize that just before war was launched by Hitler against Poland in 1939 Germany was considered one of the most developed and educated nations in the world. Moreover, Japan was the most educated and developed nation in Asia at the same time it was carrying out mass extermination campaigns in China. The killing by Nazi Germany and militarist Japan alone should caution those who believe that improving national education and wealth will decrease the likelihood of genocide and mass murder. The results of statistical analysis and case studies confirm this in general. There is no meaningful correlation of these socioeconomic characteristics and regime's overall democide or genocide specifically. This is also true even when various political controls or a regime's involvement in war and rebellion is taken into account.

The bottom line is that it is the power of a regime that accounts for its killing. The degree of a regime's power along a democratic to totalitarian scale is a direct underlying structural cause of domestic democide, including genocide. Moreover, acting through war and rebellion it is an indirect cause of foreign democide as well. The more power a regime has, the more it can act arbitrarily according to the whims and desires of the elite, the more it will make war on others and murder its foreign and domestic subjects. The more constrained the power of regimes, the more it is diffused, checked and balanced, the less it will aggress on others and commit democide. At the extremes of Power, totalitarian regimes have slaughtered their people by the tens of *millions,* while many democracies can barely bring themselves to execute even serial murderers.

In other words, the Democratic/Democide proposition is strongly supported. Democratic freedom preserves not only peace, but also life.

Notes

1. Rummel (1992).
2. Rummel (1990).
3. Rummel (1991).
4. From Rummel (1994).
5. There is, of course, the problem of separating democide during war from those killed in the war. But this is not as much of a problem as it may seem, since much of the war-time democide is as clearly democide as was the Holocaust. However, there are marginal cases, such as the dead from the bombing or shelling of an urban area, or the deaths of POWs from disease. I have used as my guide to what deaths should be considered democide the Geneva Conventions, particularly the 1977 Protocols (Bothe, Partsch, and Solf, 1982). Those deaths during military action that would be considered a war crime or crime against humanity I count as democide, such as those dead from the intentional bombing of a hospital, shooting of captured POWs, using civilians for target practice, shelling a refugee column, indiscriminate bombing of a village, and the like.
6. Rummel (1990, 1991, 1992, 1994).
7. The basic statistical analysis along with the thousands of estimates of democide gleaned from the literature are given in Rummel (1996).

Part II

Why are Democracies Nonviolent?

> *The true value of democracy is to serve as a sanitary precaution protecting us against an abuse of power. It enables us to get rid of a government and try to replace it by a better one. Or, to put it differently, it is the only convention we have yet discovered to make peaceful change possible.*
> —F. A. Hayek, *Law, Legislation and Liberty,*
> Vol. 3.

Introduction to Part II

The Democratic Peace Proposition: Democracy is a Method of Nonviolence.

Putting all the previous results together, we have found that:

* Democracies do not commit violence or war against each other.
* The more democratic two regimes the less severe their violence against each other.
* The more democratic a regime the less severe its foreign violence.
* The more democratic a regime the less severe its internal collective violence.
* The more democratic a regime the less its democide.

All this strongly suggests that there is something about democracies that encourages nonviolence. Indeed, I argue and will try to establish theoretically the Democratic Peace Proposition, the most fundamental proposition that states the most important fact of our time. It is that *democracy is a method of nonviolence.*[1]

Democracy institutionalizes a way of solving without violence disagreements over fundamental questions. Democracy promotes a culture of negotiation, bargaining, compromise, concessions, the toleration of differences, and even the acceptance of defeat ("lose today, win tomorrow"). And it unleashes forces that divide and segment the sources of violence.[2] But now we have entered the realm of abstract theory, the subject of this part of the book. But first, why has all this not been discovered before, the question I will address in the next chapter.

Notes

1. There are other methods of nonviolence, such as those presented in Ackerman and Kruegler (1994) and Sharp (1973). Although not always successful, diplomacy itself should be considered a method of nonviolence.
2. Although the end result of democratization may be peace, the process of democratization may create more violence than would stable authoritarian and totalitarian regimes. Mansfield and Snyder (1995; 1995b) investigate this statistically, and find that the *number* of wars was significantly greater for those countries in the process of democratization than for stable nondemocracies. However, this study is seriously flawed by the use of frequencies. I describe in chapter 4 the problem of using frequencies to test the Democratic/Dyadic Violence or Democratic/Foreign Violence propositions, and the same arguments hold for testing whether democratization means more or less violence.

7

A New Fact?

> By the end of the eighteenth century a com-
> plete liberal theory of international relations,
> of war and peace, had . . . developed. . . .
> Peace was . . . fundamentally a question of the
> establishment of democratic institutions
> throughout the world.
>
> —Michael Howard,
> War and the Liberal Conscience

Why has not this most important fact about democratic peacefulness been discovered before? For centuries there have been theories
and proposals about ending or moderating war and other violence. Just
in our lifetime thoughtful people who have seriously studied violence
have concluded that peace could be promoted by world government,
arms control, disarmament, proper decision making, international and
transnational institutions and linkages, diplomacy, equitable resource
distribution, conflict resolution procedures, methods of nonviolence
and civilian defense, balancing of power, collective security, education, cultural exchange, reducing poverty and inequality, and peace
research. Among all these proposals, there was no serious consideration given among scholars, practitioners, and activists to fostering
democracy as a way of dealing with violence until recently.

That democracy promotes peace is truly a matter of insight and
knowledge gained and lost among political philosophers to be redis-
covered through rigorous theoretical and empirical research. In fact, so
long ago as 1795, in what was virtually forgotten for a century,

Immanuel Kant systematically articulated the positive role of political freedom in eliminating war in his *Perpetual Peace*; and proposed therefore that constitutional republics be established to assure universal peace. This proposal has various nuances, such as those involving the difference between republics and democracies, and between political and economic freedom, but the essential idea was this: the more freedom people have to govern their own lives, the more government power is limited constitutionally, the more leaders are responsible through free elections to their people, then the more restrained the leaders will be in making war. In Kant's words:

> The republican constitution . . . gives a favorable prospect for the desired consequence, i.e., perpetual peace. The reason is this: if the consent of the citizens is required in order to decide that war should be declared (and in this constitution it cannot but be the case), nothing is more natural than that they would be very cautious in commencing such a poor game, decreeing for themselves all the calamities of war. Among the latter would be: having to fight, having to pay the costs of wars from their own resources, having painfully to repair the devastation war leaves behind, and, to fill up the measure of evils, load themselves with a heavy national debt that would embitter peace itself and that can never be liquidated on account of constant wars in the future. But, on the other hand, in a constitution which is not republican, and under which the subjects are not citizens, a declaration of war is the easiest thing in the world to decide upon, because war does not require of the ruler, who is the proprietor and not a member of the state, the least sacrifice of the pleasures of his table, the chase, his country houses, his court functions, and the like. He may, therefore, resolve on war as on a pleasure party for the most trivial reasons, and with perfect indifference leave the justification which decency requires to the diplomatic corps who are ever ready to provide it.[1]

Through the writings of Kant, Baron de Montesquieu, Thomas Paine, Jeremy Bentham, and John Stuart Mill, among others, it became an article of classical liberal faith in the eighteenth and nineteenth centuries that "government on the old system," as Paine wrote, "is an assumption of power, for the aggrandizement of itself; on the new [Republican form of government as just established in the United States], a delegation of power for the common benefit of society. The former supports itself by keeping up a system of war; the latter promotes a system of peace, as the true means of enriching a nation."[2]

These liberals believed that there was a natural harmony of interests among nations, and that free trade would facilitate this harmony and promote peace. Most important, they were convinced that monarchies, the dominant form of government of their time, had a vested interest in war. It was, in contemporary terms, a game they played with the lives of the common folk. Empower the people to make such decisions through their representatives, and they would always oppose war.

In a historical perspective that they did not have, it is clear that these classical liberals had too much faith in the masses. They did not anticipate the rise of nationalism, although the French Revolution and the Napoleonic Wars presaged what our century would behold in full glory: the total nation at arms and total war. They did not appreciate how the superheated hatred and revengefulness of majorities could drive democratic nations to war. The Crimean and Boer Wars, and the Mexican-American and Spanish-American wars were yet to occur. In democracies the clamor for war has from time to time been irresistible to ambitious politicians and special interests. The historical record now shows that the people are not only willing, but sometimes will demand to go to war. Nonetheless, the classical liberal's view of democracy's peacefulness was insightful and if followed through later in our century by scholars, practitioners, and activists might have enlarged the zone of democratic peace. But by the middle of the twentieth century, this insight became almost completely ignored or forgotten.

How did we fall off the classical liberal path to peace and fail to find it again until recently? There are several reasons for this, some ideological, some methodological. First and foremost, the classical liberal view itself fell into disrepute among intellectuals and scholars. Essentially, classical liberals believed that the government that governs least governs best. Adam Smith's *An Inquiry into the Nature and Causes of the Wealth of Nations* was their economic bible. And in current terms, they preached democratic capitalism. But beginning in the nineteenth century capitalism came under increasing attack by socialists of all flavors. First, the socialist agreed with the classical liberal that the people had to be empowered, and that this would bring peace. But what the socialist saw when the liberal creed was enacted into law, especially in Britain, was that the bellicose aristocracies were replaced by equally bellicose capitalists. Democracies and their attendant free market appeared to foster exploitation, inequality, and poverty; to enable a very few capitalists to rule over the many. Most important here, capitalism was seen not just to promote, but to require colonialism and imperialism, and thereby war.

But what was to be done? Here the socialist mainly divided into the democratic socialists, state socialists, and Marxists. The democratic socialists argued that true democracy means that both the political and economic aspects of their lives must be under the people's control, and this is done through both a representative government and government ownership, control, and management of the economy. The capitalist would be thus replaced by elected representatives, who would oversee economic planners and managers, and above all be responsive to popular majorities. With the aristocratic and capitalist interests in war thus eliminated, with the peace oriented worker and peasant democratically empowered, peace would be assured.

The state socialists, however, would simply replace representative institutions with some form of socialist dictatorship. This would assure the best implementation and progress of socialist equalitarianism, without interference by the bourgeoisie and other self-serving interests. Moreover, the people could not be trusted to know their own interests, for they are easily blinded by procapitalist propaganda and manipulation. Myanmar (Burma) still remains a good example of state socialism in practice, although state control over the economy has moderated recently.

While agreeing on much of the socialist analysis of capitalism, the Marxist added to it a deterministic, dialectical theory of history, a class analysis of societies, an economic theory of capitalism, and the necessity of the impoverishment of the worker and the inevitability of a communist revolution. However, the Marxist disagreed with the socialist on the ends. Never ultimately far from the anarchist, the Marxists, especially the Marxist-Leninist of our century, looked at the socialist state that would come into being with the overthrow of capitalism as nothing more than an intermediary dictatorship of the proletariat through which the transition to the final stage of communism would be prepared. And stripped of its feudal or capitalist exploiters and thus its agents of war, communism would mean, not the natural harmony among nations as in the liberal creed, but among all people as each works according to his ability and receives according to his need. The state then would wither away, and the masses would live in true, everlasting peace and freedom.

It should be underlined that while the democratic or state socialist believes that socialist governments will be peace loving and nonviolent, the Marxist-Leninist believed this true of only the final, communist stage of stateless anarchy. The socialist transition period might well involve war with capitalist states, but while this interstate war was to be avoided if at all possible in this age of nuclear weapons, the worldwide struggle against capitalism must be pursued by all means short of interstate war. Against capitalist states this would involve not only the arts of deception, disinformation, subversion, and demoralization, but also terrorism and domestic wars through "national liberation fronts." For the Marxist-Leninist, then, it was the communist system that was inherently peaceful, not the socialist intermediary state. This socialist stage meant the purposeful, aggressive use of force and violence to pursue the final, global stage of communist peace and freedom.

In any case, regardless of the brand of socialism from which the critique of capitalism ensued, the protracted nineteenth- and twentieth-century socialist assault on capitalism had a profound effect on liberalism and especially the theory of war. Falling into disrepute, its program seen as utopian or special pleading for capitalists, pure classical liberalism mutated among Western intellectuals and their students in the Third World into a reform or welfare liberalism that is little differentiated today from the programs and views of the early socialists. This modern liberalism, or liberalism as it is now called, has been heavily influenced by the socialist view of war. And this liberalism in turn grew widely influential in scholarly research on international relations, and thus war and peace. It must be recognized that until the 1960s such research was largely the preserve of the social sciences, and that an overwhelming number of social scientists were by the mid-twentieth-century modern liberals or socialists in their outlook.

In the early 1960s the development of peace research began to take off and is today a full discipline. In its early years it was very much an American phenomenon and also very modern liberal in its view of war. Where real factors, as apart from psychological ones, were focused upon, war was generally believed to be caused by the existence of have and have not, rich and poor nations; by poverty, unrestrained competition, and the maldistribution of resources; by exploiting multinational corporations, armament merchants, and the military industrial complex. But peace research soon became internationalized, and with this global growth the European socialist and neo-Marxist's view of capitalism and war soon dominated. The milder, American peace researcher's modern liberal view soon became passé, and in its place one began to read about Western (capitalist) imperialism and dominance; about world capitalist economic control, manipulation, and war making; and about the promotion of non-violence through material equality and a socialist world economy. Positive peace and social justice became central concepts in peace research, both meaning some kind of socialist equalitarianism.[3]

But what happened to the idea that democracy or individual freedom promotes nonviolence?[4] With the protracted socialist attack on the classical liberal's fundamental belief in capitalism, coupled with the apparent excesses of capitalism, such as sweat shops, robber barons, monopolies, depressions, and political corruption, classical liberalism eventually lost the heart and minds of Western intellectuals. And with this defeat went its fundamental truth about democracy promoting peace. Interestingly, in the 1980s there was a conservative resurgence of classical liberalism. President Ronald Reagan and Prime Minister Margaret Thatcher exemplified this, and their often-expressed views on the positive role of free institutions for peace were straight out of classical liberalism. With the end of the cold war those in the social sciences and peace research communities also began to entertain what just a decade or so previously they would have considered right-wing propaganda.

This is not to say that most peace researchers generally viewed capitalist political-economic systems as the cause of war, as asserted by hard-line socialists. Many European and Third World peace researchers generally viewed capitalism as one cause among several, although some theoretical emphasis may have been given to capitalism, as in Johan Galtung's influential center-periphery theory, which clearly lays the major blame for war on a capitalist type, competitive system.[5] Indeed, many peace researchers, and especially Americans, had until recently taken a middle position: both capitalism or socialism can be a source of peace or war, depending on the circumstances. In either case, neither was seen as a general factor in war.

Now, capitalism and democracy are not the same thing. Democratic socialist systems exist, as in Sweden and Denmark, as do authoritarian capitalist systems like Chile and Taiwan in the 1980s. Why then had the peace-making effects of democratic freedoms been tossed out with capitalism? As mentioned, these freedoms were part of an ideology emphasizing capitalism—as the ideology retreated, so did its belief in the positive role of freedom in peace. But there other factors at work here that are at least as important.

One of these factors causing social scientists and particularly peace researchers to reject democracy's peacefulness was a misreading of history. As noted, Kant and the classical liberals were writing largely in theory about freedom and war; they had little historical evidence. But by the middle of the twentieth century enough democracies had existed for over half a century for a historical judgment to be made. And that was believed to show that democracies not only do go to war often, and sometimes joyously, but they can be very aggressive. Americans alone could easily note their American-Indian Wars, Mexican-American and Spanish American wars, and of course the Civil war, the most violent war of any Western country in the century between the Napoleonic wars and World War I.[6] And even if one were to argue that the United States was dragged into both World Wars, there were the American invasions of Grenada and Panama, and the Vietnam War that many peace researchers viewed as a case of blatant American aggression.

Then, of course, there is Great Britain, which between 1850 to 1941 fought twenty wars, more than any other state. France, also a democracy for most of this period, fought the next most at eighteen. The United States fought seven. These three nations alone fought 63 percent of all the wars during these ninety-two years.[7] Of course, Britain did not become a liberal democracy until 1884 with the extension of the franchise to agricultural workers, but she was afterwards still the aggressor in numerous European and colonial wars. The historical record of democracies thus appeared no better than that of other regimes; and the classical liberal belief in the peacefulness of democracies seemed nothing more than bad theory or misplaced faith.

But all other types of regimes seemed equally bellicose. The supposed peacefulness of socialist systems was belied by the aggressiveness of its two major totalitarian variants, that of the Soviet Union and Nazi Germany[8]; and other types of regimes, whether authoritarian dictatorships like Japan before World War II, or absolute monarchies like czarist Russia before World War I, appeared no less warlike. The empirical verdict was for many social scientists an easy one—all types of political, or politico-economic, systems make war; none is especially pacific. Clearly articulated in Kenneth Waltz's widely read *Man, the State and War,*[9] this critique remains today the consensus view of American peace research,[10] and in peace research elsewhere it is the major alternative belief to that of the inherent bellicosity of capitalist systems.

A number of methodological errors accounted for researchers misreading the recent history of democracies; and for the history of wars being so misleading. First, there is that of selective attention. The many wars of a few democracies were focused upon and the total population of democracies and wars were ignored. A true comparison should involve that of all democracies against nondemocracies and for all wars, at least in this century, as has been done in recent research on war.[11]

Second, there is the error of improper weighting. As explained in chapters 3 and 4, even where such systematic comparison is done, the intensity of wars is ignored. In some such comparisons, the American invasion of Grenada and the British Falklands Islands War, among history's least violent wars, are counted as wars, and put on par with the American and British participation in, say, World War II. As I have pointed out, the proposition that democracies are more peaceful than other political systems really means that they engage in less violence, where violence is understood as a continuum, from low intensity to high. To say that democratic freedom reduces violence is like saying that aspirin reduces pain. It is not a question of the presence or absence of war, but of the degree of killing involved. The more democracy (or aspirin) the less the killing (or pain).

Another error, one I also committed in my earlier work,[12] is to atheoretically screen correlations and to ignore low ones—to claim that low correlations between political systems and violence simply show that no meaningful relationship exists. This is simply a matter of seeking mountains and ignoring hills. In truth, as a systematic screening of all the empirical and quantitative literature shows,[13] there is a consistent and significant, but low, negative correlation between democracies and collective violence, as predicted by classical liberalism. The reason for this low correlation is that democracy is not both necessary and sufficient for nonviolence to occur. That is, like democracies, authoritarian and totalitarian systems can be without violence for many years.[14] The problem here is an almost endemic one in the social sciences: drawing conclusions about a theory from exploratory data analysis in which the theory is not explicitly tested.

Even if these errors caused a historical misinterpretation of the relationship between freedom and violence, how could it be missed that democracies do not make war on each other, if true? After all, this is a point prediction whose historical truth or falsity should be obvious. The problem is simply that social scientists and peace researchers had not ordinarily thought *dyadically*. They saw nations as developed or undeveloped, strong or weak, democratic or undemocratic, large or small, belligerent or not. That is, they thought *monatically*. Thus history was and generally still is studied for the relationship between a nation's political system and *its* bellicosity, rather than of that between the similarities and differences of two nations and their behavior toward each other.

Like so much in science, this is a matter of perspective, as in looking end-wise at a cylinder and seeing only a circle. A simple change in perspective would show a cylinder; similarly, a simple shift to dyadic relations would show that when *two* nations are well-established democracies, no wars occur *between* them, the fact established chapter 2. That just for all the large or small wars since 1945, not one has involved democracies against each other; that in a world where contiguous nations often use violence to settle their differences or at least have armed borders between, democracies like the United States and Canada should have long, completely unarmed borders; and that in Europe, the historical cauldron of war, once all Western European nations became democratic they no longer armed against each other and the expectation of war among them is now zero; that all this should be missed shows how powerfully misleading an improper historical perspective or model can be.

So the socialist critique of capitalism combined with a monadic view of history and a failure to empirically and properly test these beliefs has led social scientists to accept the view that capitalist freedoms in fact were the cause of violence, or that at least there was no relationship between democratic freedoms and collective violence. But besides socialism and these methodological errors, there were still other factors at work. Since the first world war and accelerated by the second, intellectuals have strongly rejected any hint of nationalism. Nationalism was seen by many nonsocialists as a fundamental cause of war, or at least of the total national mobilization of the state and of total war when war occurred. Internationalism, rising above one's nation, seeing humanity and its transcending interest as a whole, and furthering world government, became the intellectual's ideal.

Social scientist and peace researchers, who after all are usually intellectuals with Ph.Ds, have almost universally shared this view. In fact one of the attractions of socialism for many was its inherent internationalism, its rejection of the nation and patriotism as values. Internationalists generally have refused to accept that any one nation is really better than any other. After all, cultures and values are relative; one nation's virtues is another's evils. Best we treat all nations equally to better resolve conflicts among them. As Hans Morgenthau pointed out in his most popular and still influential international relations text, both the United States and Soviet Union should have been condemned for the cold war; it was their evangelistic, crusading belief in their own values that made the East-West conflict so difficult to resolve. The following quote from Morgenthau shows well this language of *two-partyism.*

> From the aftermath of the Second World War onwards, these two blocs [centered on the superpowers] have faced each other like two fighters in a short and narrow lane. They have tended to advance and meet in what was likely to be combat, or retreat and allow the other side to advance into what to them is precious ground. . . .
>
> For the two giants that today determine the course of world affairs only one policy has seemed to be left; that is, to increase their own strength and that of their allies . . . either side must fear that the temporarily stronger contestant will use its superiority to eliminate the threat from the other side by shattering military and economic pressure of by a war of annihilation.
>
> Thus the international situation is reduced to the primitive spectacle of two giants eyeing each other with watchful suspicion. They bend every effort to increase their military potential to the utmost, since this is all they have to count on. Both prepare to strike the first decisive blow, for if one does not strike it the other might. Thus, contain or be contained, conquer or be conquered, destroy or be destroyed, become the watchwords of Cold War diplomacy.[15]

This two-partyism easily can be seen in reading the peace research and related literature of the 1970s and 1980s. There is no victim or aggressor, no right or wrong nation, but only two parties to a conflict (when this two-partyism did break down, it was usually in terms of American, or Western "imperialist aggression"). Consequently, to except that the freedoms espoused by the United States and its democratic allies led to peace, and that the totalitarian socialism fostered by the Soviet Union led to violence and war, was to take sides. It was to be nationalistic. And this for the internationalist was *ipso facto* wrong.

There was another psychological force toward two-partyism that should not be underestimated. The statement that democratic freedom fostered peace seemed not only nationalistic, but inherently ideological. After all, freedom was one of the flags in the "ideological cold war." No matter that this was a scientific statement based on rigorous theory and empirical tests; no matter that the results in favor of liberal democracy came from researchers who among themselves had different ideologies. To accept that democracies were more pacific than other types of regimes appeared not only to take sides; but to be what is worse, a right-wing, cold warrior.

For these reasons many studying violence strongly reacted against any assertion that democratic regimes do or could be a path to peace. Is it any wonder, then, that until the 1980s there had been relatively so little empirical research directly and explicitly on this question,[16] and a strong resistance to the results of such research showing the inverse relationship between freedom and collective violence, as presented in chapter 4. Nils Peter Gleditsch, the editor of a foremost journal of peace research, in typical understatement recognized this role of the cold war:

> The strong finding about the "democratic peace" may to some extent have been a victim of the Cold War. No wonder then that it fell to an 'innocent criminologist' [Babst] to observe that the emperors had no clothes. The Cold War has now ended in the real world; it should end in peace research, too.[17]

But of course there are peace researchers who reject two-partyism; and for some of these there is another factor at work, an apparently strongly emotional one hinted at above. In the 1960s and 1970s, there had grown within the peace research community a virulent anti-Westernism, often centered on the United States. Rather than being neutral between East and West, evincing a studied internationalism, this view did take sides. It was fundamentally socialist, sometimes neo-Marxist and Third World in orientation. Western democracies and in particular the United States were seen as exploiting, lusting for profit and power, and forever struggling to dominate other countries; their alleged democratic values were believed a facade behind which they manipulated and controlled poor nations. Violence was their means, their secret services, and particularly the CIA, their tool. In this view, which was held by a significant segment of the peace research community, there was nothing too evil for the West to commit in grasping for power and profit. Seemingly, anything negative was believed. For example, in a communication to the students and faculty of the Political Science Department at the University of Hawaii, such a well-known peace researcher as Johan Galtung alleged that the CIA had been carrying out "very much the same thing" as Hitler's "holocaust" against the Jews, and had "rubbed out" 6,000,000 (yes, six million) people throughout the world.[18] No peace researcher with these views could accept the possibility of Western, democratic freedoms promoting peace.

In sum, theoretical and empirical research establishes that democratic civil liberties and political rights promote nonviolence and is a path to a warless world. The clearest evidence of this is that there has never been a war between well-established democracies, while numerous wars have occurred between all other political systems; and that of the near 170 million people that governments have murdered in our century, near 99 percent were killed by nondemocracies, and especially totalitarian ones. That democracies promote peace and harmony is not a new discovery. It was fundamental to seventeenth- and eighteenth-century classical liberalism. But this truth has become forgotten or ignored in our time.

The reasons for this are many and complex, but they reduce basically to these. First, nineteenth-century socialism and twentieth-century internationalism offered influential alternative explanations of war and ways to peace that seemed to fit the contemporary history of war better than the apriori speculations of the classical liberals. This history especially seemed to show that democracies not only made war on other nations, but were at least as aggressive as any. Second, for recent generations ethical relativism (and its associated two-partyism) and anti-Westernism (or anti-Americanism) have caused many intellectuals to reject fundamental Western values, including the faith in classical democratic freedoms; and with this has also gone a rejection of any evidence that these freedoms could promote peace.

These ideological forces have been strengthened by several methodological errors. One is the tendency to see nations wholly in terms of their characteristics and behavior, and not in relation to each other. Thus the fact that democracies do not make war on each other, or that the less the democratic freedom in two nations, the more likely violence between them, was missed. Other errors were to view history selectively, without systematic comparison of all cases or wars; to seek correlations atheoretically, thus ignoring the necessarily low, but significant inverse relationships between freedom and violence; and to treat all wars as the same, no matter how different in the levels of violence.

I have now shown that democracies are a method of nonviolence. And I have also detailed why this is not a new finding. The most important question still remains. Why should democracies be more peaceful than any other regime?

Notes

1. Kant (1957, pp. 12-13).
2. Quoted in Howard (1978, p. 29).
3. Of course, much of such writing was not self-consciously socialist or ideological, but the analyses and programs were in the socialist tradition. See for example, the World Order studies, and in particular Falk (1975) and Falk and Mendlovitz (1966).
4. Keep in mind that by this time two kinds of freedom had be distinguished. To the Marxist-Leninist, it was communist freedom (in effect, anarcho-communism) that creates peace; to the classical liberal peace was fostered by individual freedom under a democratic government.
5. See Galtung (1964, 1969).
6. The Teiping Rebellion in China (1850-1864) may have cost as many as 40,000,000 lives, putting this civil war on par with the deadliness of World War II.
7. Based on Wright (1965, table 44, p. 650).
8. Hitler's Nazi party was self-consciously socialist: Nazi stood for The National Socialist German Worker's party. While not formally nationalized, big business was brought under complete Nazi government control and dictation; and the German economy was centrally directed by government ministries.
9. Published in 1954, by 1965 it had gone through six printings.
10. The consensus has been articulated specifically in the willingness to accept what a careful reading of the empirical sources should have contradicted—that democracies are no more nor less warlike than other types of regimes. See chapter 4.
11. See chapter 4 for a description of these studies.
12. See, for example, Rummel (1968).
13. See chapter 4 and Rummel (1985).
14. See chapter 2, footnote 17.
15. Morgenthau, 1985, pp. 378–79.
16. Much of the early accumulated evidence supporting the inverse relationship between democracy and violence comes from the empirical side results of research on other, often quite unrelated, topics. See Rummel (1985).
17. Gleditsch, 1992, p. 374.
18. Johan Galtung, "Memo to friends and colleagues," and published exchange of communications between Henry Kariel and Johan Galtung, Political Science Department, University of Hawaii, April, 1988. A generous interpretation of this is that Galtung was only pointing out that the CIA helped bring to power those responsible for mass murder, such as Pol Pot of Cambodia, General Pinochet of Chile, Shah Muhammad Reza Pahlevi of Iran, and the like. But Galtung made clear that by "wiped out" is meant that the CIA directly or indirectly killed 6,000,000 people.

8

What is to be Explained?

> *For once, desirable means would serve desir-*
> *able ends.*
> —Erich Weede, "Democracy and War
> Involvement"

Before trying to explain the democratic peace, I must be clear about what is in fact to be explained. We have seen that democracies not only do not make war on each other, but the more democratic two nations, the less likely they will commit violence against each other. Moreover, the more democratic a regime, the less likely it will commit violence overall, have domestic political violence, or murder its own people. One should note immediately that what is being expressed is not a dichotomous relationship, such that democracies are nonviolent and other regimes are violent. Rather, as the empirical evidence shows, there is a continuum. At one extreme we have totalitarian regimes committing the greatest violence, with democratic regimes the least, and authoritarian regimes in between. What then needs to be explained is the nature of this underlying continuum and why it should suppress all forms of violence as it does.

But this continuum cannot be well isolated unless I pay more attention to the nature of democratic, authoritarian, and totalitarian regimes than I have so far.[1] This in turn means that I have to describe the social and political bases of such regimes and the fundamental structure of relations within which they operate. I will argue that the most basic engine of behavior underlying societies and the regimes associated with them is along a socio-political dimension of freedom versus power.

117

In social and political relations *power* is the ability to get someone to do something they would not otherwise do.[2] This does not necessarily mean the use of force or coercion or authority. These are certainly alternative bases of power, but power also can operate in other ways. There is the altruistic power of love, where charismatic leaders can get their followers to do what they want by virtue of the follower's love and dedication to the leaders. There is the bargaining power of an exchange, in that one can get what one wants by exchanging it for something another desires more than what it is that you want them to give you.[3] Interest or lobbying groups in democracies use this power all the time—a legislator's promise or vote in exchange for support or campaign funds at reelection time. There is the intellectual power of persuasion, where a person comes to accept one's idea or argument because one persuades them of it. This book is an attempt to use intellectual power on the reader. And there is manipulative power, or the ability to so arrange the conditions or context of another's behavior that one can get the behavior or outcome one desires. This is the power of a committee chairman, for example, who can set the agenda, time of meeting, and control the length of a meeting such that the desired outcomes are most probable.

When dealing with societies, however, there are three basic powers (coercive, authoritative, and bargaining) or some mix of them, that function to structure social relations.[4] *Coercive power* is the use of threats of pain, negative deprivation, or some other negative outcome to get what is wanted. "Your wallet or your life." "Pay taxes or go to jail." "Obey the Lord or suffer an eternity of Hell-fire." All societies involve some coercion, but some societies are structured mainly by it. Prisons; concentration and forced labor camps; and conscript armies are examples of specific societies in which the social order is imposed coercively. At the level of nations we can also find such coercive societies, particularly those in which the political regime rules over all major institutions and groups, leaving no independent businesses, no independent church, no independent schools, and no independent farms. The regime runs all at the point of a gun.

Most of these *coercive societies* are commanded by *totalitarian regimes*.[5] There is no law above the regime and that which is not permitted the citizen is forbidden. And all that matters is controlled by the center, that is the top of the totalitarian hierarchy of power. Joseph Stalin (the Soviet Union), Mao Tse-tung (China), Pol Pot (Cambodia),

Kim Il-sung (North Korea), and Enver Hoxha (Albania) are perhaps the most egregious examples of totalitarian rulers in our century. They created social orders ruled by fear of the consequences of disobedience, insufficient enthusiasm for the regime, the violation of any one of a plethora of rules and regulations, or a simple misstep (such as accidentally wrapping fish in a newspaper showing a picture of Stalin). Typically, such societies are one nation-sized prison camp. Where geographically possible, it is circled by barbed wire, guard towers, and roving patrols along its borders, not to keep people out, but to keep citizens in. To try to escape is a crime punishable by a long term in a forced labor camp or by execution.[6]

Then there are *authoritative societies*. These are societies that are structured traditionally, according to customary rules and laws. They are spiritually rather than sensory oriented and define truth more in terms of core books and the sayings of great men rather than empirical knowledge. There is surely some coercion and perhaps minorities or dissidents that are forced to obey, but people largely do what they do because they believe they ought to. The regime is seen as legitimate, with a right to rule. Its laws codify what is seen as moral and proper. Thus the major power structuring the society is the authority of the national culture and the regime. They base their rule on the past, allow little competition for or interference with the rightful power of the regime (although they may negotiate and compromise over issues important to one or two lesser sources of power, such as the church or military), and try to enforce cultural, and often religious, norms.[7] Two centuries ago almost all major national societies were authoritarian in this sense, ruled wholly by monarchies or dynasties of one type or another. Today we have Nepal, Bhutan, Saudi Arabia, Kuwait, Bahrain, Qatar, and Oman among the few remaining examples of such authoritarian regimes and societies.

Authoritarian societies are not totalitarian. Although cultural and religious laws may be enforced on all, such as forbidding women from driving automobiles or wearing "immodest" clothing like shorts, there are still large areas in which people or groups are free. Businesses can operate, profit can be made, the arts can be pursued, science can be studied, and sports enjoyed. All this is regulated by the regime (one could not paint a blasphemous portrait of Mohammed, for example), but there is still a wide area of nonpolitical freedom.

Then there is the third type of national society, that is largely regulated by *bargaining power.* There is a central government, to be sure, along with the coercion and authority that are the essential attributes of any regime, but most relations between the regime and the society, and especially in the society as a whole, are based on exchange.[8] A largely economic free market exists and many other social relations depend mostly on what people can do for each other.[9] The regime is open and individuals are free to oppose the regime and compete for power. There is freedom of speech and the press. Churches, private schools, businesses, youth groups, and other institutions of all kinds can exist and independently pursue their interests. Politics is based on *exchange,* where politicians promise goodies in return for votes and interest groups offer support and campaign funds in return for the laws or regulations they desire. Finally, the political leadership neither tries to achieve some utopia in the future, as do totalitarian regimes, nor preserve traditions, as do authoritarian regimes, but is oriented to the present, responding to today's national problems and public demands. This is a *democracy.*[10]

We thus have three types of regimes that in effect form a political triangle, as shown in figure 9.1.[11] And as also pictured, each type of regime sits within its own type of society. Near the democratic end is the classical liberal democratic (or libertarian) type of regime that governs least, with maximum civil liberties and political rights, and within a society dominated by exchange power. Near the second end is a totalitarian regime, such as communist (or Marxist) ones, which recognize no civil or political rights, repress or extinguish all independent sources of power, and control all major aspects of society toward some end. Coercion is the governing and ordering power. And near the remaining corner of the political triangle is the authoritarian regime, traditional, bound to cultural and usually religious norms and customs, and absolutist in governance. Order is provided by the authoritative tradition and culture and outside of politics people may have considerable independence. Absolute monarchies are their purist exemplification.

With this triangle we thus have three sides and thus three continua along which regimes can vary.[12] One is from the democratic to totalitarian corners, which reflects variation in the degree of freedom from regime coercion (or conversely the degree of coercive power a regime applies), with people having the greater freedom towards the democratic corner. The second continuum is the amount of freedom people

FIGURE 8.1
The Political Triangle:
Societies and Associated Political Regimes

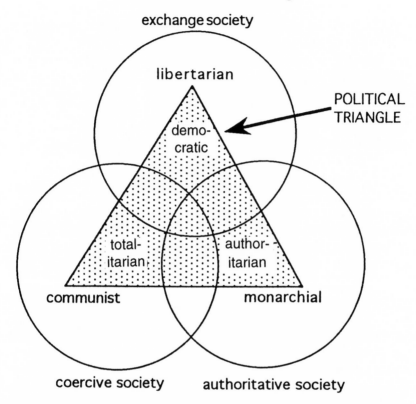

have from the authoritarian power of a regime and moves from the democratic end where people may legally act independently of tradition, cultural norms, and religious dogma to the authoritarian end where tradition, culture, and religion dominate, all maintained by the regime. It is like the difference between living in a small, one sheriff town, where everyone knows everyone else, to the freedom of living in an apartment in a large city. Finally, there is the continuum that varies from a highly coercive corner, where totalitarian regimes rule, to the authoritarian corner, with absolute monarchies. Fascist systems, like that of Juan Peron in Argentina, Francisco Franco in Spain, and Benito Mussolini in Italy would be somewhere near the middle of this continuum. Adolf Hitler's Germany—a type of fascist regime—would be closer to the totalitarian end.

There is one type of regime yet to locate in this space. That is the *oligarchic republics* that the historian Spencer Weart found almost as likely not to make war on each other as democracies.[13] First, note that Weart's historical research led him to define republics much as we would define democracy, in that there is open and competitive selection for political office and of public policies through majority voting, and those enfranchised have equal political rights. But the extent of this enfranchisement defines two kinds of republics. One is the *democratic republic* in which the franchise and equal rights extends to at least two-thirds of adult males (keep in mind that Weart was doing an historical analysis going back to the classical Greeks, and thus used a looser definition of democracy than the analyst of modern democracies might desire); the other an oligarchic republic in which the franchise and equal rights extended to no more than a third of adult males, usually a much smaller group set off by birth or race, such as of the white oligarchic republic of South Africa or Great Britain in the early decades of the last century. This is an upper class of some kind that rules, often through explicit coercion, over a disenfranchised majority. Weart found few republics that were in the gray area with an adult male franchise between one-third and two-thirds. And upon inspection, the particular nature of each allowed him to classify them as one type or the other.

As I pointed out in chapter 2, Weart discovered that beginning with the classical Greeks, well-established democratic republics never clearly made war on each other, and that well-established oligarchic republics almost never did, while each type fought wars against the other and against nonrepublics. How do these political types fit into the political triangle? His democratic republic largely corresponds to what I am calling here a democracy. His oligarchic republic would then comprise a band of regimes separating democracies from totalitarian and authoritarian types. This is all I need say about them at this point, but I will return to his distinction at the appropriate place in trying to account for the democratic peace. For I am now convinced that *any explanation of this fact must also be able to account for both peace among oligarchic republics, and for wars between them and democracies.*

Now, with the three basic types of regimes (democratic, authoritarian, and totalitarian, and recognizing what we might call the Weart addenda—oligarchic republics) and three continua, what then is the theoretical continuum along which violence moves from the least to the most? I will argue that the most relevant continuum is that along the democratic to totalitarian side of the triangle, which is that from the freedom of an exchange society to subservience to coercion and its corollary, force. As people have more freedom from government coercion the severity of political violence decreases; as the coercion exercised by government increases, violence will increase with it. Indeed, violence in part becomes the mechanism for extending the regime's power and eradicating competing centers of power within the society, as in the extensive democide of virtually all new communist regimes.

Theoretically, then, in the propositions relating democracy and violence where more or less democracy is related to foreign or internal violence or democide, what is meant is more or less freedom from coercion and force, as I will make more precise in chapters 11 and 12. The proper scale for measuring this, therefore, would have regimes at one end that are constitutionally limited, with a competitive and open political system, the election of top leaders with a secret ballot and universal adult franchise, and civil liberties such as the freedom or speech, religion, and organization. At the other end of this scale would be the totalitarian regime, with no true competitive elections for political power, with no independent sources of power allowed (such as of a church or military), and no civil liberties. In the middle, then, would be the authoritarian regime, where people are excluded from competition for political power and their civil liberties are curtailed to what is allowed by tradition and, often, the only legal religion; but outside these spheres people may have considerable freedom, as in business. All the democratic, authoritarian, totalitarian scales that I used to test out the propositions in part I were based on this continuum.

Few measurements of democracy in the literature are consistent with this continuum, and indeed, the more popular way of measuring democracy can be misleading when correlated with violence. In particular, it is not unusual to consider democracy a dimension defined by electoral related characteristics, such as the extent of the electoral franchise, whether regular elections are held, the percent of the population voting, whether the legislature is elected and the degree of its independence from an executive, whether the executive is elected and their power over the legislature, and the like. A result of such measurements is that the usual democracies (Sweden, Switzerland, Belgium, Great Britain, Canada, the United States, etc.) will be found at one end of the scale, with the totalitarian regimes in the middle, and authoritarian regimes like Saudi Arabia and Kuwait at the opposite end.[14] This is because most totalitarian systems have had some form of regular elections with a universal franchise, and at lower levels the elections may have been competitive (the ruling and only party may have put forward or allowed several candidates to run for the same minor positions). But there was no real competition for significant offices and those candidates the ruling party wanted to win might get over 95 percent of the vote. Elections thereby functioned to periodically showcase and institutionally legitimize the leadership.

However, the most authoritarian regimes and especially those with hereditary absolute monarchs usually have no political parties, no elections, and no legislatures with meaningful power. This means that basing a measurement of democracy on the existence of such structures will necessarily scale these regimes at the opposite end from democracies.[15] *This is in effect, scaling along the side of the political triangle running from democratic to authoritarian regimes, and implicitly along the continuum of nation, tradition, custom, personalism, and political absolutism.* While this is an important dimension, it is an empirically independent pattern of variation in regime characteristics from that defining the freedom from government coercion. And it is this continuum of coercion that accounts for foreign and internal violence and democide.

Defining this continuum still does not give us an explanation of violence. It is simply to say that the relationship of more or less democracy to violence means in essence more or less freedom from coercion, more or less civil liberties and political rights. Why this connection?

Notes

1. Of the many works on political systems, I have found Finer (1971) most helpful, while still pertinent to contemporary regimes. My discrimination of political characteristics reflects his typology and survey, without following it in detail. Moreover, in my view one cannot well divide these characteristics into different regime types without careful attention to the underlying political ideologies. On this, see O'Sullivan (1989); Minogue (1985); and in particular Ebenstein and Fogelman (1985).
2. In Rummel (1976, chapters 19–21) I have considered a variety of definitions of power, including those by Russell (1938, p. 18); Bierstedt (1950, p. 733); Simon (1957, p. 5); Dahl (1957, p. 202); Cartwright (1959, p. 193); Kuhn (1963, p. 317);

Schermerhorn (1961, p. 12); Jouvenal (1962, p. 96); May (1972, p. 99); and, of course, the most conceptually systematic of treatments, Lasswell and Kaplan (1950, p. 76). As a result I have treated power as a family of physical and social powers. The social are defined as intentionally producing effects through another's will, and involves coercive, authoritative, bargaining, intellectual, altruistic (or love), and manipulative powers, which I will discuss in the text. For an excellent general treatment of power and related questions, see Barry (1989) and Baldwin (1989). For a recent radical view of power, see Wartenberg (1992).

3. Social exchange is not only the basis of bargaining power but a basic type of social interaction. In my work it is one of a handful of central variables. On social exchange, see Baldwin (1989); Cook (1987); and Gergen, Greenberg, and Willis (1980). For an analysis of events in Maoist China in terms of social exchange, see Nee (1991).

4. I have developed this idea in Rummel (1976, chapter 30). As to whether these societies in fact exist, I have summarized the relevant empirical analyses done by myself and others in Rummel (1976, section 34.3). I concluded that three separate clusters of nations well representing these three types of societies is delineated by the cross-national factor analysis of hundreds of socio-political, economic, cultural, and behavioral characteristics. See particularly Russett (1967); Cattell (1950); and Rummel (1972).

5. The distinctions to be made among totalitarian, authoritarian, and (liberal) democratic regimes are discussed more fully in Rummel (1976, chapter 31). They are based on four fundamental political characteristics: the degree to which regimes are open or closed (allow competitive elections for top offices and have freedom of speech and organization); allow groups outside of politics to be free; follow traditional or positivistic norms; and follow backward looking (e.g., maintaining past customs), forward looking (e.g., mobilizing the population to achieve some goal), or presentist policies (e.g., satisfying public demands). A variety of factor analyses show that the three major types of regimes—democratic, authoritarian, and totalitarian—derived from these four characteristics also emerge from these and a variety of other characteristics on which regimes can be measured. For a summary of these see Rummel (1976, section 34.2). Also see the subsequent factor analyses simultaneous done over years, nations, and variables (called super-p factor analyses) in Rummel (1979b, pp. 42–44).

6. Totalitarianism has been a disputed concept in political science, although not among those who have suffered under such regimes, such as Aleksandr Solzhenitsyn (1973). Among the best treatments if this type of regime, see Arendt (1966) and Friedrich and Brzezinski (1965). For a twentieth-century history of totalitarianism, see Taylor (1993). For a treatment of totalitarianism consistent with my democratic, authoritarian, totalitarian typology, see Ebenstein (1962).

7. In Sorokin's (1937–1941) useful and important distinction between sensate and ideational cultures, authoritative societies are ideational. For particularly useful works on authoritarianism as a type of political regime, see Germani (1978) and Perlmutter (1981).

8. The exchange and coercive societies are alternative types of what Sorokin (1937–1941) calls sensate cultures in his great work.

9. Von Mises (1963), one of the top economists of this century, has generalized the exchange basis of the free market to all social relations. I am doing the same here, but for a particular kind of society. The term *exchange* also captures the essence of the type of society Friedrich Hayek, Adam Smith, John Stuart Mill, and Jeremy

Bentham had in mind, and which is the ideal of contemporary libertarians (the inheritors of classical liberalism), such as Friedman (1962); Rothbard (1962); and Hospers (1971).

10. I have much discussed democracy as a type of regime in chapter 2 and described the various definitions used among those testing in particular for the relationship between democracy and war. For recent and helpful theoretical discussions of democracy going beyond definitions, see Barry (1989); Benjamin and Elkin (1985); and Stankiewicz (1981).

11. This political triangle is empirical and has been delineated by the factor analyses cited in notes 4 and 5. Moreover, in Rummel (1996, chapter 17) I did a component factor analysis of seventeen political scales and regime characteristics on about half of the over 400 regimes that existed or have existed in this century. A large number of sources were used for the scales, including Banks 1971; Arat (1991); and Gurr (1990)—I could not use the scales referenced below in footnote 14 because they only were for regimes for years around 1960. The largest orthogonally rotated factor, accounting for about 50 percent of the variance, was a democratic versus totalitarian dimension; the second was an authoritarian versus totalitarian dimension accounting for 20 percent of the variance, and the third, taking an additional 14 percent of the variance, was monarchical. In effect, these dimensions empirically verify further the political triangle, since the first two dimensions that together reflect 70 percent of the variation among all the political indices and characteristics comprise the two sides of the political triangle. Because the political triangle exists in a two-dimensional political space, where the two dimensions are democracy versus totalitarianism, and democracy versus authoritarianism, a line drawn from totalitarianism to authoritarianism in the two-dimensional space completes the triangle. That is, the third side is implicit in the other two.

12. There are of course many political mixtures that fall within the triangle, without being at the corners. For example, utilizing Finer's (1971) classification of political types, we could define direct or indirect military, facade-democratic, and quasi-democratic mixtures. Or using an alternative classification by Coleman (1960) we could locate in the triangle systems that are political, tutelary, terminal, or colonial democracies; and modernizing, colonial and racial, conservative, or traditional oligarchies. For an excellent more recent analysis of political types, see Bebler and Seroka (1990). There is no point here is getting so specific about the mixtures, examples of which are given in chapter 12. It is sufficient to designate the corners of the political triangle and the connecting continua.

13. Weart (1994, 1995).

14. For example, for a political democracy index developed by Bollen (1980), the country most opposite from democracy is Yemen, then followed by in decreasing order Saudi Arabia, Afghanistan (before the communist coup), Cuba, and Iraq. See also his latest scales (Bollen, 1991). For Smith's (1969) index of democracy, the most opposite country is Saudi Arabia, followed by Ethiopia (under Emperor Haile Selassie) and Afghanistan (before the communist coup of 1978). For Cutright and Wiley's (1969, appendix C) political representation index, the most opposite to democracy is Saudi Arabia, followed by Nepal, Afghanistan (before the communist coup), and Iraq. There is also the liberal democracy scale of Coulter (1975), which has as the most opposite from the democracies the UAR, Iraq, Sudan, Kenya, and Pakistan. In spite of the apparent similarity of these scales, their correlations are low. For example, the variation in common among scale

values for Bollen's index and that of Smith is 69 percent (this is the product moment correlation squared times 100), with Cutright and Wiley it is 72 percent, and for Coulter it is 62 percent. This is for scales presumably measuring the same thing for about the same years.

For my purposes, the best scale is that developed by Raymond Gastil (1991) for Freedom House. It measures the degree of freedom by civil liberties and political rights and ends up placing totalitarian regimes at the opposite end from undoubted democracies. The amount of variation in common between the Freedom House scale values for freedom and Bollen's index of democracy is 70 percent, for Smith it is 47 percent, for Cutright and Wiley 51 percent, and for Coulter 51 percent. Clearly, these scales are all measuring different aspects of political systems, and one therefore must be theoretically clear about the choice of scale.

15. As in fact has happened on a number of scales developed in the literature. See note 14.

9

First-Level Explanation: The People's Will

> *[If] the consent of the citizens is required in order to decide that war should be declared . . . nothing is more natural than that they would be very cautious in commencing such a poor game, decreeing for themselves all the calamities of war.*
> —Immanuel Kant, *Perpetual Peace*

I will divide explanations of the democratic peace into three levels, each more abstract and fundamental. By more abstract I mean further from what we can immediately perceive and immediately know. The first level—and that closest to a popular and historic understanding of why democracy should promote nonviolence—has to do with the representative nature of democracies and the costs of violence. In his seminal *Perpetual Peace,* as quoted in the epigraph and the previous chapter, Immanuel Kant was the first to advance this explanation. In sum, he argued that it is the people who suffer from war, and not the monarchs that can play at war without danger to themselves. And people in general do not want to die or lose their loved ones and property in war. Dean Babst also assumed this explanation when he presented his statistics, the first ever, showing that democracies don't make war on each other. As he put it, "the general public does not want war, if it can choose."[1]

Therefore, where there is a government by elected representatives who can be run out of office if they oppose the will of the people, it will be most reluctant to start costly and lethal wars, or to bear the continuing costs of such wars it was forced to fight or mistakenly got into. A more general way of putting this is as D. Marc Kilgour does. On the basis of game theory he hypothesizes that "decisional constraints discourage war initiation. . . . [And the] existence of an effective opposition discourages war initiation."[2]

And there is some empirical evidence for all this. Kurt Gaubatz argued that if the above is true,

> in a democracy we would expect the power of the society relative to the state to vary within the election cycle. The closer the society is to an impending election, the greater will be the societal restrictions on the courses of action the state can follow. Thus the electoral cycle gives us a dynamic picture of the effects of social constraints on state action.[3]

For data on sixty-nine cases of seventeen different democracies fighting in forty-five wars, 1838 to 1973, twenty three of which involved fewer than a thousand battle dead, he found that

> there is a relationship between democratic election cycles and the timing of war entry in the past 200 years of democratic experience. In the post election period, when public power is hypothesized to be lowest relative to the power of the government, democracies are not only more likely to start wars, but are more likely to be the targets of others aggressive aims. Even more surprising, in the preelection period, when public power is hypothesized to be highest relative to governmental power, democratic states seem not only to resist the international pressures to start wars, but also somehow to defuse the international pressures that would lead others to start wars against them. These results, I believe, are quite unambiguous and are significant and interesting in and of themselves. They would appear to add some validity to the liberal argument that public control will have distinct influence on the war-making behavior of democratic states.[4]

Related to this explanation is that the people tend to choose for their leaders those who are nonviolent, who tend to compromise and appease. This was the way Quincy Wright explained why democracies should be more peaceful than autocracies. After pointing out that "Democracy has inherent possibilities of being the more peaceful form of government," he explained that

> autocrats, especially those who have achieved their own position, tend to be aggressive types of personality, to consider themselves above the law, to regard universal ideals as useful only for propaganda, to value military preparation and the institution of war as instruments of both internal and external policy, and to value power above welfare. Democracies, on the other hand, tend to give leadership to personalities of a conciliator type, to attach importance to respect for law, to oppose military preparation and war, and to value liberty, humanity, and welfare above power.[5]

Ernst-Otto Czempiel also provides a related first level type explanation for democracies being more peaceful in their international relations. He gives three reasons:

> First, they do not have the tradition of violence because in their domestic context they work by compromise and consensus. Second, for this lack of use they do not have the military means at hand. Democracies usually have command over only residual military forces, as was the case in the United States in the 30s and as it was preparing to do again before the outbreak of the Gulf war. Third, because of high degrees of domestic consensus, democracies do not depend on external tensions and military pressures to produce artificially the necessary consensus. *This consensus does exist because political values are being distributed equally. Everybody is content with what she/he gets.* Power is not concentrated but decentralized; its benefits can be consumed generally.[6]

In contemporary research the first-level explanation focuses on democratic institutions. It argues that competitive and periodic elections for the highest offices, a wide franchise, a secret ballot, and freedom of speech create a regime responsible to the people and less likely to engage in violence. One can argue this in two ways or in both. One and the usual approach, as already seen, is to treat *popular will* as a constraint.[7] It inhibits and pressures representative leaders from deciding for violence. T. Clifton Morgan and Sally Howard Campbell put this theory clearly, when they write that

> the greater the decisional constraints on a dispute participant, the lower the probability that the dispute will escalate to war. The causal mechanism linking domestic structure to conflict behavior specified in this theoretical argument focuses on the degree to which various segments of a society constrain the decisions of a state leader. It seems reasonable to assume that these constraints increase in severity as does the visibility of the situation requiring decision. The general public is usually completely ignorant of decisions regarding the initiation of disputes, and even most legislators can be unaware that such decisions are being considered. Thus, the only constraints that should operate on such decisions are those that operate through a leader's perception of how the decision will affect his ability to remain in power (which we have argued is the least direct and least important constraint and which is of some concern to all but the most entrenched and powerful dictators).[8]

The second approach is to view popular will as background to an "incentive explanation." That is, as Nehemia Geva, Karl DeRouen, and Alex Mintz summarize it,

> one of the major reasons why democracies do not fight each other is because their leaders have very few political incentives to do so. The political incentive explanation of the democratic peace phenomenon suggests that leaders of democratic

states do not use force against other democracies because such an action is perceived by the public as a *failure* of foreign policy. The political leader can not claim credit for it. There are only costs to the use of force, no political benefits. The net gain is therefore negative. . . . We argue that this democratic state conciliatory process is therefore due to lack of certain *political incentives* which overshadow constraints, norms, pluralistic foreign policy or some shared pre-conception towards peace in determining conflict escalation. . . . [And] nested within the political incentive explanation of democratic peace is the expectation that leaders of democratic states will not fight other democracies because this may be perceived as a foreign policy failure.[9]

Regardless of which form this explanation takes, each is ultimately based on popular will and has to be understood as a statistical and not absolute explanation. That is, democratic peoples have become jingoistic on occasions and enthusiastically favored war, as against Spain in 1898. They can also be aggressive today, pacific tomorrow. One need only contrast the popular support for American involvement in Vietnam from 1963 to 1966, to the vigorous hostility among intellectuals and opinion leaders to a continuation of the war in 1969. Of course, it is also true that the people can be stubbornly opposed to what they perceive as bellicose policies, no matter what their merits may be. Thus, President Roosevelt felt constrained by isolationist public opinion from giving all-out military aid to America's fraternal ally Great Britain in 1940–1941, the time when her survival from air and submarine attacks by Nazi Germany was very questionable, indeed. Yet, in deference to massive public opposition to American involvement, Roosevelt could only aid indirectly, discreetly, or illegally under the table, this last Western European bulwark against Nazi tyranny, aggression, and genocide. Vietnam and World War II are paradigm cases, for they represent what on balance is true about democratic peoples: they usually have been reluctant to go to war or to continue to fight costly wars they once supported. And if one focuses on war alone, popular will seems a simple and direct way to understand why democracies are pacific.

But that the explanation does focus wholly on war is a problem. It is, of course, applicable to lesser international violence, such as American military interventions in Panama and Grenada. Comparatively, in prospect and actuality, each involved relatively little violence, nothing like even a minor war. The American public and politicians largely ignored them and the subsequent election campaign was fought without reference to them, thus signaling the American foreign policy elite that there was considerable freedom of action to decide on such limited interventions, if they could be won rapidly and with few American casualties. One might thus predict from the public will that democracies would be more inclined to engage in low level military action and minor wars than those that are severe, as in fact is true.[10]

Moreover, this explanation is also applicable to extreme repression, genocide, and mass murder. This is put to the point, for example, in the writings of Milovan Djilas, a former member of the Yugoslav politburo, after his renunciation of communism. Writing about Goli Otok, one of the most barbarous of the Yugoslav concentration camps built in the late 1940s, and to which 15,000 purged communist party members and Soviet sympathizers (called Cominformists) were sent after Tito defected from the Soviet camp, he says:

> A substantial number served time simply because of having expressed pro-Soviet sentiments among friends. Some were entirely innocent. . . . Very few, if any, returned from Goli Otok unscathed. Not so much physically, perhaps, as psychologically and intellectually. Many were bitter, depressed, shattered. Even wise and well-intended ideologically reeducation—let alone the forced methods of Goli Otok—leads inevitably to aberration and tragedy if it goes on without public control. *Public control is the only control.*[11]

Djilas later makes the same point in a different context and in a way to stress the essence of the explanation in terms of the public will. At a politburo meeting he

> urged that some thought be given to dissolving [Goli Otok], that those who were guilty should be, instead, handed over to the courts. Kardelj was the first to oppose my recommendations. "We need the camp now desperately!" If I remember correctly, Rankovic remarked that it would not be so easy to settle accounts with the Cominformists through normal procedures. Tito was silent, reflective, then he dismissed my proposal, probably on the ground that it was premature. And so we reacted in the *typical fashion of politicians who are above public control*—in pursuit of political goals, arbitrarily and without overriding concern for human conditions, human suffering.[12]

But the explanation by popular will is not easily applicable to internal collective violence. Often such violence is provoked and launched by some domestic group, either seeking to overthrow the political leadership, change the system of rule (as by a Marxist or Maoist guerrilla war), or alter public policy. The decision of such groups to fight the government is not one made by elected representatives, and indeed, were the representatives not to approve responding with force to such violence they might by turned out of office for not maintaining order, or for cravenly submitting to violent demands. And where government itself violently attacks one group or another, or carries out a democidal campaign against a minority, this could be well argued to reflect the will of the majority. After all, rule by a people is rule by some majority and a majority can well turn on a minority in spite of the costs. Note the internment in concentration camps during World War II of West coast Japanese-Americans by the American government for no other reason than their national origin. Then note also that after the French Revolution a committee of the elected parliament of the First French Republic killed up to 20,000 people in the Terror,[13] many losing their heads to the guillotine, and carried out a campaign of genocide in the Vendée in which some 117,000 men, women, and children may have been slaughtered.[14]

Moreover, over some extremely vital national issue, a majority could provoke a minority to take up arms, as in the American Civil War.

In other words, the explanation in terms of the cost perceived by a democratic people is not sufficiently general to explain why democracy should be a method of nonviolence.[15]

Nor does it explain Weart's addenda, why an oligarchic republic should not make war on those of its own kind. After all, in such a republic governance is in the hands of a minority who, while among themselves they have equal rights, repress the majority. That is, even were a majority strongly opposed to war or any other kind of violence or repression, the elite are free to exercise their will.

But there is also a second reason to question this explanation. Its basis lies in the electoral machinery of a democracy, which assumes that the more representative a regime, the less inclined to severe violence. This in effect says that those regimes without any electoral mechanisms should be the most warlike, which would be the absolute monarchies like Saudi Arabia. But this has not been found (nor as later explanations will argue, should it be found) to be the case. It is totalitarian regimes that are the most warlike, and although their electoral machinery and legislatures are run by or wholly dominated by one party, they have the facade of democratic government and thus would be predicted to have less foreign violence than authoritarian regimes, which is not the case.

In sum, the first-level explanation is really along the continuum of democracy to authoritarianism, rather than the more relevant continuum of democracy to totalitarianism. This mistake is understandable, since when this explanation was first proposed by Kant in 1795, totalitarian systems of the modern variety did not exist. Except for the newly republican United States and revolutionary France, the world was almost wholly made up of authoritarian monarchies. Nonetheless, it does give an easily understandable partial explanation for the interdemocratic peace, one that is most applicable to the most democratic of regimes most of the time.

Notes

1. Babst (1964, p. 9).
2. Kilgour (1991, p. 282). Russett (1990, pp. 9-14) has a relevant and insightful section on "How domestic politics matter, " which deals in general with the public restraints on the American president.
3. Gaubatz (1991, p. 213).
4. Gaubatz (1991, p. 232).
5. Wright (1942, p. 847). For more on how public opinion works in democracies, see Dalton (1988).
6. Czempiel (1992, p. 262, italics added).
7. I do not mean by popular will that which the people would truly want were they to know all the facts and what is good for them (as in Jean Jacques Rousseau's General Will), but rather the opinions and attitudes of the people as would be expressed through public opinion polls, attitudinal surveys, focus groups, and particularly in elections.
8. Morgan and Campbell (1991, p. 195).
9. Geva, DeRouen, and Mintz (1993, p. 218). They believe they "confirmed" this through simulation experiments (Ibid., p. 224). See also Mintz and Geva (1993, p. 498), who, importantly, found in their simulation experiments that "the most important finding . . . is that public approval of the use of force is contingent upon the regime of the adversary. Although the use of force was perceived appropriate when associated with a nondemocratic state, it seemed significantly less appropriate when it was targeted against a democratic regime" (Ibid., pp. 500–01).
10. See chapter 4.
11. Djilas (1980, p. 87, italics added).
12. Djilas (1980, p. 88, italics added). He subsequently makes freedom of information the intermediary variable between public control and regime repression. He wrote, "The ban on freedom of information is the source of evil in Communists regimes, and in Tito's and Yugoslavia's. This evil permeates society, seeps into its pores, prevents organic development, impels dictatorial authority to terror and violence" (p. 89).
13. Medvedev (1971, p. 269); Burns and Ralph (1955, Vol. 2, p. 95); Sydenham (1965, chapter 8).
14. Ladouce (1988, pp. 686, 690).
15. For critical treatments of the supposed sovereignty of public opinion, or that public opinion will work against centralized power, see Schattschneider (1960) and Ginsberg (1986).

10

Second-Level Explanation:
Cross-Pressures, Exchange Culture,
and In-Group Perception

> *(a) Democracies rarely fight each other . . .
> because (b) they have other means of resolv-
> ing conflicts between them and therefore do
> not need to fight each other . . . and (c) they
> perceive that democracies should not fight each
> other. . . . By this reasoning, the more democ-
> racies there are in the world, the fewer poten-
> tial adversaries we and other democracies will
> have and the wider the zone of peace.*
> —Bruce Russett,
> *Grasping the Democratic Peace*

There are several other explanations for the peacefulness of democracies that go beneath the immediately observed institutions of democracy and public will. One emphasizes democratic *culture*, another the
diversity or *pluralism* created by democracies. And a third the *perception of others* as of the same kind, part of one's group.

The culture argument is as straightforward as that focusing on representative institutions. It has been nicely summarized by T. Clifton
Morgan and Valerie Schwebach, which is that

liberal democracies are more peace loving than other states less because their
citizenry have a direct influence on specific policy decisions than because of the
norms regarding appropriate methods of conflict resolution that develop within the
society. Adjudication and bargaining are viewed as proper methods of resolving
disputes while the use of force is disdained. Citizens of democracies believe that
they, as individuals, should behave in this way *and* they expect similar behavior

137

from others. The expectation is important. By reducing the incentive to "draw first" it increases the likelihood that disputes will be resolved peacefully. State leaders of liberal democracies are drawn from the citizenry that hold these values. They believe that disputes can and should be settled without resort to violence and these norms are carried over into the international arena. Thus, conflicts of interest between democratic countries are resolved peacefully. Even the most ideologically committed liberal democrat recognizes that the leaders of non-democracies do not conform to these norms of behavior, however. When a democracy becomes involved in a dispute with another type of state there is no expectation that the other will rely on peaceful means of conflict resolution. Hence, liberal democrats are able and willing to lead their countries into war with other types of states; and, in fact, their ideological beliefs can serve as a motivation for aggression (i.e., to bring others into the liberal fold).[1]

To put this more generally, democracy creates a political culture in which opposing groups and representatives must constantly make compromises.[2] Negotiation, concessions, splitting the differences, and the toleration of different views and ideologies is necessitated in a system of governance where simply to carry out the functions of government and respond to national issues and problems there must be a give and take among representatives of different constituencies, regions, and ideologies. Moreover, and particularly important, there must be a willingness to lose on vital issues, to regroup, and fight within the system to win the election or vote the next time or the time after that.

Democracy breeds this culture of negotiation, compromise, and toleration by virtue of its institutions, and by virtue of the exchange society of which it is a part. Exchange, as in economic relations, of necessity requires bargaining and compromise. Politics and society work together to produce and reinforce the democratic culture and it is this culture that inhibits the reluctance of democratic peoples and representatives to engage in violence.

This is a persuasive argument. Where by virtue of their institutions democratic people must, to maintain democracy, negotiate and compromise rather than fight, this becomes part of the cultural heritage.[3] It is the way people come to naturally behave, perceive, and expect. And since we deal with others through a cultural matrix, it is also natural for democratic people to perceive other regimes in these terms, to believe that all basic issues between nations can be settled by people sitting down at a table and talking them out, and to tolerate the existence of other regimes and ideologies that do not openly threaten one's democratic way of life. More formally, Bueno de Mesquita and Lalman derived from their expected utilities model something like this and put it in the form of a proposition: "Democracies confronting one another are less likely to engage in violence than are mixed dyads because each believes the other is likely to be averse to using force (that is, to be dovelike), and each state is more likely to be dovelike. Leaders averse to using force who confront rivals also believed (with sufficient confidence) to be averse to using force do not use force."[4] And they found empirically that democracies are more inclined to use negotiation and be "generally adverse to using force."[5]

With a slightly different slant, Bruce Russett expressed in outline the same explanation:

Violent conflicts between democracies will be rare because: . . . In democracies the relevant decisionmakers expect to be able to resolve conflicts by compromise and nonviolence, respecting the rights and continued existence of opponents. . . . Therefore democracies will follow norms of peaceful conflict resolution with other democracies, and will expect other democracies to do so with them. . . . The more stable the democracy, the more will democratic norms govern its behavior with other democracies, and the more will other democracies expect democratic norms to govern its international behavior. . . . Violent conflicts between nondemocracies, and between democracies and nondemocracies, will be more frequent because:. . . In nondemocracies decisionmakers use, and may expect their opponents to use, violence and the threat of violence to resolve conflict as part of their domestic political processes. . . . Therefore nondemocracies may use violence and the threat of violence in conflicts with other states, and other states may expect them to use violence and the threat of violence in such conflicts. . . . Democratic norms can be more easily exploited to force concessions than can nondemocratic ones; to avoid exploitation democracies may adopt nondemocratic norms in dealing with nondemocracies.[6]

Bruce Russet and William Antholis tested this culture-norm explanation on the wars between city-states in classical Greece. They in fact found even in those days, as imperfect as Greek democracies were, that

ties of common democratic culture therefore offered some restraint on wars between Greek democracies. That restraint, certainly rooted in self-interest, also exhibited elements of normative restraint. For the restraints to operate, however, it was necessary for states and peoples actually to perceive each other as democratic.[7]

Consider also William Dixon's norm based explanation of why disputes between democracies should rarely, if at all, escalate to violence. He argues that the

international disputes of democratic states are in the hands of individuals who have experienced the politics of competing values and interests and who have consistently responded within the normative guidelines of bounded competition. In situations where both parties to a dispute are democracies, not only do both sides subscribe to these norms, but the leaders of both are also fully cognizant that bounded competition is the norm, both for themselves and their opponents. Democracy, after all, cannot be conducted in secret. When democracies do confront other democracies, these shared norms of bounded competition will provide a mutual basis for contingent consent, suggesting that disputes between democracies should evolve somewhat differently than do disputes between states not sharing these norms (i.e., between democratic and nondemocratic states or between two nondemocratic states).[8]

Dixon tested this explanation on a global sample of 264 post-World War II disputes[9] and subsequently retested it in a more refined manner.[10] He found that with the increasing democratization of a regime its management of conflict improved, consistent with his prior conclusion that "the empirical results proved to be remarkably stable under a variety of alternative specifications. The overall implications are exceedingly clear: Democracy does carry the systematic positive influence on the probability of conflict management expected of it."[11]

Finally there is the culture-based argument of historian and physicist Spencer Weart. In explaining why he cannot find one clear war between well established democracies throughout all of history, including the classical Greek city-states, he says that

(1) Republican political culture (a shorthand for beliefs tied up with the whole social complex including norms, institutional constraints, civic society, etc.) teaches people to negotiate and make reciprocal concessions as equals with other people, provided these are members of their ingroup, the "people like us." (2) It also teaches them that the ingroup of equals includes almost anybody who follows their own political principles, even foreigners. The only people who may legitimately be coerced are ones who reject republican principles: those are seen as criminals or perhaps, like tribal peoples, incompetent. Democratic leaders will try to negotiate with anybody who seems like a democrat—they will even try to negotiate with the Hitler's and Saddam Husseins of the world until disabused.[12]

This also applies to the lack of wars between oligarchic republics that Weart found throughout written history, where although the larger majority may have second class citizenship, the ruling minority have equal rights among themselves. They negotiate and bargain, compromise and peacefully accept losing. In other words, they share democratic norms, and apply these equally to other regimes like their own and expect their conciliatory behavior to be reciprocated. They see other such republics as of their own kind, as members of their ingroup, their moral universe.[13]

The virtue of the cultural norm-based explanation is that it is applicable to not just war, but all kinds of violence, including domestic collective violence or democide. Why is there very little democide and the least collective political violence in democracies? Because of the internal inhibitions ("it is not the way one should settle issues") and behavioral patterns—compromise, negotiation, and the like—inherent in democratic culture. Why less foreign violence by democracies? Because democratic leaders and peoples are least inclined to fight before exhausting avenues of diplomacy that are natural to democrats. Why do democracies not fight each other? Because two democratic peoples and leaders perceive each other as democratic and thus see their relations wholly in democratic terms, and are correct. Both use negotiation and compromise as the avenues of conflict resolution and besides, have a basic cultural sympathy toward each other.

Related to this is the argument of John M. Owen. It is a liberal ideology (the belief in freedom, equality before the law, and democratic practices) working within a liberal structure that accounts for peace between democracies. Within a democracy there may be elites that might favor war against another country, but when liberals perceive the other as governed liberally, they work against war. Since in a democracy such liberals dominate, they are able to prevent war against democracies. This also explains why democracies are more cooperative among themselves. In general, as Owen puts it:

> Liberal ideas are the source—the independent variable—behind the distinctive foreign policies of liberal democracies. These ideas give rise to two intervening variables, liberal ideology and domestic democratic institutions, which shape foreign policy. Liberal ideology prohibits war against liberal democracies, but sometimes calls for war against illiberal states. Democratic institutions allow these drives to affect foreign policy and international relations.[14]

As for Weart, note particularly Owen's emphasis on perception. Democratic leaders to Weart, and democratic liberals for Owen, *perceive* the other country like their own or as sharing their liberal ideology and thus work to resolve their conflicts without violence.

Those who believe democratic culture or ideology helps account for a democratic peace often see this as a dichotomy. There is an opposition posed between democracy and nondemocracy (or in Weart's case, to republics and nonrepublics) such that within each type of regime the conditions of peace and violence are similar, particularly the existence of a nonviolent culture of democracy versus the lack of such a culture for nondemocracies. This dichotomy has been fed by the findings that democracies don't make war on each other and the mistaken consensus that democracies are neither more nor less warlike than other regimes. As has been shown and argued in chapter 4, the latter belief is not tenable. Nonetheless, acting on it, some have found the democratic culture explanation the best way to square these "inconsistent findings." Democracies will not make war on democracies because they both have democratic cultures and each expects the other to act in a democratic way—to talk, negotiate, and compromise. But with other regimes that have no democratic culture, there is no such disposition and it is conflict, violence, and war as usual. Even the term *democratic* culture assumes something unique about it that is not shared with other regimes.

But there are good reasons not to treat democratic culture as a dichotomy. We might begin by simply changing the term to an *exchange culture,* noting that this is a culture that develops wherever there is the art of bargaining and exchange over goods, services, and ideas, as in business, science, or the community of scholars. Wherever a regime allows a fair amount of exchange there has to be likewise the arts of bargaining, negotiation, and compromise, as in those fully or partly authoritarian societies with a high degree of capitalism, such as the mixed (partial authoritarian, partially coercive) regimes of Taiwan and South Korea before they democratized, Thailand, Chile under Pinochet, Pakistan, Malaysia, Jordan, Liberia, Gabon, and Mexico, among others.

Moreover, authoritarian or mixed authoritarian-totalitarian regimes (like Mussolini's Italy or Franco's Spain) do not stand alone in power. Although there are no real institutional means of settling vital issues by the ballot or legislative voting, leaders of authoritarian regimes are not absolute inside or outside of politics. They monopolize coercive power, but their rule is also partly (or in the case of absolute monarchies, mainly) based on authority and legitimacy. Although autocratic, although there is no oligarchic elite with whom they share equal rights, to maintain their legitimacy they must contend and bargain with church officials, diverse foreign and domestic business leaders, ethnic, religious, and linguistic minorities, regional leaders, the military, and factions within the regime itself. Through all this bargaining it is reasonable to expect that authoritarian regimes will share certain aspects of a culture based on exchange. Moreover we can say that where all independent sources of power have been liquidated, where dissidents in and without the regime are periodically purged, and where an absolute leaders stands in uncontested power, with control over all, as of Kim Il-sung in North Korea or Stalin over the Soviet Union, then there is no need to bargain on important issues. When force and coercion are the fundamental engine of order, then we can expect that there will be little of an exchange culture. *We can thus think of an exchange culture as being on a continuum, with authoritarian regimes lying somewhere between the democratic and totalitarian types.*

A virtue of the culture argument is that it can accept that people by themselves are prone to violence and can even kill for what they desire; that all of us can be both angels and devils. And that democratic people by themselves are genetically and psychological no more nor less prone to genocide, mass murder, and war than any other people. But the nature of a democratic system and exchange society is that it disciplines our dispositions; it requires that we learn the ways of nonviolent conflict resolution if we are to get along and prosper. Significantly, in such an exchange society one generally is neither forced to behave in a certain way or given a road map of desirable behavior by tradition, but through trial and error, interaction, and conflict with others, one learns to adjust, negotiate, and compromise. Of course, the institutions of a democracy magnify all this and that helps them to be least violent.

Culture is one thing. Another is the social, economic, and political diversity of society that acts to restrain and isolate violence. Before getting into this I need to clarify the meaning of *constraint,* which is an important concept in much theorizing on democracies not making war on each other. For example, Bueno de Mesquita and Lalman even derive theorems—democratic constraint propositions—from their expected utilities model:

> Nations like the average democracy that face a high and visible domestic political cost for using force utilize force to avoid exploitation either by initiating violence or by retaliating for the use of force by rivals who do not face a relatively high domestic political constraint.
>
> The probability that A will resort to the use of force depends on A's probability of success and on A's domestic political constraints such that these two variables bear an inverse relation to each other if B is expected to capitulate to A's use of force or if B expects A to capitulate to its use of force. If B anticipates a war begun by A, then B's probability of success can be positively or negatively associated with its domestic political constraints.[15]

What is the source of such constraints? For Gaubatz it is the public will: "The closer the society is to an impending election, the greater will be the societal restrictions on the courses of action the state can follow. Thus the electoral cycle gives us a dynamic picture of the effects of social constraints on state action."[16] This kind of constraint was discussed on the last chapter.

For Zeev Maoz and Bruce Russett, however, while no doubt recognizing public will, focus on a different kind of constraint: "The structural version [of the theory] emphasizes the constraints on political leaders in democratic states with regard to dispute and war initiation. These constraints include the division of power and other legal restraints on executive power; they would be magnified in the case of a pair of democratic states in a possible dispute."[17]

For Domke the constraint involves effective interest groups: "Only when domestic interests opposed to war have effective means of influencing the actions of government does constraint exist."[18]

In a slightly different way, Bueno de Mesquita and Lalman also see this as a constraint: "Liberal democratic institutions ensure that opponents of government policies incur lower costs for their actions than in nondemocratic states. This makes it easy for domestic political opponents to mobilize, including mobilization to oppose the use of force. Such mobilized opposition increases the political constraints in democracies."[19]

For Kilgour the decisional "constraint" lies in the political competitiveness of democracy: "The existence of an effective opposition discourages war initiation."[20]

And Morgan and Campbell discuss three types of constraints: the method of selecting executives, nature of political competition, and the degree to which the executive shares decision-making power. Of these they say that "the method of executive selection and, to a lesser extent, the nature of political competition variables constrain decisions only indirectly. Their effect is felt through the leader's perceptions regarding the likely domestic political consequences of particular actions. This can certainly influence decisions, but not to the extent of a direct constraint such as that imposed by the requirement that other people and/or institutions be included in the decision process."[21]

Institutional constraints therefore can be of many different kinds, such as of the public will already discussed, institutional checks and balances within government, social diversity that cross-cuts and cross-pressures interests, or the plethora of groups produced within a democracy that pressure and lobby representatives for or against policies and laws. I mean by constraint all of these. Moreover, there are not only constraints, but positive inducements for leaders to behave. The constraint argument is that democratic leaders are inclined to choose violence were it not for these restraints. But it also may be that the complex and extended process of campaigning and working one's way up through lower elected positions selects the personality type less disposed toward violence. Moreover, those in office may also have positive inducements to avoid violence.

Such has been focused on by Mintz and Geva, who theorized and, they believe, empirically supported through their simulation experiments, that the "democratic avoidance of aggression is not only a function of fear of normative and structural constraints, but also relates to lack of potential benefits from the use of force."[22]

Now, with an exchange society with a democratic government (as discussed in chapter 8), people are largely free to follow there own interests. They can invent businesses, write books and articles, produce movies and television programs, organize special interest groups, even start a new political party. In short, they can create, organize, and associate as they find people of like mind or interests. All such free activity generates a diversity of corporations, organizations, groups, and individuals interests. This social diversity occurs regardless of whether the society is ethnically, racially, or religiously homogenous. It is a superimposed diversity of activities and of interests, and it is a pluralism in the citizen's concerns, stakes, commitments and obligations that comes with the freedom of cultural, social, and economic exchange.

As with democratic culture, this is a diversity that acts to contravene the worst consequences of the potentiality for violence within all of us, democratic people or not, and thus within all regimes, which after all simply comprise people empowered to govern. It does this by segmenting interests, statuses, and activities such that the tendency to violence is tied down by numerous bonds, such as to church, to professional associations, to unions, to sport or recreational groups, to political parties, and to businesses. But more important than these bonds is the dividing up of interests this produces. That is, with diverse statuses, commitments and benefits, it is difficult to become impassioned about any one interest to the exclusion or detriment of the others. One is therefore *cross-pressured*.[23] To overly push one's interests in an antiabortion law may effect legislation on health care that one favors. The result is to be cross-pressured. One may be disposed to oppose a candidate for office because of their race but also know that person has a position on the issues congenial to one's own views; cross-pressured again.

Relevantly, one way democracies inhibit violence is by co-opting those potential revolutionaries who oppose the system altogether or certain basic policies and institutions. In groups and on college campuses these radicals may strongly and sometimes violently express their revolutionary spirit, as did the student and social rebels in the 1960s. But these rebels were soon absorbed into the system, within which they found an outlet for their beliefs. Many become journalists, educators, and legislators, and the tendency to pursue their radical beliefs, even through revolution and violence, is now moderated within the social system. Some may still remain radical in beliefs, but they now have too much to lose in influence and benefits by being openly revolutionary and particularly violent. They are cross-pressured.

What about foreign violence? Democratic nations with their shared democratic ideas and largely exchange societies develop between them a variety of bonds, connections, and transactions, not the least of which are bilateral foreign relations between different government agencies, bureaus, and departments and common membership in intergovernmental and nongovernmental organizations. The diversifying and segmenting of interests across national boundaries is not much different than that within an exchange society. The upshot of this multitude of ties is that they make it difficult for a people or regime to consciously promote one interest to the level of violence because of the negative effects on other interests; cross-pressures here also.

It should be obvious that even for authoritarian regimes the existence of independent areas of exchange, such as a relatively free market, foreign trade and investment, and scientific, technological, and cultural exchange, make for transnational bonds that transcend the regime. As in the case of democracy, these link it in ways to other countries that can influence its disposition to escalate foreign conflict to a level of violence that would severe the advantages the regime and other power centers in the society enjoy.

But the dynamics of interaction and thus the influence of cross-pressures in authoritative societies differ from those for the exchange society of a democracy. In a democracy there is the constant friction of interaction and exchange between groups and individuals as they adjust to new situations, new demands, and new issues. *This makes for a high level of nonviolent conflict across the society, the stuff of democratic politics.*[24] But there usually is no conflict front that traverses society. Because of the multitude of diverse groups and separate interests, because of the lack of coincidence of interests across groups and issues, if political conflict escalates to violence it is usually limited to an issue or so, a neighborhood or urban area, or particular individuals.[25]

For an authoritative society, however, the society is held together largely by custom, cultural norms, tradition, and the legitimacy of the rules of the authoritarian regime. As a result nonviolent conflict may be less than in the near free-for-all of the exchange society and democratic regime. But when the crust of tradition is broken, as by rapid economic and technological change or a modernizing ruler, like the Shah of Iran in the 1970s; or conflict occurs over the legitimacy of the regime, as currently provoked by Moslem Fundamentalists in Egypt or Algeria; or the conflict is even over the political system itself, as when the rebels Pancho Villa and Emiliano Zapata triggered the Mexican Revolution in 1910; a national conflict front traversing all groups can form, causing nationwide conflict and escalation to extreme violence and even revolution.

With totalitarian regimes and their coercively imposed order, however, there are no independent groups to either establish transnational linkages and bonds, nor are there the independent domestic groups and centers of power to moderate and isolate domestic conflict over major issues. All that matters is a matter of government control. Ultimately, then, all becomes a question between those who command and those who must obey; of them and us. In foreign affairs, then, no international issue or conflict is too little to concern the regime and become a question of regime power, honor, credibility, and other interests of state. And any significant domestic conflict can easily become a matter of deep political significance, questioning the regime's or ruler's power or programs, and thus a matter for the army and secret policy, and purges, repression, and renewed arrests and executions.

There is one more related explanation to consider, that based on positive expectations. Dixon puts this well:

each party to a purely democratic dispute is secure in the knowledge that its opponent is also normatively proscribed from violent and coercive means for reconciling divergent values and interests, at least in the domestic political arena. These norms are externalized to foreign affairs only if the practices underlying them are sufficiently robust to foster mutual expectations of congruent behavior beyond borders. Accordingly, we would expect highly democratic opponents to be constrained from resorting to violent and coercive means at the earliest stage of their disputes no matter how severe or contentious the underlying grievances.[26]

This is a variant of the explanation in terms of culture, where now we focus on the norms and culturally influenced perceptions and expectations of a decision maker that dispose them toward negotiation rather than violence. But here I should be more precise about this, especially since Spencer Weart has made a similar argument the central explanation of why throughout history well established democratic and oligarchic republics have not or rarely made war on each other. He says that

the republican custom of accommodation applies only within a group who recognize one another as equals. In some oligarchic republics, such groups have included only a few hundred men. Even democrats hold that coercion is legitimate against anyone who is unable or unwilling to abide by the law, such as children and criminals. The leaders of a state will not necessarily be accommodating to foreign leaders unless they see them as people who are due equal treatment, in the same sense as domestic citizens.

We meet here the universal human tendency to divide people into "ingroup" and "outgroups"—a tendency that anthropologists and sociologists have long identified as central to war-making. People normally use one set of attitudes and norms for behavior with their ingroup, and a different set, often far more suspicious and belligerent, with outgroups. That may matter little for authoritarian cliques and autocrats, who demand submission and use coercion even among their colleagues and kin. But republican political culture—or at any rate the aspect of it that concerns us—mandates continual efforts at peaceful conciliation of anyone seen as fellow citizens.[27]

There is a common psychological mechanism operating here that has been well identified in the literature on genocide.[28] Those that are *perceived* as like oneself in norms and behavior will be treated as a member of one's group and one will *expect* them to behave in a similar way. Those that are perceived different will be treated differently, perhaps suspiciously, warily, and even aggressively. This is not a matter of social, economic, and psychological distances.[29] Nor is it a matter of political similarity, for two communist nations can be at each other's throat (as for China and Vietnam in the later 1970s). It is a matter of norm sharing, of seeing the other as behaving like oneself.[30] Thus, democratic and oligarchic republican decision makers and those who matter in politics see other like regimes as willing to talk, negotiate, and compromise expect this behavior, and thus act in a way to encourage this. There is a reinforcing circle here of perception, expectations, and behavior among these regimes. However, if the other is viewed as not only having different norms, but an antagonistic political system, then perception and expectations can work against conciliation and for the escalation of conflict.

But do authoritarian and totalitarian systems also see each other as the same? Yes, and this works for the increasing conflict and violence than against it as in the case of republics. For the rulers of such regimes treat others as subordinates, are used to command and not negotiation and compromise among equals, and will often use prisons and concentration camps, torture and executions, to keep the masses in their place. As Weart puts it, "They do not accept as in-group anyone outside their own skin (many monarchs killed even their own brothers)."[31] Often outright murderers, rightfully paranoiac about those around them, they have no reason to expect that other rulers of regimes like theirs will be any different. Indeed, as I pointed out in part I, not only should we expect more violence between and by such regimes, this is in fact what we find empirically.

So far, however, there is one major problem with this explanation, and that is it that treats nonrepublics as all alike. But as I have shown in part I, there is an underlying continuum here. On the average, violence between two regimes will scale upward the less democratic they are. While the cultural explanation can take account of this scale, as I have shown, that extension of the cultural explanation to in-group/ out-group dynamics cannot. Nor was it meant to be as developed by Weart, who tied to primary historical sources that hardly provided the detailed information available for contemporary regimes, could not in any case distinguish the degree of violence between different types of regimes.

To conclude, then, at the first level, that of popular will, we have an explanation in terms of the natural desire of people to avoid the loss of their property, their loved ones, and their own lives, and thus the reluctance of their representatives to favor violence. As problematic as this explanation is, it still provides some direct understanding of why there is a democratic peace. At the deeper level of social structure and culture we can point to the violence dampening and fractionating effect of the social, economic, and political pluralism created with the increased freedom of a people, and a concomitant culture such that the more the democracy the more the culture favors negotiation, compromise, and tolerance. In particular, this means that when democratic leaders and citizens deal with other democracies, they see them as like themselves and thus behave to resolve conflicts.

There is, however, yet a third level of explanation. That is of social fields and antifields, of freedom and exchange versus coercive power. This is the subject of the next chapters.

Notes

1. Morgan and Schwebach (1992, pp. 306–07).
2. Culture is a form of behavior that individuals learn as members of a group and that includes generally followed customs, morals, mores, norms, and beliefs. On culture in general, see Carrithers (1992) and Featherstone (1992). The idea of culture has been central in social theory, as it should. On this, see Archer (1988).
3. The nature and role of negotiation has, of course, been much studied in international relations. This has been largely ignored in the study of social conflict generally, however, until recently. On this, see Pruitt and Carnevale (1993).
4. Bueno de Mesquita and Lalman (1992, p. 155, italics omitted).
5. Ibid., p. 157. Their chi-square test of this was significant at .0005 (table 5.1—I give the highest significance level compatible with their specification of p = .000).
6. Russett (1993, p. 35). In one study Russett with Maoz (1993, pp. 81-82) measured democratic norms by the political stability of a regime and the extent of its internal violent political conflict and political executions. See also Maoz and Russett (1993, p. 625), who put the normative model explicitly: "NORMATIVE ASSUMPTION 1. States, to the extent possible, externalize the norms of behavior that are developed within and characterize their domestic political processes and institutions.
   NORMATIVE ASSUMPTION 2. The anarchic nature of international politics implies that a clash between democratic and nondemocratic norms is dominated by the latter, rather than by the former" (italics omitted).
7. Russett and Antholis (1992, p. 429).
8. Dixon (1994, p. 4).
9. Dixon (1993).
10. Dixon (1994).
11. Dixon (1993, p. 64).
12. Personal communication. Also, see Weart (1994, 1995).
13. The analysis of social and international conflict in terms of in-group versus out-group perception has a long tradition. See in particular the work of Sherif (1966) and Sherif and Sherif (1953). For the overall social psychology of conflict, see Worchel and Simpson (1993); Fisher (1990); and Stroebe (1988).
14. Owen (1994, p. 93). Owen's argument is based on the study of a dozen case studies of crises involving the United States from the 1790s through 1919. See Owen (1993).
15. Bueno de Mesquita and Lalman (1992, pp. 158, 164; italics omitted).

16. Gaubatz (1991, p. 213).
17. Maoz and Russett (1992, p 246). See also Maoz and Russett (1993, p. 626) where they elaborate their structural model: "STRUCTURAL ASSUMPTION 1. International challenges require political leaders to mobilize domestic support to their policies. Such support must be mobilized from those groups that provide the leadership the kind of legitimacy that is required for international action. STRUCTURAL ASSUMPTION 2. Shortcuts to political mobilization of relevant political support can be accomplished only in situations that can be appropriately described as emergencies" (p. 626, italics omitted).
18. Domke (1988, p. 185).
19. Bueno de Mesquita and Lalman (1992, p. 148).
20. Kilgour (1991, p. 282).
21. Morgan and Campbell (1991, p. 192).
22. Mintz and Geva (1993, p. 486).
23. The idea of cross-cutting groups and cross-pressures has a long history in sociology. A basic work on this is Simmel (1955). See also Coser (1956). Social scientists have made much use of the concept to explain voting behavior or the intensity of interests. See, for example, Lipset (1963); Campbell, Converse, Miller, and Stokes (1960); and Dahl (1966, 1971). The empirical tests of this idea on domestic societies have been mixed, as shown for example in Powell (1976). As I use it here cross-pressures is a psychological concept that goes well beyond the simple cross-pressures felt, say, by a practicing liberal Catholic who is both inclined to vote for the conservative Catholic Republican and the liberal Jewish Democrat. It includes, for example, the dissonance in perception when the enemy of one's friend is also one's friend, cross-pressuring behavior toward both of them. It also includes the social dissonance felt by a person high on one status, such as wealth, and low on another, such as power or prestige. Such status incongruence is a common feature of democracies, where a government bureaucrat may be lower middle class in wealth but have tremendous regulatory power over a wealthy businessman. The result is that behavior is also cross-pressured, for one's inconsistent tendencies is to both behave along one's highest status and to reciprocate that behavior of another responding to one's lower statuses. On this, see for example, Galtung (1966, pp. 159–60); Malewski (1966, p. 305); and Hewitt (1970, p. 21). On the relationship between status disequilibrium and cognitive dissonance, see Sampson (1963). In fact, "Many of the behaviors that political sociologists ascribe to 'cross-pressures' may possibly by subsumed under the concept of status discrepancy" (Svalastoga, 1959, p. 66). In an inventory I did of empirical research on international relations, I found (Rummel, 1979, p. 290) that the results tended to support the proposition that cross-pressures inhibit intense violence. For a recent application of the idea to intergroup bias, see Marcus-Newhall, Miller, and Holtz (1993). For an empirical examination of cross-pressures and revision of the concept consistent with my theoretical use here, see Sperlich (1971).
24. For this reason, among others, I insist that to empirically analyze the relationship between democracy and a scale of both violent and nonviolent conflict obscures the important inverse link between democracy and violence.
25. Even for democracies, however, such a conflict front can form when divisions on several vital issues coalesce into one. For instance, the American Civil War increasingly loomed in the 1840s and 1850s as several issues between northern and southern states combined into one huge divide—conflict front—separating them on such vital questions as slavery, states rights and sovereignty, and foreign trade.
26. Dixon (1994, p. 4).

27. Weart (1994—this is from a preprint of his article).
28. Fein (1979, 1984) has put this in terms of excluding another from one's moral universe. For how this can account, in part, for ordinary people carrying out genocide by their own hands, see Browning (1992).
29. This is not to say that such distances are unimportant in other ways. I have much emphasized social (including status) distances in my theoretical and related empirical work on international relations and conflict in general, including status distances. I found (Rummel, 1977, 1979b) that these distances between nations in their diverse attribute dimensions accounted for about one-third to one-half of the variation in their bilateral international behavior. However, distances on democracy versus totalitarian and democracy versus authoritarian dimensions did not even moderately well account for foreign conflict and violence. The reason for this is now clear from the text. Democracies and oligarchic republics do not fight their own kind while authoritarian and totalitarian regimes do. That is, political distances do account for violence, *but only when the parameters are specific to the type of regime.* The first theoretical use of social and other distances to explain war was by Quincy Wright (1942, chapter 35). See note 7 of chapter 11.
30. This is the important point made by Sorokin (1969, p. 143), in what I still regard as one of the most important sociological works.
31. Personal communication. Also, see Weart (1994, 1995).

11

Third-Level Explanation I:
Social Field and Freedom

> *We believe that the greater the freedoms in
> other countries the more secure both our own
> freedoms and peace.*
> —President Reagan, May, 1988
> speech in the USSR

The third level is the most encompassing and powerful explanation
of why democracy is a method of nonviolence. It comprises the ideas
of social field and antifield, which provide a conceptual model of this
proposition, and a way of understanding it. This level is thus basically
philosophical and meta-sociological.[1] For this reason I should begin
with the assumptions that underlay this explanation.

First, I argue that mind and matter, our perceptions, expectations,
interests, and needs, and the material reality external to us form a
seamless tapestry. We introduce scale and perspective into this reality,
we actualize its potentiality and give it purpose through our biophysi-
cal capabilities and social perceptions, expectations, and interests.[2] We
give this reality significance and importance through our *meanings,
values, and norms.*[3] Most basically, then, the fundamental questions of
human behavior, as for social and political violence and their causes,
have to do with mentality and not material things. That is, it is not
material wealth or poverty, or armaments or sheer physical size, or
human density or number of people that basically explain violence.
Rather, it is how these things are perceived or valued, what meaning
they have, or their relationship to expectations and interests that are
the nexus for understanding violence.[4]

Moreover, this assumption necessarily implies a focus on the individual. Groups and institutions and nations or governments do not perceive or have expectations. They are abstractions only given meaning and value in the minds of individuals. As the saying goes, you can't kick a regime, only its leader. The core of any explanation of democracy's effect on violence, therefore, has to be the *individual*. And specifically this has to be the individual's *mental field* within which they define their purposes, gains and losses, and their achievements and failures, whatever these may mean to them.

Second, a person's mental reference point is not absolute, but one constantly evolving in terms of their experiences, learning, and specific subculture. It is *relative*. Some living in poverty may be satisfied with what they have, particularly if they live only among the poor and believe that those with more wealth deserve what they have.[5] Some with great wealth may be quite unhappy with what they have, envying the one with millions more and believing that market or government machinations has deprived them of their due. Moreover, a nation wealthy in material goods in 1900 may be a poor nation by comparison to nations in 1990. It is often the status of an individual or nation in wealth, power, or prestige that effect their behavior and not a particular amount of wealth.[6] Moreover, it is the differences and similarities—what may be called *social distances*—in wealth, power, prestige, values, and norms between individuals and nations that effect the behavior between them and not the actual material levels in money, physical property, resources, size, or strength.[7] It is the comparative that is important, unless it can be shown that there is something about a certain level of wealth or education or physical size, and the like, that effects individual mentality in a way to change behavior.

Third is that any explanation of violence must take into account that violence is part of a social and historical *process*.

Fourth, violence is a form of *discontinuous behavior*. It is not part of a behavioral continuum of ever-increasing nonviolent conflict acts that merge into violence, which itself escalates to some peak, then gradually dies off and merges back into nonviolent behavior. This may seem to be so by measurements of some sort, as of the number killed in a conflict, which may over days move from zero to one, five, fifteen, thirty-three, and then decrease to sixteen, nine, and soon zero again. This treats the movement from zero to one killed or injured in violence as if it were the same as the movement from two to three or

101 to 102. Of course, the statistically sophisticated might suggest that we simply transform the data to logarithms so that the escalation in conflict from one to two killed has about the same importance (weight) as that from ten to twenty, or 100 to 200. But any such transformations are smoothly done along some continuum, while the point here is that *violence is a jump*. Not a smooth change, but a sharp discontinuity in behavior that has profound meaning and value.[8] If as a teacher, for example, I have an argument with a student over their grade, and it becomes heated with raised voices and some regrettable things being said, that is one thing, although bad enough for a teacher to let it get to this level. However, were I then to punch the student, in no way could this be considered simply a continuation of the argument by other means. Even with one punch and just in the shoulder, let us say, it is a jump in behavior that is so profound, a boundary crossed that is so meaningful and valued, that either suspension as a teacher or outright firing is possible. Similarly, for individuals or political leaders to purposely initiate the assassination or murder of opponents is to leap into a new dimension of conflict, one with utterly new meaning, unless such behavior has already been regularized in the system, as for Stalin or Pol Pot, or in bilateral relations, as for the regular shelling of Chinese Nationalist held Quemoy and Matsu Islands by the communist Chinese that began in 1958 and went on for years, so many shells at such and such a time each day.

Fifth, this discontinuity of violence is a breakdown of a *social equilibrium* among individual perceptions, values, meanings, interests, capabilities, and wills. That is, all societies, whether as large as that of the global system of nations, or as small as our family and friendship groups, are at one time or another in a social equilibrium. This equilibrium reflects the peculiar history of the individuals involved in it and the adjustments that they have made to each other. A breakdown in this equilibrium usually occasions social conflict and will only cause a jump to violence under particular conditions to be described.[9] The assumption here is that we all have, and therefore our groups and nations manifest, a disposition to equilibrium. Indeed, we can say that a cooperative and well-functioning social order at any one time is such an equilibrium, maintained by a structure of expectations that makes such cooperation possible. A disposition to equilibrium means that we tend to behave in such a way as to create and maintain a social order of whatever kind, whether of a family, clan, tribe, village, or nation.

Sixth, the breakdown of this equilibrium and jump to violence may be *triggered* by minor events or actions. That is, the precipitating event may physically appear insignificant compared to the violence it unleashes. The assassination of the Austrian Archduke Franz Ferdinand in Sarajevo in 1914 by a Bosnian Serb nationalist precipitated World War I and the death in battle of nine million people, and caused the death of millions of others, including the near 21 million people[10] who died in the war-caused great flu epidemic of 1918. The not guilty verdict against four policemen being tried by the beating of Rodney King in Los Angeles provoked a riot in 1992 killing several dozen people and causing millions of dollars in property destroyed. Probably in each of our lives we can point to very minor events that incited a big fight with a family member.

The reason minor events can have outcomes far out of proportion, even monstrously out of proportion to the event, as in the case of World War I, is that the social equilibrium that underlies one's relationships, or that between group or nation decision makers, is ripe to collapse. The triggering event or action is not so much a cause as an excuse. But the point here, to put this technically, is that the distribution of the conditions underlying violence can be bimodal. The same conditions may not be related to violence at one time and yet appear to bring the violence about at another. This is because it is not the events or conditions per se that trigger violence, although we may use that language for convenience, but the mentality of those involved when these things occur—the perceptions and associated meaning and values with which these physical occurrences are endowed.

Seventh, I assume that the effect of the various conditions and causes contributing to violence or nonviolence is greater than the sum of their parts. That is, they form a *gestalt* over and above what one would find by simply looking at them individually. This is much like the effect of a charismatic political personality, an Adolf Hitler, Martin Luther King, Jr., John Fitzgerald Kennedy, or a Mahatma Gandhi. It is not just what they say and the way they say it, nor their facial expressions and gestures, nor their manner of dress, and the like. There is something electric, something that is a field of expression that compels attention, love, and devotion. As I will argue, a social field is such a gestalt transcending the social parts of which it is comprised.[11]

Finally, I assume that people are not wholly good or bad, but that within all of us lies the potential for extreme violence and democide.

Common people with no particularly ideological bent or sadistic side to them can carry out mass murder.[12] They do it because they are told to do so by someone in a position of authority or they are afraid of what their friends or those they respect will say if they don't.[13] I believe that human nature is the same for all races or cultures and that under the proper circumstances, Americans or British, or any other nationality that prides itself on its civilization can do what the Germans did to the Jews, the Turks to the Armenians, or the Japanese to their prisoners of war and forced laborers.[14] I therefore argue that what prevents democratic peoples from doing to each other or foreigners the worst that lies within us is an arrangement of social institutions and the development of an associated culture such that this dark side of us is strongly inhibited, and if it does emerge it is only given very limited room within which to act (as in atrocities by American soldiers on foreign battlefields or isolated torture-murders by individuals in civil society).

Now, to pull all these assumptions together I will use three central theoretical concepts: *social field* and its opposite, *antifield,* and that of a *conflict helix.* The idea of a social field is not new, and has at one time or another been widely used in the psychological and social sciences[15] and Quincy Wright even summed up his life-long understanding of the nature and conditions of international relations through such a concept.[16] As used here, by social field I mean all the spontaneous social relations comprising a society (examples of societies are families, social and work groups, nations, international organizations, and international relations) and the underlying individual mentalities that gives them significance and importance. If we wish to be technical about this field we can conceive and indeed measure its dimensions in terms of the distinguishing psychological, cultural, and social characteristics of individuals in that society and the diverse behaviors they manifest.[17]

To make this idea of a social field clearer, we can look at three alternative ways of conceptualizing social relations and particularly causes and effects. One is to simply explain nonviolence, Y, as a consequence of cause X. The relationship between the two is assumed such that either Y does not occur without X being present (X is a *necessary* condition or cause of Y), Y always follows from X (X is a *sufficient* condition or cause of Y), or Y will occur if and only if X occurs (X is a *necessary and sufficient* condition or cause of Y). In the social sciences, these logical relations are usually reduced to probabilities and correlations, but the underlying logic is still clear. Thus we have said that at the first level of explanation popular will is related to nonviolence, such that the people are unwilling to bear the costs of war and their representatives in a democracy will therefore likely be inhibited from waging war. That is, if I may torture the English, empowered popular will is positively related to nonviolence, such that empowered popular will is, probabilistically, a necessary and sufficient cause of nonviolence. This is a simple, commonsense, and often effective explanation. But as mentioned it does not account for many anomalies, particularly the fact the popular will has sometimes directly led to international and civil war.

A second way of accounting for nonviolence is to pose *interacting multiple causes* such that their impact on each other and together cause nonviolence. For simplicity, let me focus just on the explanation of nonviolence in terms of an exchange culture and the cross-pressured interests created by democratization. I have argued that democratization necessarily entails negotiation, compromise, and toleration within government and the society, and that this becomes instilled in the culture. And when leaders and the people perceive another nation as of the same democratic or republican type, they treat them as though of their own group, people with whom one can comprise and negotiate differences. Moreover, the greater the democracy, the more a society is cross-cut by diverse groups and interests that isolate and cross-pressure dispositions to conflict and violence and impede their escalation. But the greater diversity and interaction between different groups and institutions further extends and strengthens the culture of negotiation, compromise, and toleration. We thus have democracy and its exchange society as variables promoting culture and diversity, with culture then a condition of democratic nonviolence, and diversity causally impacting both this culture and nonviolence. Both culture and cross-cutting groups can be considered, probabilistically again, sufficient causes of nonviolence in general.

A third way of explaining violence could be in terms of the *system of relations* within democratic societies. System-level explanations are popular and pervasive in the social sciences, although one has yet to well explain war. A simple analogy may help here to understand how a system works. Consider a watch. It has various precise pieces that work with each other in various ways to uniformly turn the hands of the watch to keep time. Notice that a watch has precisely integrated and causally related pieces. When properly working together its pieces form a system that causes the hands of the watch to keep time. No one piece does it alone; no subset of them do it together. The moving of the watch's hands is therefore a causal effect within the system of correctly interconnected working watch parts. Violence might be looked at in the same way, where the various parts of society, its groups, institutions, culture, economy, politics, and the regime, interact in specific ways to create a system that produces either violence or nonviolence. That is, violence and nonviolence could be seen as an outcome of the operation of a system of interrelationships, conditions, and causes, where these conditions and causes are thought jointly sufficient for nonviolence.

The concept of a social field is essentially different from that of a single or multiple cause explanation or that of a social system just as a watch or other mechanical device is a causal complex different from that of a magnet, gravity, the flow of heat or electricity in a solid, or the dynamics of a stream of water or gas. For one, in a social field the idea of a precise cause-effect relationship between specific parts, all together contributing to violence or nonviolence, is replaced with the idea of a medium in which forces of some sort operate and which forces continuously vary depending on the region of the field. Moreover, unlike a watch, the field transcends the units that compose it. It is a gestalt of individuals, groups, and their relations. To understand violence within a social field, therefore, is not to separate it out as a mechanical effect of some specific causes, but to see it as part of a field, itself contributing to the gestalt. Finally, parts of the field may be conceptually distinguishable, as of the Catholic Church, prime minister, or IBM, but in causes and effects, behavior and attributes, conditions and entities, the social field is a seamless merging of them all.

I will argue that *the idea of a social field is the most appropriate theoretical perspective for understanding why democracies are pacific.* In doing this I do not want to overburden the reader with distinctions and unnecessarily multiple concepts that have little bearing on the purpose here, which is to explain at the most basic level the relationship between democracy and nonviolence.[18] To this end we should understand that the medium of the social field, that within which social forces are imbedded, comprise the shared *meanings, values, and norms* of individuals within a society.[19] These convey and carry what is important and significant, at its most basic that an individual is willing to fight over and even die for. These are the loci of social forces toward or away from an equilibrium in the field. By meanings is meant such a thing as interpreting two pieces of wood laying across each other as a cross; or the American flag as symbolizing the nation and way of life; or seeing those who favor welfare reform as racist, that is as against African-Americans receiving welfare payments; or interpreting a man opening a car door for a women as sexist. Values refer to the moral weight one gives to facts or ideas, as to whether they are good or bad, ethically right or wrong, such as welfare, gun control, socialism, and democracy itself. Norms are standards by which we orient ourselves physically, such as by north and south, up and down, hot and cold, centimeters and inches, thin and fat; and more relevantly here, those standards of behavior that are considered right and proper, such as going the extra mile of negotiation and compromise before fighting.

Now—and this is the critical point—the field is produced by individuals (including individuals acting in some authoritative capacity on behalf of groups) cooperating or conflicting according to *their* meanings, values, and norms. What gives specificity to these—and, thus, focus to the forces involved—is the *perceptions, expectations, dispositions, capabilities, interests,* and *wills* of these individuals. *The field is thus a gestalt of a spontaneous society, one in which people are largely free to act as they see fit or wish.*[20] We have a concept for this type of society in the economic realm, which is of a free market. This is a field specific to a spontaneously formed division of labor and the free production of goods and services. The generalization of this to society as a whole should not be strange. The social field is a social free market in which individuals spontaneously follow their own interests, mainly restricted by the interests of others and abstract rules[21] that have evolved to facilitate interaction.[22] This is in fact what we usually mean by a free society or nation, and what I have been calling an exchange society.

Within such an exchange society, that is a social field, individuals and groups freely learn about and adjust to each other's interests, and expectations are developed that evolve and accrue to the society as a whole. We can then talk of a society as having customs, mores, and abstract rules, that are nothing more than the development of an equilibrium across the society evolving from the adjustments, trial and error, and learning among individuals. I will focus on this when I describe the conflict helix. The important point here is that the social field is created by the spontaneous interaction among individuals.

As a result *the social field it is criss-crossed and cross-cut by the natural product of individuals acting spontaneously.* This is a great multitude of different corporations, partnerships, family businesses, churches, schools, unions, institutes, parties, leagues, clubs and other associations, institutions, and small groups. All are organized to satisfy or further the particular shared interests of individuals. Moreover, there is no one society. Societies themselves are nested within each other and overlap. There is the core family, extended family, and possibly the clan; the informal friendship group, the interaction among professionals within a certain specialty that constitutes an invisible college; the regular get togethers of people to play tennis or soccer or bowl; the small town and urban societies; and the national and international societies. And within these societies and among groups and individuals there develop in a process yet to be described, *structures of expectations* (agreements, contracts, compacts, settlements, arrangements, or implicit understandings) that traverse society and knit it together. No one group wholly dominates this free society. As Frederick Hayek says,

> It is in fact very misleading to single out the inhabitants or citizens of a particular political unit as the prototype of a society. There exists, under modern conditions, no single society to which an individual normally belongs, and it is highly desirable that this should not be so. Each of us is fortunately a member of many different overlapping and interlacing societies to which he may belong more or less strongly or lastingly. Society is a network of voluntary relationships between individuals and organized groups, and strictly speaking there is hardly ever merely one society to which any person exclusively belongs.[23]

In national, urban, or provincial societies their governments monopolizes force, of course, and in that sense would appear to sit at the center of their societies. But even for a modern liberal democratic government within a national society, even with its extensive laws and regulations controlling aspects of economic and social behavior, such as through a minimum wage, pollution controls, educational grants, and laws against gambling, prostitution, drugs, education, and racial and sexual discrimination, its leaders still must bargain, negotiate, compromise, internally—agency by agency, bureau by bureau—and externally in their relations with interest and lobbying groups and those they regulate. The government is not the primary source of expectations that organize and structure a largely exchange society and its spontaneous behavior. It is just one of many groups that enter into the fundamental expectations tying a national society together. Most social relations and intercourse, most of what people and groups do with regard to each other can be done in such a society without recourse to or being regulated by the government—the state.

This separation between society and the state has been noted by Hayek, who also correctly points out the tendency to overlook this critical distinction. The confusion over this, he writes,

> is due to a tendency (particularly strong in the Continental tradition, but with the spreading of socialist ideas growing rapidly also in the Anglo-Saxon world) to identify "state" and "society". The state, the organization of the people of a territory under a single government, although an indispensable condition for the development of an advanced society, is yet very far from being identical with society, or rather with the multiplicity of grown and self-generating structures of men who have any freedom that alone deserves the name of society. In a free society the state is one of many organizations—the one which is required to provide an effective external framework within which self-generating orders can form, but an organization which is confined to the government apparatus and which does not determine the activities of the free individuals. And while this organization of the state will contain many voluntary organizations, it is the spontaneously grown network of relationships between the individuals and the various organizations they create that constitutes societies. Societies form but states are made.[24]

As this separation becomes less so, as government regulation and control extends to cover more social and economic activities, then the government expands to absorb and determine more of the expectations comprising the society and thus moves toward its center. That is, as government becomes larger in its control, as government commands replace individual and group negotiation and compromise and their determination of their own agreements and contracts, the society is less based on exchange power and more on coercion. People act less spontaneously and more by the dictation of government decrees, laws, and bureaucratic regulations and rules. There comes to be only one major group, the government, and other social and economic groups are either eliminated by the government, restructured to be within it, as in the nationalization of large businesses, or allowed to exist on the periphery of society, as of a tennis club, reading club, or mom and pop grocery store.

In effect, the society has been turned into an *antifield*. The natural tendency of people to act spontaneously in terms of their own perception and interests has been confined within narrow and isolated social regions, while all major and essential social activities are now commanded. The social field has been largely replaced by an organization of society built and structured by government. *It is this organization that turns a state into an antifield.*[25]

There is nothing strange in this idea. Place a magnet under a sheet of paper and a spoonful of metal filings on top and one can see the effect of the magnetic field as filings line up according to the forces within the field. But place a cardboard lattice on the paper first and then spread the filings across the lattice, and in reacting to the underlying field the filings are then confined within the cells of the lattice. The lattice is the antifield. At the lesser social level within a state, democratic or not, a factory exemplifies an antifield. While at work the spontaneous behavior of individuals is limited and constrained by the tasks they are required to do and by the many rules and procedures that govern their work time. As a young man I worked in several factories as a laborer and I can say that I was not able to wander around, socialize with my fellow workers when I felt like it, come or leave work as I wished, listen to the radio when I wanted, or even eat when I was hungry. I lived for eight hours a day within a command structure organized to achieve a purpose, a profitable product. It was an antifield. When a political regime so organizes much of society to achieve some purpose, whether economic development, equality, religious orthodoxy, racial purity, or victory in war, this part of society is turned into such an antifield.

Social field and antifield are linked antonyms that I will now use to explain why democracies should be nonviolent. Within a social field people and groups develop among themselves those expectations that best fit their own situations as they see them and in terms of their own wants and goals. If conflict develops and escalates to violence it is limited to the situation and issues that generated it. Moreover, since in a social field there is across individuals the development of diverse groups and manifold issues, interests are spread out and attenuated. It is difficult to focus entirely on any one issue to the exclusion of others, and even were an interest sufficiently strong for some individuals or groups to carry a conflict to the level of violence, as over abortion in the United States, one must carefully consider how many other interests will be sacrificed in favor of the one at stake in the violence.[26] But still, even if the violence escalates, it is unlikely to spread across much of society. For the diversity of groups and individual interests will surely isolate and contain the violence largely to its source. And where interests stand in such a relation that the attempt to satisfy the one by violence will mean a lose on some others, people will be cross-pressured about contributing to or escalating the violence.

Moreover, individuals will apply to the operations of government and its domestic and foreign relations the nonviolent attitudes they develop in their own spontaneous interaction. Joseph Schumpeter in his classic *Capitalism, Socialism and Democracy* recognized this power of the spontaneous society, although he limited his discussion to one region of it, the free market, or capitalism. "Capitalist civilization," he writes,

is rationalistic "and anti-heroic." The two go together of course. Success in industry and commerce requires a lot of stamina, yet industrial and commercial activity is essentially unheroic in the knight's sense—no flourishing of swords about it, not much physical prowess, no chance to gallop the armored horse into the enemy, preferably a heretic or heathen—and the ideology that glorifies the idea of fighting for fighting's sake and of victory for victory for victory's sake understandably withers in the office among all the columns of figures. Therefore, owning assets that are apt to attract the robber or the tax gatherer and not sharing or even disliking warrior ideology that conflicts with its "rational" utilitarianism, the industrial and commercial bourgeoisie is fundamentally pacifist and inclined to insist on the application of the moral precepts of private life to international relations. It is true that, unlike most but like some other features of capitalist civilization, pacifism and international morality have also been espoused in non-capitalist environments and by precapitalist agencies, in the Middle Ages by the Roman Church for instance. Modern pacifism and modern international morality are nonetheless products of capitalism.[27]

There is more to a spontaneous society than simply diversity of expectations and interests and the pacifism associated with a free market. Recall that the medium of a social field within which is transmitted its social forces is made up of the meanings people give to the social and physical world about them, the value with which it is endowed, and the norms (standards) according to which it is evaluated and structured. For each individual these meanings, values, and norms comprise a *cultural matrix* through which reality is perceived and interpreted. It is within this matrix that individuals develop their expectations of each other, and as these expectations are determined freely between individuals and groups they link into ever larger clusters until they finally span the society and hold it together as an evolving, ever-changing field of social behavior.

Another key to violence, therefore, is the role of this cultural matrix for *expectations* and *perception*. We perceive subjectively depending in part on what we want and are able to perceive, and the power of an external reality to impose a particular perception on us, as of a clap of thunder or the screaming of a child in pain. Our perception is thus a balance between ourselves and reality, and an integral part of this balance is the meanings, values, and norms that our cultural matrix gives to the sensory stream of colors, shapes, lines, sounds, smells, tastes, and tactile feelings it receives. Doubtlessly, much of what we see is a consequence of our culture and its associated language that conceptually maps reality.[28]

But second, how we define our expectations about what will happen in reality and the behavior of others is in part also a matter of the meanings, values, and norms we give social and physical reality. In conflict, for example, we are disposed culturally to accept certain ways of resolving conflict, and come to expect others within our culture to behave similarly. We may by custom consult a headman or religious mediator, or enlarge the conflict to the clan so that all can gather around and come to a consensus for resolving the conflict, or we may make it a test of will and sharpshooting in a duel, or talk it out. Whatever, our way of conflicting and resolving a conflict is mainly a cultural given. And most important here, as through our cultural matrix we perceive another nation as being of the same kind, democratic (or oligarchic republican) like us, then we expect them to behave like democrats and are thus *disposed* to act toward them as democrats.[29]

The spontaneous social field of constantly interacting individuals and groups, all pursuing their own interests, is a field of continuous *nonviolent* conflict.[30] Interests, expectations, and perceptions are in continual confrontation and competition. *This is the friction of freedom and associated exchange.*[31] If one has difficulty in thinking of all this nonviolent conflict as natural to a spontaneous social field, observe the free market of goods and services. Businesses of all sorts compete to sell their wares, in the process of which they are continuously engaged in making agreements, signing contracts, hiring people, and establishing rules among manufacturers, producers, suppliers, warehouses, shippers, and real estate agents. Correlatively there are the disputes, the broken contracts and agreements, the misunderstandings, the fraud and abuse, the strikes and lockouts, and the suits in the courts. All this is part of the living, changing, field of the free market. When this field is extended to include most behavior within the greater society, then, there develop necessarily standard ways all this conflict becomes settled. And this evolves into cultural norms—abstract rules of just behavior.

These norms are those of the exchange society; of bargaining. Conflicts are resolved through negotiation and compromise, and this becomes the expected way of settling them. And these concern means and not ends. That is, they govern the conflict and facilitate the associated negotiation and bargaining between individuals and groups without defining the outcome. They are like the court rules and procedures that regulate a trial, but do not specify who will be found innocent or guilty.

For the social field that encompasses a democratic nation-state, its regime constitutionally guarantees fundamental civil liberties and political rights and is primarily limited in its use of coercive power to enforcing abstract rules of just conduct.[32] Indeed, democracy itself can be defined procedurally and not substantively, as a method for settling conflict over who will rule and what their policies will be. And the norms of bargaining infuse politics within the government and in its external relations to groups and citizens. As these abstract rules for a society or regime begin to define ends, as they do, for example, in socialist systems, they increasingly define a storm front of serious conflict, and most likely violence.[33]

At this point it will be useful to give an empirical example of a social field with a very limited government, that of our largest society, the global *world society*. A standard way of conceptualizing this society, most often called international relations, is as an anarchy. This means that the global society has no government that monopolizes force, and its constituent units—nation-states since the treaties of Westphalia that ended the Thirty-Years War in 1648—are free to act in terms of their national interests. But this is not an anarchy without laws, customs and norms of behavior, nor without a division of labor, or system of communication. This anarchy does not mean chaos or the tooth and fang rule of the jungle. Nor does it mean a continuous state of war, of each nation-state against all others and all against each.[34]

First, one should not be confused by the use of "nations" or "states" or "nation-states" to denote the units of international relations. Actually, this social field comprises individuals acting in various authoritative capacities on behalf of nations, transnational groups (such as multinational corporations and international societies), and governmental and nongovernmental international organizations. It includes individuals moving across borders for personal reasons (for example, tourists, foreign students, scientists, businessmen, criminals, terrorists). All that has been said about a social field applies to international relations, such as the cross-cutting and cross-pressuring of interests and the development of the norms of bargaining, known more familiarly for this global society as the arts of diplomacy and negotiation.

There is as well a constant and continual nonviolent conflict—the noise of free societies—as, for example, between the United States and Japan over trade, and between members of the European Union over a common currency and import restrictions. And, there is a most limited government, the United Nations. It functions under an international constitution, the Charter of the United Nations, and through it and other multilateral treaties, there is an international recognition of the most basic civil liberties and political rights of nations, their sovereignty, independence, and equality. Moreover, this government is basically democratic with respect to nation-states. Virtually all nations have representation in the United Nations and its basic policies are established by majority vote, with the exception of the veto power of the United States, France, Great Britain, China, and Russia in the Security Council, the only nondemocratic body of the UN.

There is some dispute as to whether the United Nations and allied international organizations can be called a government, however. If we accept that a regime must monopolize force within a society to deserve being called a government, then obviously the UN is not. But if we recognize that this regime has a bicameral legislature (the General Assembly and Security Council), an executive (the Secretary General) and associated bureaucracy, and judiciary (the World Court), and if we note that under UN auspices coercive action has been taken against members because of their violation of commonly accepted international law, such as the Gulf War against Iraq for invading and occupying Kuwait, the Korean War against North Korea for invading South Korea (it was fought under the United Nations flag), the intervention in Iraq to feed and protect the Kurd Minority, and the threat to bomb Serbian artillery emplacements surrounding Sarajevo in Bosnia-

Hercegovina, then we must accept that we have, while not a government monopolizing force, one nonetheless functioning as a government of the world society.

With all this noted, consider that the level of violence in international relations is far less than one would expect for a world society made up of independent and armed nation-states. Given the enormous size of this social field and the tremendous power of some of its members, international violence between them is relatively rare. For example, F. S. Northedge and M. D. Donelan published a study of fifty international disputes occurring between 1945 and 1970 and concluded that,

> in contrast [to those disputes within states], the disputes between states were much less marked by violence. . . . Many included some form of breach of relations. Some led to fighting. But, on the whole, the remarkable feature of these disputes, for all the drama, bitterness, disruption and waste that they caused, was how little bloodshed was suffered and how little physical damage the antagonists did to each other or even sought to do.[35]

Indeed, there is more extensive and deadly violence within a few nations than there is between all of them. The total number of people killed in battle in all foreign wars between 1900 and 1980 is close to 29,200,000, while all those killed in battle in civil wars of one type or another during the same period and democide between 1900 and 1987 amounts to near 174,000,000.[36] Just one nation, the Soviet Union, from 1917 to 1987 has had about 56,500,000 citizens killed in civil wars and democide, close to 94 percent *more* than all those killed in all international wars for all nations in this century up to 1980. And this does not even include the deadly civil wars and democide in China, Mexico, Spain, Ethiopia, and elsewhere. The reason that the largest of all societies, the world, is not near as deadly as even one of its constituent units is that it is a social field, where the norm of exchange and the dividing up and cross-pressuring of interests play a central role; whereas the Soviet Union was an antifield, dominated by the rule of one man, with virtually no room for independent interests, small groups, institutions, and associations.

The key to all this is the freedom of the nations, groups, and individuals in our world society and of groups and individuals in national of subnational societies to pursue their own interests. This creates the exchange society and thus, the spontaneous social field. And its product is one of limited, constrained, and cross-pressured interests, and the norms of negotiation, compromise, and tolerance. Whether freedom comes first, as it has in international relations with a democratic regime, the United Nations, gradually emerging from it, or the regime comes first through a constitution granting considerable freedom to a people, is academic. *In either case the freedom of the people and their groups is the central and prime factor. At the level of social fields, it is the explanation for the democratic and oligarchic republican peace.*

To further understand why this should be so, it is time to deal with the dynamic of the social field, the *process* connecting cooperation and conflict.[37] In interaction, individuals and their groups have a *psychological disposition* toward an equilibrium in their interests, their capabilities, and their wills. In the international social field, this equilibrium is known as a balance of power, but such balances comprise societies at all levels.[38] This may seem strange at first read, since the tendency is to see power in terms of coercion and force, and to neglect that there are exchange, intellectual, authoritative, and altruistic powers that also may contribute to or constitute an equilibrium.[39]

This equilibrium is made up of three forces that largely define the dynamics of the social field. First is that which motivates individuals and energizes their purposes, which is their *interests*, their active, living, throbbing wants and goals. Second is their mental and physical *capabilities* to achieve their interests. And third is their resolution, their determination to achieve their interests, what we should call will power, or *will* for short. These three forces, interests (I), capabilities (C), and will (W) determine for each individual and group a *power equation*, such that an individual's power in a particular situation = I × C × W. If any of these components are near zero, then the person's power in that situation is not much different than zero.

For a teacher it is easy to illustrate how this equation works. I have had numerous students that have had high intelligence (capability) and a well-focused interest in some aspect of political science, but have simply been unable to bring themselves to do that required to get a higher degree (such as reading and note taking from works that one must know and remember to be a well-rounded political scientist, even if one has no interest in them). They simply lacked the will, and for this reason did not have the power to succeed. I also have had students of moderate or average intelligence, reading, and conceptual ability who while hardly noteworthy in capability, were so sure about what they wanted and would prepare so diligently that they worked through to the Ph.D. What they lacked in capability they made up for in interests and especially in will.

What is true about students is true about the power we see in all situations. At the international level, Israel in her wars with her Arab neighbors was on paper far inferior to the combined Arab armies. By their military capability alone they should have defeated Israel. But what the Israeli's had, which the Arabs did not, was a burning passion to survive as a nation and people. Israelis perceived their very existence at stake. And they had an iron will, forged by the history of Jewish persecution, the Holocaust, and the historical claim, right or wrong, to the Jewish homeland. It was this that defeated the Arabs in each of the four wars they have fought against Israel, although certainly military training, generalship, and national moral and support played a significant role.

An *equilibrium* between individuals and groups, such as nations, in a social field is a balance between their power equations, what in international relations is called the balance of power.[40] It is a simultaneous solution to the different interests, capabilities, and wills of the parties involved. And associated with this equilibrium is a *structure of expectations* that allocates among the relevant individuals and groups who does or gets what, when, and how.[41] In other words, the equilibrium defines for these people and groups the social order within which they associate and cooperate. At the highest level, the customs, laws, and rules that govern society as a whole are based on an equilibrium between the power equations of the most important groups and individuals (just as international law is based on a balance of power among the major Powers).[42]

But this is a static perspective and the field is dynamic. Equilibriums change and break down, and indeed, I will argue, when this happens in certain circumstances, there will be a leap to violence. Over the next several pages let me sketch the process involved. First, any social equilibrium between individual or group power equations is one phase in the process of adjustment and learning between individuals and groups within a social field, the process I call the *conflict helix*.[43] Moreover, any equilibrium is but one of many that have occurred sequentially within a particular conflict helix.

Second, at its beginning a social equilibrium is congruent with a particular structure of expectations, which may be codified in contracts, treaties, agreements, or which could be implicit or unwritten understandings. Whatever, these expectations govern relations and define the social order between individuals and groups. But then this congruency between the equilibrium among power equations on the one side and expectations on the other will change. And because social expectations change slowly and with difficulty, the usual source of this change will be in the components of the power equations themselves.

Third, interests, capabilities, and wills do in time change, together or singly. People no longer want the same thing or they want more of it, their capabilities increase or decrease as they change or lose jobs, get college diplomas, fail at business, or become handicapped. Moreover, for one reason or another, their resolution or dedication strengthens or weakens. Any such change is a shift in their power equation and a resulting alteration in the equilibrium of power with others.

But, fourth, the structure of expectations based on the original equilibrium is unlikely to change accordingly. Expectations, particularly those written into law, rules, contracts, or agreements are very slow to change. They have, so to say, high social viscosity. As a result the structure of expectations becomes more and more incongruent with the underlying and supposedly supporting power equations. Expectations hang in the air. What people and groups are required to do by their previously understandings, agreements, and the like, is no longer supported by what they want to do, are capable of doing, or have the will to perform.

Fifth, this gap is like an explosive gas. It creates tension in a social relationship, such that the larger the gap the greater the tension. One just does not out of the blue discard an agreement, but yet the gap between it and the power equations becomes increasingly uncomfortable.

Sixth, then, the larger this gap the more likely some event will finally trigger a breakdown in expectations (the breaking of a treaty or contract, the disavowal of an agreement, the violation of an understanding) and conflict will result. Conflict within this context should be understood as a disagreement over expectations (again, as to who does or gets what, when, and how) due to a change in the underlying power equations, and more basically a disruption of the equilibrium between the individuals or groups within the social field. This conflict is a jump in behavior[44] out of the cooperative mode that had been the norm as long as the structure of expectations were in place.

This conflict is also a new phase in the conflict helix. In human terms conflict may be disagreeable, possibly full of emotion, loud words and unfortunate phrases, strong and coercive actions, and even tears and violence. But theoretically, this conflict is a mechanism for working out a new structure of expectations more congruent with the changed power equations. That is, conflict is but a means for reestablishing the social equilibrium; it is a way of adjusting the need for cooperation among people to the underlying facts of what they want, can, and will do.

Seventh, consequently, a new equilibrium and associated congruent structure of expectations is established through conflict. At first this is congruent, but also in time a gap will form again, there will be trigger, another conflict, and yet once more through conflict still another equilibrium and structure of expectations. And so on and on.

Eighth, this repetitive process of conflict and cooperation, order and disorder, equilibrium and disequilibrium, and continuity and discontinuity in behavior, is a process ever-winding upward through conflict and cooperation, achieving ever more adjustments and learning in the interrelationship.[45] People remember and learn from previous conflict and cooperation. The history of the process becomes the mental base for the readjustments necessary to bring expectations in line with changes in the power equations. As this process works through numerous expectations and conflicts, the cooperative phases become longer and more solidary, the conflict shorter and less severe. Eventually, like a couple who have been married for thirty years and have lived a quiet and uneventful life, they move from one day to another fully in synchrony. They know how to read each other, they know what to expect of each other, they have fully adjusted to each other, and their frequent and sometimes violent conflicts of the earlier years are past.

Ninth, rarely does this process work out to all but eliminate conflict. For usually there is a change in the conditions or environment underlying a particular helix. People may become handicapped, get a new job, or fall out of love with their mate. Families may have their first child, move to a new state, or their in-laws may move in. Groups may gain many new members, be confronted with new competition, or get new leadership. Nations may suffer a revolution, get an ideologically different regime, lose a war, or become enriched by the discovery of vast new oil fields. The learning and adjusting process of conflict and cooperation is always within a context of certain givens.

Some important things remain constant, such as occupation or career, the basic physical condition of the parties, their personalities, and such. If for some reason these change, as when the first child is born into a family, then the conflict helix is set back, a whole range of new expectations are required, and renewed conflict will occur.

There are thus two kinds of changes within the social field that effect the equilibrium between individuals and groups. One is the change in the power equations underlying a social relationship, ultimately causing a breakdown in association expectations, and conflict that serves to readjust expectations to the new interest, capabilities, and wills of the parties. But this change takes place against a backdrop of relatively unchanging basic conditions underlying the relationship. The second change is in these conditions and is more fundamental. It effects the process of adjustment itself, sets back the helix, and requires a new process of adjustments. As a result conflict may sharply rise over what it was before and cooperation may become more limited and difficult to achieve.

One example of the second type of change is among students who get married while students working their way through college. Initially the adjustments will be very difficult for both, quite obviously, but through time, love, empathy, discussion, arguments, perhaps more severe conflict, and a growing ability to read each other, by the time they graduate they may well have developed a solid and deeply satisfying structure of expectations of each other and related cooperative activities. However, once they graduate it is a whole new world for their marriage, whether one or both go to a graduate school elsewhere or work. The conditions (both being undergraduates and working at the same time) of the regular process of adjustment between them, the conflict helix, has now fundamentally changed. Whatever they decide to do, a new sequence of adjustments to each other within a wholly new environment is required.

A second example is of the Cuban-American bilateral relationship. The United States had intervened in Cuba numerous times in this century (1906, 1912, and 1917) and had exercised much influence over politics in the country. With a new constitution, Cuba was marginally democratic from 1940 to 1952, when Fulgencio Batista overthrew the regime and reinstituted authoritarian rule. Relations between the Unites States and the new Batista regime were difficult at first, but Batista welcomed American tourists and investments, and supported the United States in the cold war. By 1957 the United States and Batista had worked out a structure of expectations that both were comfortable with. However, this became strained as opposition against Batista's rule strengthened and virtual civil war broke out. By 1959 an insurrection emerged in the mountains led by Fidel Castro and succeeded in overthrowing Batista and establishing, as soon became evident, a communist regime moving to ally itself with the Soviet Union.

This was a fundamental change in the conditions of the Cuban-American relationship and all but destroyed their structure of expectations. New and severe Cuban-American and associated American-Soviet conflict and violence was the result, with the disastrous American prepared and financed invasion of Cuba at the Bay of Pigs by some 1,500 Cuban exiles, and the Cuban Missile Crises in 1962 during which a misstep by either the United States or Soviets could have triggered nuclear war. Eventually the violence and more extreme conflict between the United States and Cuba disappeared as through successive American administrations a structure of expectations and limited cooperation was worked out with Fidel Castro.

And tenth, the nature of the expectations that are part of a particular conflict helix have much to do with the occurrence of violence once they are disrupted. At the core of a structure of expectations are those expectations that an individual or group consider vital. These are felt or seen to be at the very center of one's existence—they concern one's self-preservation, prized property, loved ones, basic principles, honor, reputation, and self-image. When such vital expectations are disrupted and conflict over these essential interests ensues, violence may be seen as the final resort to protecting or advancing these values. Collective and political violence entail danger and high risks to those involved. It is a jump into the unknown, for no one can predict with any certainty what the specific outcome for each party will be. Whatever, as for conflict generally, violence will resolve the who gets or does what, when, or how, and a new structure of expectations will be formed more congruent with the interests, capabilities, and wills of the parties.

In a spontaneous society this process is primarily between two individuals, either representing or acting on behalf of themselves or a group, and this is what makes for a social field. Jane establishes expectations with Bob and each separately with John, and the three of them develop their own with Jim, an automobile insurance agent, in order to insure their cars, and meanwhile Jim works out his expectations with Mary, an agent for another insurance company regarding its coverage for an accident that one of her clients had with one of his, and so on and on, throughout all the different relationships that tie a free society together. It is often said that power is personal. This is an apt description of this process of cooperation and conflict, of the underlying generator of expectations—the power equations—and of the social equilibrium.

As these expectations overlap and reinforce each other, and as they become models for new relationships and are increasingly accepted as standard expectations to govern relationships, they become abstracted from particular relationships and generalized into customs, norms, mores, and rules of behavior. They are like the informal rules that evolve to regulate automobile and truck traffic on roads, so that when to dim one's lights at night, who turns first at an intersection, how fast one can go above the legal speed limit (about five miles per hour in Hawaii), and when to move over to the slower lane, are all governed by expectations that evolve between drivers, and that new drivers are either told about or soon understand through near misses, horns beeping at them, and other drivers shaking their fist.

Violence between any individuals is in regard to their vital expectations and over their power equations. It is their social equilibrium that is disrupted. Of course, violence may spread across conflict helices that are closely tied into each other, as all members in two families or two clans can be drawn into the violence between a member of each. But the diversity of these structures of expectations, their distinctness, and their fundamental tie to individual interests, capabilities, and wills, serve to inhibit the spread of violence.

Now, without collusion or even knowing each other, many in some locality or area or over some issue or event may similarly perceive a vital opportunity or threat, or be triggered to act alike due to what the issue or event means to them. For example, a particular structure of expectations may have evolved among dwellers, businessmen, police, and politicians in an inner city. It comprises an urban equilibrium within which business is conducted, people can go about their personal affairs, and there is law and order. However, beneath the surface there may have been growing frustration among the residents about crime, their treatment by local businesses, unemployment, poverty, the bias of and abuse by the police, and inaction by politicians. These are vital issues. With the inner city equilibrium, the social order, incongruent with the underlying interests, capabilities, and wills of the residents, it only takes some trigger to cause a breakdown of the social order and violence. This happened in Los Angeles when the not-guilty verdict of four White policemen tried for the beating a black, Rodney King, triggered a section of the inner city of Los Angeles to erupt into bloody violence.

But note that this violence did not spread to other areas of Los Angeles, to the countryside, or to many other inner cities elsewhere. Although hellish for those directly involved, the violence was contained and limited. Those elsewhere did not share the same expectations, were not part of the same social equilibrium, and did not have the same underlying power equations.

The key to all this, again, is the freedom of individuals, good or bad, human monsters or angels, to pursue their own interests to the point where they meet the interests of others. Then they and these others are largely free to establish their own mutual structures of expectations. And when these collapse, which they are sure to be doing between some people and their groups somewhere at some time, and if vital expectations and central interests are involved, then violence may result. However, this same freedom has (a) furthered the development of independent, diverse, and cross-cutting interests; and (b) created a tightly inter and cross woven tapestry of associated personal expectations between them; such that (c) violence among some at one place at one time cannot easily spread across society.

Moreover, as people are free to work out these expectations, and as common expectations must be developed in order for people to cooperate, an imperative of any society, then discussion, negotiation, and compromise become means for resolving conflict and determining what the expectations will be, even concerning the resolution of vital issues, core values, and fundamental principles. What become accepted techniques for resolving conflict and establishing expectations soon develop into customs and rules of behavior. This is to say that from freedom evolves a field of checks and balances that tends to localize and inhibit violence while also creating a culture of nonviolence.

But while this may explain internal collective violence, it does not yet explain why two such societies are more peaceful. Why in this view do not democracies or oligarchic republics make war on each other? Before answering this let me give an example of how this peace operates and of the conceptual confusion that tends to hide what is going on. Michael Doyle, who I have mentioned in chapter 2, was along with Dean Babst and myself the first to point out and empirically test that democracies don't make war on each other. He observed that,

> during the nineteenth century, the United States and Great Britain engaged in nearly continual strife; however, after the Reform Act of 1832 defined actual representation as the formal source of the sovereignty of the British parliament, Britain and the United States negotiated their disputes. They negotiated despite, for example, British grievances during the Civil War against the North's blockade of the South, with which Britain had close economic ties. Despite severe Anglo-French colonial rivalry, liberal France and liberal Britain formed an entente against illiberal Germany before World War I. And from 1914 to 1915, Italy, the liberal member of the Triple Alliance with Germany and Austria, chose not to fulfill its obligations under that treaty to support its allies. Instead, Italy joined in an alliance with Britain and France, which prevented it from having to fight other liberal states and then declared war on German and Austria. Despite generations of Anglo-American tension and Britain wartime restrictions on American trade with Germany, the United States leaned toward Britain and France from 1914 to 1917 before entering World War I on its side.[46]

First note that once the United States, Great Britain, France, and Italy became democratic they not only began to negotiate their disputes and join the same sides in war, but also Italy changed from the side it was obligated to fight on to line up with the democracies. This interdemocratic peace among democracies was established empirically in chapter 2. However, note that by convention and sometimes rhetorical necessity, history is given in terms of *states*. The problem in explaining the democratic peace is in part due to this usage. It is conceptual.

In dealing with international relations we tend to focus primarily on the behavior between states, as between Russia and the United States, or between their leaders or administrations, such as between presidents Yeltsin and Clinton. Whichever, this characterizes the relations between the United States and Russia as dyadic, as though between two individuals, and implicitly we thus tend to think in terms of one process of cooperation and conflict, one conflict helix, between the two states.

Moreover, the tendency is to see international relations as an anarchy, a governmentless jungle of nation-states ever in competition and dependent only on their own resources for their defense and pursuit of justice. But as Ernst-Otto Czempiel points out, "Even the anarchical structure of the international system is not an independent objectivity.

Of course, the structure is anarchical. But the effects of this structure are being defined by political systems which, in turn, are influenced by their relationship to their societal environment."[47]

Between two democracies, however, the relationship is far more complex even than this. It is the merging of the social field of each into one, which now contains the two regimes and the diverse multitude of groups and individuals that exist in each national social field. All that has been said about individual-to-individual, group-to-group equilibrium, structures of expectations, and associated equations of power holds for the combined field as well. And we find the web of cross-cutting, intersecting, and cross-pressuring expectations and interests as well.

Granted this, then still why has no official violence erupted between democratic regimes within their combined social field? One reason is, of course, related to the public will discussed in the last chapter and the ability of groups opposing each administration or its policy. As a result, as Bueno de Mesquita and Lalman have shown empirically, "democratic leaders on average, apparently expected to experience greater political opposition to the use of force than did their nondemocratic counterparts."[48] This not only applies to the citizens and domestic groups of the one regime, but in the joint society as well where cross-regime costs are incurred. Private groups and corporations in the United States, for example, may well let their views be known to and pressure the leaders of the other democratic regime, as regularly do American Jewish groups about Israeli policies.

Second is that democratic regimes, whether presidential or parliamentary systems, are composed of multitudinous agencies, departments, and bureaus that check and balance each other's power, and these individually have established expectations with those of the other regime. All these linkages and bonds serve to inhibit violence. Moreover, since they recognize each other as democratic, we can draw on Bueno de Mesquita and Lalman's proposition derived from a game theory type analysis. Defining doves as those who prefer negotiations to the exploitation of rivals (itself defined as compelling capitulation), they say, "With common knowledge of types, Doves with a conflict of interest always negotiate."[49] Bueno De Mesquita also derived a Democracy Corollary: "Democratic institutions signal higher than average domestic costs associated with using force, implying that adversaries confronting a democracy hold an unusually high prior belief that the democracy is Dove-like. Consequently, democracies confronting one another are unlikely to use force, whereas democracies confronting non-democracies are likely to use force."[50] Moreover, we can also draw on Spencer Weart's historically based argument that once democracies recognize each other as being of the same kind, then they do not expect to fight, but rather to negotiate.[51]

Doyle has captured part of the linkages and bonds between democratic regimes in reference to a largely free international market among democracies, where

> the international market removes difficult decisions of production and distribution from the direct sphere of state policy. A foreign state thus does not appear directly responsible for these outcomes; states can stand aside from, and to some degree above, these contentious market rivalries and be ready to step in to resolve crises. Furthermore, the interdependence of commerce and the connections of state officials help create crosscutting transnational ties that serve as lobbies for mutual accommodation. According to modern liberal scholars, international financiers and transnational bureaucratic, and domestic organizations create interests in favor of accommodation and have ensured by their variety that no single conflict sours an entire relationship.[52]

Third, the culture of negotiation, compromise, and tolerance that grows out of the spontaneous field no less effects relations between parts of the two regimes. And fourth, parts of each regime have developed multiple relations with individuals and groups within its own national society and that of the other that serve to check and balance, limit and inhibit violence.

In effect, the democracies within their combined social field form the kind of peace league Immanuel Kant envisioned in his Perpetual Peace. As pointed out by Volker Rittberger,

> there is even more, however, that emerges from a further evaluation of the international relations of liberal-democratic states. Aside from the fact that they show the highest rates of participation in the totality of international organizations, they are characterized by intensive organized as well as informal political ties which are based on voluntariness and consensus. One can see from the example of the European Community and to a lesser extent with regard to the trans-Atlantic alliance system that another core thought of Kant's theory can be sustained, i.e. that liberal-democratic states are more or less capable of institutionalized associations through which they exercise a peaceful balance of their respective interests as well as cooperation. There can be no doubt that the democratic constitutional states united in the European Community or in the Council of Europe in their internal relations constitute a *de facto* peace league.[53]

Indeed, looking at historical alliances between democratic regimes there is clear evidence that they only do not only fight each other, but also negotiate enduring alliances among themselves, more than one would expect from the operation of a global or regional balance of power system, but as would be predicted from the logic of their combined social fields. For example, Timothy Cole analyzed the relationship between democracies and their alliances for the period 1580 to 1815. He concluded that regardless of balance of power considerations, democracies among themselves

> end up on the same side when threat is perceived and counteractive action is taken. Therefore a nascent democratic structure can be discerned within the context of defense alliances formed by democratic states. . . . We can state this a bit more strongly, because few constant threads hold together the very complex and shifting European diplomatic picture in this period. Reading the history of the diplomacy of the era takes a keen eye; it is difficult to follow precisely because so many "flip-flops" occur in alliance relationships, where former antagonists now are seen to be in alliance and former protagonists drift apart. None of this "flip-flopping," however, had much of an effect on the nascent democratic structure of alliance relationships discernible in this period.[54]

Cole then looked at the alliances between democracies for the years 1815 to 1980, a period when there were clearly many more democracies, and thus a stronger test of this question. Again, regardless of balance of power considerations, Cole says that "the finding is quite striking." He goes on to write that

> in no cases have democratic states allied against one another in this period. . . . Where several democracies perceive threat and form counteractive alliances, they again end up on the same side. Democratic states clearly do not ally only with other democracies; however, when responding to threat in situations where other democratic states are involved, they do ally together. . . . Democratic states, in terms of threat perception, reaction to threat, and interest definition, seem to make the same sorts of choices and respond to challenges in a manner suggesting "democratic empathy."[55]

Others have also found that historically democracies ally with each other more than one would expect by chance.[56] Weart found the same thing through the history of democracies, beginning with the classical Greek city-states.[57] It should be no surprise, then, that Doyle concluded from his study of democracies and war, from the eighteenth century on, that "a liberal zone of peace, a pacific union, has been maintained and has expanded despite numerous particular conflicts of economic and strategic interest."[58] This liberal zone of peace, this pacific union, is the joint social field.

This pacific union has been maintained even during one of the most dangerous times in international politics, when a major world power is being overtaken by another. The so-called power transition theory would argue that this is a time of greatest crisis between the two, for it most likely when war will break out between them as the one tries to maintain the status quo that favors it and the other attempts to restructure the status quo in favor of its growing power status.[59] Yet early in this century this transition took place between the democratic United States, the challenger, and democratic Great Britain, without war or even a deep crisis. Doyle describes this transition well:

> New power challenges old prestige, excessive commitments face new demands; so Sparta felt compelled to attack Athens, France warred Spain, England and Holland fought with France (and with each other), and Germany and England struggled for the mastery of Europe in World War 1. But here liberals [democracies] may again be an exception, for despite the fact that the United States constituted Britain's greatest challenger along all the dimensions most central to the British maritime hegemony, Britain and the United States accommodated their differences. After the defeat of Germany, Britain eventually, though not without regret, accepted its replacement by the United States as the commercial and maritime hegemon of the liberal world. The promise of a peaceable transition thus may be one of the factors helping to moderate economic and political rivalries among Europe, Japan, and the United States.[60]

Schweller in fact tested the power transition theory for all Great Power preventative wars since 1665 and a sample of ten Great Power transitions that did not end in war. He showed that

> only nondemocratic regimes wage preventive wars against rising opponents. Declining democratic states, for a variety of reasons . . . do not exercise this option. Instead, when the challenger is an authoritarian state, declining democratic leaders attempt to form counterbalancing alliances; when the challenger is another democratic state, they seek accommodation.[61]

That two democratic political regimes, now very large and complex law-making, law-administering, and law-judging organizations within the combined social field should avoid official violence and cooperate is not unique. Of course, regardless of laws against violence, individuals do commit murder or assault on each other. And there are Mafia families and diverse gangs among which turf wars may occasionally erupt. However, it is at least very rare and I cannot think of a single case in the national social field that is the United States, where two major independent and legitimate organizations committed intentional violence against each other. Of course, violence has occurred between unions and their corporations, but this is a form of intraorganizational violence.

However, has General Motors ever committed violence against Ford Motor Company or Chrysler? Has any Catholic Church attacked a Methodist or Presbyterian one?[62] Has any University launched violence against another one, or any other major organization? Indeed even the asking of the question seems ridiculous. But I'm not thinking of a frontal attack with guns, which would obviously and immediately trigger government intervention and prison for those involved, but a covert attempt to sabotage, assassinate, and otherwise try to violently weaken a competing organization or those which one's own is at odds. Perhaps such have occurred, but not a single example comes to mind, nor can I find any by browsing through some American political and economic history books. The lack or rarity of such violence shows the power of a social field in suppressing violence, as between two democratic regimes.

Now extend the international relations between two democratic regimes to those among many, including Canada, the United States, Australia, New Zealand, and all of those in Western Europe. Now the social field of each has been collapsed into one social field, and within this each of these regimes is one group among many. The structures of expectations, power equations, and processes of adjustment checking and balancing, limiting and inhibiting the behavior of the parts of each regime and thus the regime as a whole has now been vastly multiplied.

Rather than the probability of violence breaking out among any two of them being greater the more regimes that are in the overall social field, which would be a standard way of looking at the likelihood of international violence, *the probability of violence should decrease the more democratic the regimes*. This is because these regimes are not independent of each other, but the more the number of regimes and correspondingly the larger the social field incorporating all, then the greater the multiplicity of linkages and bonds, the tighter the web of expectations and interests that block violence from occurring at all, and the more other regimes can act as mediators in conflict. We have something akin to this at the level of individuals, where those most likely to commit violence against each other are the young, single, unemployed males. Those young males who are well-integrated into an extended family and neighborhood and have a regular job are much less likely to murder or violently assault each other.

One more point: in effect the people of the respective democratic societies are now merged into one largely spontaneous field. They thus view each other as closer to them in values and norms than for those outside the common field, then for authoritarian and totalitarian societies. Evidence for this comes from public opinion polls. Russett has nicely summarized one of these with regard to the interdemocratic peace.

A *Euro-baromèter*... survey asked citizens of each country in the European Community whether the people of every other country in the community, and citizens of six other states (China, Japan, the Soviet Union, Switzerland, Turkey, and the United States), were "in general very trustworthy, fairly trustworthy, not particularly trustworthy or not at all trustworthy." At the time, all twelve members of the EC [European Community] were democracies, as were three of the others (not China or the Soviet Union, and Turkey's democratic processes had been largely suspended under military rule). In six of the twelve EC countries, Russians, Chinese, and Turks—in different orders—rated as the three least "trustworthy nations," after all fourteen democracies. Either the Russians or the Turks were last on everyone's list, and eight of the twelve listed the Chinese on the untrustworthy side of the balance. Some country quirks are evident, but it is not just a matter, for example, of trusting their fellow EC partners. (Italians rated nine nations as on the untrustworthy side, and were not rated terribly high by others either). Only two countries considered the Japanese to be on balance untrustworthy. Whatever the quirks, political system type is a very strong correlate of trust, and it was generally the democratic nations that were trusted.[63]

And this is the clue to understanding why oligarchic republics and democracies make war on each other. Oligarchic republics, it is recalled, have a minority of male adult citizens that share equal rights and democratically participate in governance. Nonetheless, this minority comprises a social field that incorporates the enfranchised minority of other such republics, and all that has been said about why such a joint field militates against regime violence applies here. But then would not there also be such a joint field between democracies and these republics? The answer is largely no, and the relationship between democracies and South Africa may help to exemplify this. Ties were restricted, trade was boycotted, and people-to-people exchanges frowned upon. As the democracies leveled economic boycotts against South Africa and severally restricted exchange, there could not be a spontaneous field tying democracies and oligarchic republics together.

Rather, what was created was two different fields largely interacting through their respective political regimes. Not only was the freedom of interaction between these societies thus limited, but each saw the other as not only competitive, but as a natural political enemy.

In sum, *a key to understanding peace within the social field is the freedom people have to run their own lives,* whether through exchange or by tradition and custom, consistent of course with a like freedom of others. This not only creates the social diversity that isolates and moderates violence, but also a culture of negotiation and accommodation. And as democratic or republican leaders see other regimes as similar in this regard, they nearly always choose negotiation to fighting.

Now let us look at an antifield.

Notes

1. In *Understanding Conflict and War* (Rummel, 1975) I summed up my philosophical perspective, which I call *intentional humanism.* In summary, I argue that truth is a manifold of intuition, reason, and empirical experience. Reason structures and organizes our experience; intuition provides direction, insights, and initial hypotheses. Reality itself is a seamless whole where differences and dependencies shade off into each other, here physical, there mind; here potentiality, there actuality; here a field, there free will; here culture, there instincts; here the individual, there physical nature. Whether this is in reality true or not, we cannot know. We can treat it as provisionally true, however, draw out its implications in the search for inconsistencies, apply its suggestions, and pragmatically test its conclusions. Within the constraints of our empirical knowledge, we can choose to interpret reality in the light of one's own values and act within such an interpretation to achieve them. We thus comprise an intentional field at the center of which is our mentality, which is distinguished by its intellectual and creative abilities and moral capacity. And nature is given scale and perspective only by our meanings, values, norms, and intentions. Not all of this is relevant to explaining the democratic peace, of course, but that which is will be summarized in the following pages.
2. Bound up within this sentence is a perspective on reality as a complex of manifestations, potentialities, and latents; of dispositions, determinables, and powers. While this is not the place to go into this except as relevant to the democratic peace, I have employed these concepts and related ideas elsewhere to understand what I call the dynamic psychological field (Rummel, 1975).
3. For the importance and role I give to meanings, values, and norms I owe much to Pitirim Sorokin's great work, *Society, Culture, and Personality* (1969).
4. I treat interests as the fundamental motivation of individuals. Relevant work on this is Axelrod (1970); Petri (1986); and Bolles (1975). For my approach to motivation and thus interests I rely in particular on Cattell (1966) and associated work therein.
5. This is the theory that deprivation is relative. On relative deprivation, see for example, Gurr (1970); Davies (1973); and Runciman (1966).
6. There is a wealth of literature in sociology on social status, but comparatively little done on international relations. Galtung (1966) was one of the first to look at

this and stimulated much research on the behavior between high and low status nations. I have tried to integrate status theory into the social field theory to be later described (Rummel, 1977, chapter 9).

7. The idea of social distance, similarity and difference, has played a large role in empirical and theoretical sociological work. See for example the empirical references in Davis (1966); Heider (1958); Burgess and Wallin (1943); Sorokin (1969, chapter 7); and Berelson and Steiner (1964, pp. 305–09, 313). Even Plato in his *Republic* noted: "And so iron will be mingled with silver, and brass with gold, and hence there will arise dissimilarity and inequality and irregularity, which always and in all places are causes of hatred and war." Wright (1942, 1965, chapter 35) has made international social distances a central part of his explanation and theoretical model for war. Social distances has been a central part of my social field theory, and indeed, I treat them as the lines of force accounting for social and international behavior. See Rummel (1977; 1977b, chapter 6; 1979). See also note 28 of chapter 10.

8. For this reason and some other assumptions, such as that of conflict taking place within an historical process, I model this process—called the conflict helix—by Catastrophe Theory (see Rummel, 1987). There now have been several applications of Catastrophe Theory to political and social systems. See, for example, Morris Davis (1979); Diener (1980); Smirnov and Ershov (1992); and Adelman, Taft, and Hihn (1982). For a basic treatment and overview of Catastrophe Theory, see Majthay (1985) and Poston and Stewart (1978).

9. The idea here is close to that of Chalmers Johnson (1966), who argued that a harmonious society is one in equilibrium, a synchronization between values and the division of scarce resources and labor. When these get out of synchronization due to technological change, global communications, rise of external reference groups, and so on, and homeostatic devices fail, as in the normal way social and political conflict are resolved, then a revolutionary situation is created and violence is possible.

10. McWhirter and McWhirter (1977, p. 435).

11. Another widely recognized political gestalt is when an American president's administration takes on a character that is beyond the simple contribution of each member and their behavior—one can in this way, for example, talk about the Nixon administration or the Clinton administration. The importance of social and political gestalts in understanding behavior is one reason I prefer the social *field*, as will be discussed, over a social *system* perspective on behavior. There is another aspect to a gestalt that also is relevant. This is the idea that within the field there is a *dynamic process* through which the field is organized and an equilibrium created and maintained, and that people innately by perception and behavior try to bring things into equilibrium and maintain it. For gestalt theorists this applies particularly to perception. I argue that it also applies to a social field as seen through the *conflict helix* to be later described. In this I have been particularly influenced by Koffka (1947) and Köhler (1942). Perhaps because of my own background in art, I found especially helpful and stimulating Ushenko's (1953) excellent theoretical analysis of the gestalt phenomena in painting. For my discussion of gestalt theory within the context of field theories, see Rummel (1975, chapter 3). Gestalt theory has been particularly applied in psychotherapy. See, for example, Shub (1992) and Korb, Gorrell, and van de Riet (1989).

12. For an important study of why in the early 1940s the ordinary German with no particularly ideological bent or antisemitism could shoot to death helpless Jewish women and children, see Browning (1992).

13. See Haney, Banks, and Zimbardo (1983), and Milgram (1974), for experiments that show that even Americans having been acculturated to democratic norms and values can knowingly inflict pain or subject others to barbarous treatment if (1) an authoritative person in an authoritative situation instructs them to do so, or (2) they are put into a social structure facilitating and encouraging such behavior, as in simulating being a prison guard. These and other confirming experiments well show the potential that lies close to the surface even within democratic societies. It is my argument here that the social field of which democracy is a part, and the forces associated with and unleashed by this field, largely keep these tendencies in check.

14. After years of searching out all cases of democide in this and previous centuries, I have been particularly struck by how, given the right circumstances—as of the American army fighting Philippine rebels, the British army fighting a mutiny in India, or the French army fighting an uprising in Algeria—people from every culture, religion, and nation can massacre their fellow human beings in cold blood. For many cases of this, see Chalk and Jonassohn (1990), and Rummel (1994).

15. See, for example, Köhler (1942); Koffka (1947); Lewin (1951); Tolman (1951); Brown (1936); Mannheim (1940); Yinger (1965); and Mey (1965). The most systematically philosophical, wide-ranging, and profound use of field theory outside the natural sciences is developed in four books written by the philosopher Andrew Paul Ushenko (1937; 1946; 1953; 1958). These have had much impact on my thinking about social fields. I have tried to sketch the philosophical and theoretical history of physical, psychological, and social fields in my *The Dynamic Psychological Field* (Rummel, 1975, part 1). I show that as developed in the literature, there are three types of fields: relational, equilibrium, and dynamic. That which I am describing here is a mixture of equilibrium and dynamic fields. For recent work on social field theories, see Wheelan, Pepitone, and Abt (1990), and Stivers and Wheelan (1986).

16. Wright (1955, part V).

17. I have tried to do this for international relations through the separate factor analysis of national attributes and behavior and then by linking (through canonical analysis) the resulting between nation distances in attribute space to the location of dyads in behavioral space. This was in the way of operationalizing and testing a field theory model, which tests were largely positive (see Rummel 1977; 1979; 1979b).

18. As completely as I could, I have dealt with a variety of aspects of social fields in relation to peace, violence, and war in my *Understanding Conflict and War* (1975; 1976; 1977b; 1979; 1981). Social field theory was the basic theory of those five volumes.

19. See footnote 3.

20. The idea, nature, and role of a spontaneous society has been well-developed in Hayek's excellent three volumes on *Law, Legislation and Liberty* (1973; 1976; 1979). Although he does not use the concept of social field, his discussion of a spontaneous society is as though it were a social field in my terms.

21. These are what Hayek (1973) calls "Just Rules."

22. These abstract rules operate like a traffic policeman at a busy intersection. The policeman is only interested in facilitating the passage of vehicles through the intersection without collision or undue delay, regardless of the drivers destination, character, or interests. Similarly, abstract rules are those applicable to all regardless of purpose, race, religion, or socioeconomic status. Etiquette is an example of

such rules, as are rules of the road, dating norms, or those governing business, such as confirming an agreement with a handshake. Many such abstract rules are passed into formal laws, as for example, those defining murder, incest, or statutory rape.

23. Hayek (1979, p. 140).

24. Ibid.

25. I have not been able to find the term *antifield* used elsewhere in the social and psychological sciences. But the idea of a hierarchical, command-driven *organization* as the opposite of a spontaneous society or free market is not new. Its best development and consistent application is in Hayek (1973; 1976; 1979). Moreover, there is some similarity to Michels' (1949) "iron law of oligarchy," where the tendency to well-defined positions of command by a few freezes out field processes and increasingly emphasizes coercion as apart from authority. Also, the small college turned large public university, the political discussion group turned successful political party, and the small business turned large industry manifest the growth of command-driven organizations (antifields), as noted by the elite theorists, like Mosca (1939) and Pareto (1963). At a more general level, the idea is consistent with the notion that command-power breeds command-power. It is in the nature of such power to aggrandize, to grow until limited by other powers, as so well described by de Jouvenal (1962). See my chapter on "fields and antifields" (Rummel, 1976, chapter 22).

26. On cross-cutting and cross-pressures, see chapter 10, note 23. Note that this idea was central to Secretary of State Kissinger's attempt to link different issues in negotiation and treaties with the Soviet Union. This indeed defined in practice the foreign policy of détente. See Kissinger's memoirs (1982, chapter VII).

27. Schumpeter (1962, pp. 127–28). See Doyle (1986, p. 1153) for a relevant discussion of Schumpeter's view.

28. Obviously, how one perceives within a cultural matrix is critical to understanding conflict. This is not the place to go into perception in great detail, which I have tried to do elsewhere (Rummel, 1991c) consistent with a field approach. My view of perception owes much to the gestalt psychologists (e.g., Köhler, 1942; Koffka, 1947; and Rogers, 1961) and the philosophical work of Ushenko, particularly on art (1953). For a more general and conventional approach to perception, see Goldstein (1989) and Rock (1983).

29. This is not the place to discuss dispositions in detail. I see an understanding of dispositions as theoretically fundamental, where the disposition to behave in a certain way within a situation is a result of perceptions and interests. How one actually behaves is a result of situational expectations of the outcome of how one is disposed to behave. For a full specification of this, see Rummel (1979, chapter 5). For a full work on dispositions, see Prior (1985).

30. There is a tendency among works on democracy and conflict to conflate nonviolent and violent conflict. I argue that these are distinctly different kinds of behavior sharing a similar process (the conflict helix, still to be discussed), but with different general causes and conditions, as for a contract dispute between two corporations, and a guerrilla attack on a police station.

31. It is an empirical question whether exchange societies (social fields) manifest a characteristic type of conflict we might label turmoil or pluralistic conflict. Such has in fact been found in the studies of Adelman and Morris (1973); Gurr (1969); Sorokin (1957); Bwy (1972); and Banks (1972). Moreover, numerous factor analyses have found three dimensions of conflict, one of which is clearly a turmoil type. See, for example, Bwy (1972); Hibbs (1973); Morrison and Stevenson (1971);

and Wilkenfeld (1969). I discuss and compare these and other studies with regard to this and related questions in Rummel (1976, chapter 35). I have not kept track of more recent and relevant factor analyses, but those I happened to read do not depart from this. Virtually always turmoil is a dominant and distinct dimension of domestic conflict and violence.

32. Of course modern and especially social democratic (or democratic socialist) regimes have passed many laws regarding welfare, taxes, health, conservation, and the like, that specify outcomes and transfer incomes. These are not abstract rules, but legislative laws meant to organize society in a particular way to achieve some social purpose, such as greater equality. As these laws gain in number and scope over abstract rules society is turned more into an antifield. However, I argue that the distinguishing feature of democracies—their civil liberties and political rights—assure that abstract rules and thus the social field (exchange society) dominates.

33. See Hayek, (1976, pp. 3–4, 38). Indeed, Hayek's whole discussion of abstract or Just Rules in his three volumes (1973; 1976; 1979) within a spontaneous society is relevant to this point.

34. For a treatment of the global society from this perspective, see Hoffman (1965), who in fact titles his work *The State of War*. See also Glenn Snyder (1971, pp. 73–74), who argues that this state of war due to an international anarchy creates a "security dilemma." He says that "the dilemma arises because states can never be sure that the security measures of others are intended only for security and not for aggression. Consequently, each state's effort to gain security through power accumulation do tend to increase the insecurity of other states, stimulating them to enhance their power, which then leads to further apprehension and power accumulation by the first states, and so on." See also Herz (1959). As shown empirically in part I, the empirical error in such arguments is that they do not take the type of regime into account. The security dilemma or state of war does not hold between democracies, for example. On the resulting change in views of international theory, see for example Kegley (1993).

35. Northedge and Donelan (1971, p. 145). For years I coded the daily *The New York Times* and collected clippings from all the major American newspapers and news magazines on conflict events of any sort. It was with some amazement that in time I noted that the frequency of such events was but a small fraction of the cooperative events and flows, such as trade, between nations. Others have also noted this. McGowan (1973), for example, found that for all international cooperative, participatory, and conflict events among thirty-two black African states, conflict comprised only 17.7 percent. For all international events, McClelland and Hoggard (1969) found 31.5 percent were conflictful. And Hermann (1975) discovered that for 11,589 events between thirty-five states between 1959 and 1968, only 3 percent were hostile.

36. Battle dead total from Small and Singer (1982); democide data from chapter 6.

37. I adopt a conflict model of society rather than a consensus one. I see the change and adjustments in society as a function of conflict. Thus, conflict is normal and not an aberration in a supposedly normatively and consensually structured society. On the debate between the conflict and consensus models, see Bernard (1983).

38. In much of my earlier work on the conflict helix, perhaps influenced by the international relations literature where the term "balance" of power, rather than "equilibrium" of power is standard, I used the term balance in place of equilibrium. This has created some confusion, since to many readers a balance of power connotes relative power equality.

39. If it is still difficult to think of an equilibrium of power in any other terms than

coercion and force, note that the price of a product in a free market is an equilibrium of bargaining powers, the consensus among scientists about a theory is an equilibrium of intellectual powers (based on persuasion), the international aid given to famine victims is an equilibrium of altruistic powers, the accepted dogma of a church an equilibrium of authoritative powers, and the relationship between lovers is an equilibrium of altruistic powers. On power, see chapter 9.

40. The operation of the balance of power among nations is a particular example of the process being described here. For a study of the historical operation of this, see Gulick (1982). Simowitz (1982) provides an incisive critical analysis of the concept.

41. For the most recent research on interpersonal expectations, see Blanck (1993). The idea of an equilibrium in expectations has played a strong role in economic theory. See, for example, Kollintzas (1989); Hamouda and Rowley (1988); and Torr (1988). Also for the expression "who gets what, when, how," see Lasswell (1958).

42. I have attempted to measure this equilibrium and associated structure of expectations for the cold war bilateral relations among the United States, Soviet Union, and China in Rummel (1987c), and between Pakistan and India (Rummel, 1987). I also have employed them (Rummel, 1984) within a conceptual framework for understanding the cold war.

43. I call the process a conflict helix because behavior between two people, groups, or regimes, cycles upward in mutual learning and successive adjustment, each cycle involving deeper cooperation and milder conflict, thus metaphorically creating the shape of a helix. The idea and model of the helix developed over a dozen or more years as I tried to make sense of social violence. I gave it near final form in Rummel (1976, chapter 29) and applied it to international relations in Rummel (1979). I give a simplified characterization of the helix and its supporting principles in Rummel (1991b). There is no one person or small group of theorists on whom I can blame it. Perhaps the closest in idea is that of Chalmers Johnson's (1966) dynamic theory of revolution, in which a growing value-environment disequilibration creates a revolutionary situation. In its emphasis on a dialectical conflict model of society it also owes something to the dialectical (social) materialism of Karl Marx, but without the materialism and in fact a return to something like the idealism of Hegel; and in its view of conflict and cooperation as a continuous process, it leans to some extent on Sorokin's work (1957, p. 537; 1969, pp. 481–82). Also see for example Simon (1957) and Coleman (1964). For international relations, Richardson's arms race process model (1960) had some influence. For other related process models, see Barringer (1972); Wright (1942; 1955; 1965; and in particular 1965b), and Northedge and Donelan (1971). I have used Catastrophe Theory (Rummel, 1987) to model the dynamics of the conflict helix (see footnote 8). For an interesting economic approach to social process, see Roberts and Holdren (1972).

44. This is a "jump" as modeled in Catastrophe Theory. See footnote 8.

45. That conflict is a form of learning or trial and error has not been until recently a popular view among social psychologists. This was largely because of the widely held view in the 1950s and early 1960s that conflict was a social aberration and dysfunctional. Now it has become well recognized that not only do participants learn from conflict, but that it is a real world laboratory for learning how to manage change. See, for example, the training handbook of Hart (1981).

46. Doyle (1986, p. 1156).

47. Czempiel (1992, p. 259). His following sentences are: "It is interesting to note

that democracies have never waged war against one another. The anarchical structure is weakened if the system is composed of democracies. Against non-democracies, however, democracies have been no less warlike than non-democracies. This implies that the system of government is not the only variable which explains foreign policy behavior. It is, however, the most important one." (Ibid.)

48. Bueno de Mesquita and Lalman (1992, p. 154).
49. Bueno de Mesquita and Lalman (1989, p. 260).
50. Bueno de Mesquita (1993, p. 156).
51. Weart (1994, 1995).
52. Doyle (1983, pp. 231–32).
53. Rittberger (1989, p. 50).
54. Cole (1990, p. 17).
55. Ibid., pp. 17, 19.
56. Siverson and Emmons (1991).
57. Weart (1994, 1995).
58. Doyle (1983, pp. 213–15).
59. See Organski (1958) and Organski and Kugler (1980) for a positive test of the power transition theory.
60. Doyle (1983, p. 234).
61. Schweller (1992, p. 236).
62. Of course the Catholic Church carried out bloody crusades against Protestants and Muslims in the Middle Ages. However, this was when the Church was protected by and a handmaiden in absolute monarchies.
63. Russett (1993, pp. 129–30).

12

Third-Level Explanation II:
Antifield and Power

> *No one thinks his justice is not universal. As
> Marx observed, no one is opposed to freedom
> in general, only to that freedom which jeopar-
> dizes his own power. Tito was for such selec-
> tive freedom. . . . If that were not so, Tito would
> not have been faithful to himself, to his Com-
> munism and his power. For Tito was faithful
> to pure power. That power enabled him to put
> his stamp on every aspect of social and na-
> tional life.*
> —Milovan Djilas, *Tito: The Story from Inside*

Possibly the best way of conceptualizing an antifield is to outline a
typical organization that is constructed to achieve a task, let us say to
manufacture widgets.[1] There is a president, vice presidents, treasurer,
host of secretaries and heads of divisions, foremans, skilled workers,
and ordinary laborers. That is, there is a hierarchy of coercive and
authoritative power represented by the organizational chart for the
business. For eight or more hours a day, people are integrated into and
directed in their tasks by rules and commands issued from the top
down, all with the purpose of most efficiently and cheaply producing
widgets and marketing them. This is a society, to be sure, but it is not
a spontaneous one. Between individual members of the organization
while on the job there is little freedom to develop their own expectations according to their own power equations. In the organization, and
particularly if they are the mass of workers at or near the bottom of the
hierarchy, they have to work at particular jobs at particular locations

in the organization. They must eat or take a break at particular times. And they seldom have a choice of who they must work with, whether they like the person or not or have large or small differences with them.[2]

Of course, even in the most tightly organized company there will be room for some free interaction and the working out of individual to individual expectations, and each worker to some degree will also establish social expectations with the bosses immediately above them. But the major substance and lines of behavior between people are passed down from above, not as a result of free interaction between those who command and those who obey, but by higher ups who decide what is to be done.

Thus we have in the organization the example previously given for an antifield. The hierarchy and the commands that pass down from top to bottom and govern most behavior between individuals in the organization are like a cardboard grid placed on top of a piece of paper under which there is a magnet. As noted in the previous chapter, sprinkle iron filings across the grid and they will respond to the magnetic pull only within the confines of each cell of the grid. The overall social field has in effect been purposely reduced to separate little fields within an overall antifield, the organization, in order to achieve some common task.

This has several consequences for conflict and violence. First, since the structure of expectations governing relations and behavior within the organization are given by commands to the multitude of those near and at the bottom of its hierarchy, there develops a clear conflict front between bosses and workers. This creates two classes within the organization: those who command and those who must obey.[3] This forms a social storm front within the organization along which its major conflicts will occur. There is little to moderate or inhibit this latent conflict between bosses and workers, except the belief of the workers that they are being treated justly on the one side, and on the other the fear that their wages will be docked, they will be punished with a less desirable task, or they will be fired altogether.

This is not an abstract conflict front, a theoretical construct. It is an empirical front that is well defined in most task-oriented organizations and in even in some universities and colleges. It is the line between management and workers, where in many organizations unions have grown to represent workers against management and to bargain collectively for higher pay and benefits and better conditions of work. Within this antifield a relatively minor issue in one part of the organization or even a conflict between an executive and a worker that leads to the worker being fired can become a matter to be fought out along the union-management conflict front within an organization. Workers or their union representatives may see this as an issue of worker rights and demand that the worker be rehired, and which if not done may be met by a work slowdown or a strike against the firm. If the issue is perceived as vital to union power and worker rights, and management is intransigent, the strike could involve violence.

Note the flow of expectations, conflict, and the power equations. Unlike a social field where the flow is multidirectional, aligned only with the constantly evolving patterns of expectations and interests among individuals and groups within a society, in a tightly managed organization it is polarized up and down the hierarchy. For the workers the direction is up; for the bosses the direction is down. What is thus created across the organization is one governing structure of expectations and two usually balanced power equations. One of these is the power of the workers, often reflected in their interests as defined by their union and its demands on management; its membership, treasury and reserve funds; its leadership and ability to bargain; and its willingness to strike. On the other side is management—the bosses—and their interests; the profitability of the organization and support of local politicians and police; its ability to withstand a long strike; and the determination of management to hang tough. If expectations—agreements between management and workers or their union, and the nonnegotiated commands and rules that management lays down—get out of sync with the two power equations, if a gap between the two grows bigger and bigger, then some trigger, perhaps a worker getting injured or fired or a unilateral change in some work rules for just one part of the manufacturing process, can disrupt the management-worker equilibrium. And some or all of the workers may then go on strike.

Such a society of perhaps a thousand or so people is an antifield within which the larger process of cooperation and conflict, order and disorder is mainly as though between two individuals. This antifield has been created by the power of a few or one person to build an organization in order to achieve some goal, hire those who become its members, and command and control them. Power has created the antifield.

Work within such organizations today is usually not forced or slave or indentured labor. Members are theoretically free to quit. Of course, how free depends on the situation of the worker and whether the organization is a small-town monopoly, or within a highly competitive market at a time of low unemployment. And of course these variables will effect the type of power employed, but let us assume the worker is fairly free to quit his job. Then the hiring of a worker is a negotiated contract between the applicant and management (bargaining power). Moreover, the worker will do much of what is commanded within the organization's rules because they believe they ought to do that for which they are getting paid (authoritative power). Finally, there will be rules and commands that the worker obeys only because they carry the threat of sanctions or firing for nonperformance (coercive power). The mix of these depends, of course, on the organization, time, and place.

In contemporary, largely free markets these powers may be well mixed, with exchange and authoritative power being as important if not more so than coercive power. However, there have also been such organizations entirely run by coercive power, as on many late nineteenth-century Mexican *hacienda,* where Indians who were tricked or seduced into owing money were sold to the plantations and from then on forced under lash, beatings, and the threat of death to labor in the fields. They were often worked to death, and those who were caught trying to escape could be beaten to death as an example to the others. Those who got much beyond the plantation were hunted by the police and if caught would be returned to the plantation, regardless of their fate. Coercive power and associated fear ruled.[4]

The idea of an antifield thus has practical and empirical meaning and captures an essential aspect of some societies, specifically those organized in a tight hierarchy of power. The antifield begins with trying to impose on a society some common goal or task, no matter what it may be. This initiates the conflict front that may span the society and along which violence may occur. Using a different language and different focus, Hayek nonetheless had a similar idea in mind when he wrote in the second volume of his *Law, Legislation and Liberty* that

> the savage in us still regards as good what was good in the small group but what the Great Society [spontaneous society] must not only refrain from enforcing but cannot even allow particular groups to enforce. A peaceful Open Society [social

field] is possible only if it renounces the method of creating solidarity that is most effective in the small group, namely acting on the principle that "if people are to be in harmony, then let them strive for some common end." This is the conception of creating coherence which leads straight to the interpretation of politics as a matter of friend-enemy relations. It is also the device which has been effectively employed by all dictators.[5]

Now I can deal with the opposite of a democratic political regime and associated exchange society, which is the totalitarian one and the coercive society it organizes. I will first sketch the structure of one such society, Cambodia under the Khmer Rouge, 1976 to January, 1979.[6] I could just as well exemplify this with Stalin's USSR, Mao Tse-tung's China in the first decade and a half after the communists took over all of mainland China, Hitler's rule over Poland, Hoxha's Albania, Ceausescu's Rumania, Kim Il-sung's North Korea, and Poland, East Germany, Hungary, Bulgaria, Yugoslavia, Czechoslovakia, or Castro's Cuba in the first decade of their communist rule.

In Cambodia the Khmer Rouge seized power over the country when the authoritarian Lon Nol regime collapsed from their military defeats by the Khmer Rouge. Once in power the first thing they did was to evacuate all cities newly under their control. No matter the population, all residents and refugees were required immediately to leave their homes, businesses, hospitals, and schools for unknown destinations in the country. Resisters were shot; those refusing to hand over to the Khmer Rouge whatever they demanded were also shot.

The crowds on all the roads leading out of cities were guided at gun point by Khmer Rouge soldiers, and in gradually thinning columns over many days directed to one village or another, or stopped to build where they stood a village with their own hands, sometimes in a virgin forest. However settled, they all were put to work as common peasants to farm or create fields. But first, in many cases, those who were former military officers were executed, as were those who had been officials in the former government of Lon Nol, or who had worked for foreigners. Moreover, often those who could speak a foreign language, particularly French (Cambodia had been a French colony), Vietnamese, or English were killed. So were many professionals, such as lawyers, doctors, engineers, and others that the Khmer Rough thought might be therefore ideologically polluted. The search for such people went on throughout the near four-year history of this regime, and whenever they were discovered among the former city dwellers and now new peasants they were killed. Moreover, the regime systematically murdered Vietnamese and Vietnamese-Cambodians, Chams (a Muslim-Cambodian minority), Buddhist monks, and other minorities and possible sources of countervailing power.

As for the peasants, new and old, the task was to produce food for the regime and do as commanded, under threat of severe punishment and often execution. Rules were draconian, and life virtually limited to one's twelve- or fourteen-hour work day. There were no newspapers, no television, no school (except for some teaching of farming), no hospitals (there were "clinics" run by untrained "nurses"), no mail, no travel. There were no private businesses. All and everything was either fully under Khmer Rouge control or had been eliminated. In many parts of the country people were not even permitted to own pots and pans, to eat alone, or to scrounge in the fertile Cambodian forests for food. Secreting and eating a banana could mean execution. They had to eat communally and for this they may have been allowed their own spoon.

There was only work, and that was done under strict supervision by gun-toting soldiers or cadre. All the products of their work in the field were taken by the Khmer Rouge, a portion subsequently to be rationed out. One had to have a pass to leave the village. Even laughter and informal conversation, or holding hands with a loved one, or hugging a relative could be dangerous, for that showed less dedication to the regime and the revolution. To try to escape from Cambodia meant death if caught, and except for the almost inhospitable and inaccessible mountain range between Thailand and Cambodia, the border was mined and patrolled by the regime. The whole country had been turned into a prison of slaves.[7]

There was a purpose to all this. Under the leadership of Pol Pot, the Khmer Rouge wanted to create post-haste a true communist society. In the process they were trying to eradicate the "mental and spiritual pollution" of capitalism and reeducate those minds that had been so "contaminated." The way of doing this, they thought, was through work in the fields as a peasant, for the peasant life and working the soil was the source of ultimate knowledge and happiness. Moreover, they were intent on making Cambodia self-sufficient, to end what they perceived as the exploitation of Cambodia by her neighbors and the major powers. That is, to achieve their goals, they had reconstructed Cambodian society into a hierarchical organization based entirely on coercion, that is the threat of torture, severe sanctions, and execution. All alternative sources of power within Cambodia, such as the Buddhist church, the military, and a traditional aristocracy, had been eliminated, and in order to maintain power there was a constant purging and execution of even high Khmer Rouge officials.

All meaningful and important issues between Cambodians had been turned into that between the Khmer Rouge and the old and new peasants, or the Pol Pot faction in power and other Khmer rouge factions. And throughout the country there was really only one overall structure of expectations, and two organizing powers—that of coercion and raw physical force exercised by the Khmer Rouge leadership over all others. And these expectations constantly broke down. Since virtually all was seen as vital to the survival of the regime and the revolution, Pol Pot and his clique and their opponents commonly resorted to violence. There were numerous coup attempts, possibly several regional rebellions, and the documented outright rebellion of the Eastern Province as Pol Pot attempted to purge its top Khmer Rouge.[8] And many high Khmer Rouge ended up tortured in the infamous Tuol Slen prison in Phnom Penh to reveal "who they had colluded with" against Pol Pot[9] (of the many thousands incarcerated there, only fourteen may have survived[10]).

The number of overall executions of former soldiers, government officials, professionals, former urbanites, and peasants carried out in the process of establishing and maintaining this antifield is impossible to calculate. The number of deaths in coups and rebellions is also incalculable, but must exceed 100,000 dead. But when those who died of disease and starvation due to slave labor, mistreatment, and neglect by the regime are also taken into account, a reasonable figure is something close to 2,000,000 Cambodians, or near one-third of the Cambodia population.[11]

Cambodia had been built into a hierarchical organization to achieve a purpose, the communist nirvana. It was the strongest kind of antifield. Even honeyed words between loved ones could, if overheard, be the cause of punishment and death.[12] Only the most trivial conflict helices could be worked out individual to individual. What people did with each other, even often marriage, was commanded by this totalitarian regime. And accordingly violence was a way of life, execution always a possibility. And the regime warred on its neighbors, engaging the Thai army several times along the border and invading Vietnam in a number of places, massacring tens of thousands of Vietnamese in the process. Indeed, the regime seemed to believe it could win a war against the vastly more superior Vietnamese and recover ancient Cambodian land long part of Vietnam by making each soldier responsible for killing several dozen Vietnamese. In any case, Vietnam tired of this and put an end to it by a full force invasion of Cambodia in January, 1979 and defeat of the Khmer Rouge within a few weeks.

There still is a tendency in the social sciences to think of any description of a regime as totalitarian and the society it creates as wholly coercive as hyperbole. Some like to point to differences among the elite and to factions that oppose the regime's policies. Moreover, they find it almost impossible to believe that any regime could be so absolute as to control nearly everything that goes on in society. True, there were divisions among the Khmer Rough, for which opponents paid with their lives. True, the governors of some provinces were less harsh than others and there was considerable variation across the nation in cruelty and lethality. But the regime ruled, it did try and largely succeeded in controlling all normal social behavior, and its rule was by force and coercion. And as I pointed out when I began this example, there were many other regimes that were as totalitarian, if not more so, although perhaps not as barbarous and deadly. North Korea under Kim Il-song was an antlike society utterly controlled and managed under either his absolute rule or, increasingly before his death, by his son. There was none of the visible disunity within his regime that was seen within the Khmer Rouge, although top officials were still periodically purged and executed up to his death.[13]

As these examples show, one does not need to invent an abstract ideal type to describe an antifield. They exist now and have existed in the past.[14] And most relevantly here, they are the most violent societies. As shown in chapter 6, totalitarian regimes have been willing to accept the greatest number of killed in war to pursue their aims and have had the most severe domestic collective violence. The world's most total and costly war was launched in Europe by totalitarian Hitler and in Asia by the near totalitarian Japanese military. Moreover, as far as my statistics go, fascist, communist, and other totalitarian regimes have murdered near 134,000,000 people in this century, which is 83 percent of all people killed in genocide and mass murder by one national regime or another.[15] Stalin, one of the most absolute of dictators controlling by force and coercion the whole Soviet empire from

1928 to 1953 is responsible for the murder of some 43,000,000 citizens.[16] Antifields created by human will over national societies and ruled by coercion are the most violent and lethal.

One thing remains to be clarified. What about the international relations between such regimes? Recall that relations between democratic regimes are, in practice, within a common social field. But there is no social field for totalitarian regimes, but rather two entirely independent organizations within each of which there is a tight hierarchy of power. The cross border movement of people and goods, the relationships between the parts of one totalitarian regime and that of another are thoroughly controlled by the leadership. To assure this control their secret agents spy on what their citizens do abroad, and if for reasons of state or diplomatic purposes they must be allowed to travel abroad, other agents are assigned to spy on these spies.

In fact *the usual view of international relations as that between states fully applies to such totalitarian systems, for literally nothing done between these states is not controlled (commanded, permitted, spied on) by their regimes.* As a result, the whole set of relationships between any two such regimes reduces to the conflict helix between their rulers, such as between Hitler and Stalin or Stalin and Mao Tsetung. And all that applies to violence within any conflict helix is relevant. That is, a breakdown in the core expectations concerning fundamental values is likely to lead to violence as a way of resolving which of them gets or does what, when, or how. There are few, if any, moderating, inhibiting, cross-pressuring, balancing linkages or bonds. To be sure, relations with third and forth countries and the effect of violence on one's long run capability will influence the decision for violence. But these are considerations that enter into a decision, and are not the same as multiple and cross-cutting expectations and interests. Without such inhibitors and checks to violence, the relations between two totalitarian rulers is as though they were playing a game of chess against each other, moving their pieces and keeping track of their power until they can take advantage of the other's stupid moves.

It is in this case that game theory, the favorite tool of some analysts of international relations and conflict is most applicable.[17] Depending on the cost and benefits (marginal utilities) of various moves each can make under various assumptions, such as complete rationality or perfect information or that one will minimize losses, one should be able to determine the most likely move each will make, or define a conflict situation for which neither can find a rational solution (such as in the so-called prisoners dilemma). The argument here is that such game theory is most applicable to totalitarian regimes, not democracies operating in a common social field. In such a field democratic regimes do not respond to each other as calculating game players in general, but as though the output of multiple interconnecting committees.[18] For this, among other reasons, they tend to be less aggressive. Domke established this empirically for war, from 1816 to 1975. He found that

> seventeen decisions for war of conquest were undertaken by invaders with closed political structures. Although six decisions to invade were by governments with legislative parity, no decision to wage war of conquest was taken by a government with institutionalized political competition.[19]

Even authoritarian regimes, as shown in chapter 2, are willing to bear a greater cost in war. Although the larger society may be near free, the regime is autocratic and well able to play the war game. Authoritarian Portugal, for example, tried to keep control of its colonies in the face of bloody guerrilla wars of independence. In 1968 alone it spent 6 percent of its gross national product on its African wars, twice as much as the United States at the height of the Vietnam War,[20] just before the establishment and elite began to turn against the war.

Besides the rulers of antifields playing at war and peace and lacking domestic constraints, there is another reason that they tend to be more aggressive and violence prone in international relations. This is well put by Czempiel, who writes:

> Since those dictatorships habitually use violence in their relationship with their domestic societies, they will not hesitate, if necessary, to use violence also in foreign policy. There is no institutional and/or traditional barrier which would keep them from doing so. Without being able to instrumentalize a "Primacy of Foreign Policy," they might not be able to survive. Therefore, they are bound to have external conflicts with at least a threat of military violence. The East-West conflict demonstrates that communist regimes nourished the military confrontation in order to consolidate and to protect their rule over the societies.[21]

In sum, then, as social fields are converted into antifields a spontaneous society is turned into an organization. There is then a strict hierarchy of power, members are clearly divided into those who command and those who must obey, and coercion and force are the glue holding the organization together. By the very nature of this antifield, violence, democide, and war is its most likely outcome. Such is theory. The evidence supports this. As shown in part I, war, domestic collective violence, and democide are significantly and highly correlated with the degree to which a regime is totalitarian, and thus has created an antifield.

Notes

1. There has been much work among sociologists and political scientists to understand the social functions of organizations and the role of power within them. See Mintzberg (1983); Clegg (1990); Hassard (1993); and Hodgetts (1991).
2. On work within organizations, see Czander (1993). One of the major current concerns about organizations is the role, function, and nature of cultural diversity within them. For the latest work on this, see Cox (1993).
3. At this point I should express my intellectual debt to Dahrendorf's stimulating and provocative *Class and Class Conflict in Industrial Society* (1959). I depart from his ideas in many ways and he might not have recognized his influence on these pages, but his work provided the idea wedge into the problem of societal conflict and antifields and a way of understanding class conflict consistent with the conflict helix. For related works, see Parkin (1971) and Calvert (1982).
4. See Fehrenbach (1973) and especially Turner (1969). The conditions and life expectancy of forced laborers on the worst of the Mexican haciendas apparently was on par with the Soviet gulag.
5. Hayek, 1976, p. 149.
6. For various treatments of this incredible period of Cambodian history, see Becker (1986); Hawk (1984); Jackson (1989); Kiernan and Boua (1982); and Vickery (1984). I have written a case study of the Cambodian democide in Rummel (1994).
7. This may seem exaggerated, but consider that not only were Cambodians made to labor at the point of guns, not only were they often killed for the slightest infraction or even implied criticism of the regime (as in showing grief over the execution of a loved one), but also all their social affairs were dictated by the regime or ruled by the fear of discovery or disapproval. On all this, see the autobiographies of Yathay (1987) and Ngor (1987), or the biographical based account of Stuart-Fox with Ung (1985).
8. Stuart-Fox with Ung (1985, p. 123) and Kiernan (1982, p. 278; 1990, p. 39).
9. Puddington (1987, p. 20); Stuart-Fox with Ung (1985, p. 165); and *Kampuchea: Political Imprisonment and Torture* (1987).
10. Wain (1981).
11. I arrived at this figure after a quantitative and qualitative comparison of all the estimates I could find in the literature. I also checked it systematically against polynomial regressions of what the population should have been and was over the years 1976 to 1979. See Rummel (1996, chapter 3).
12. Haing Ngor (1987, pp. 216–25) reports in his autobiography that he was overhead by spies calling his wife by a term of endearment. Interrogated for this and other transgressions he was told "the chhlop [spies] say that you call your wife 'sweet.' We have no 'sweethearts' here. That is forbidden." He was then imprisoned,

where he was severely tortured, including having a finger cut off and his ankle sliced with a hatchet. He almost died.

13. See Sin (1991). For current human rights practices, see Chira (1989). And for past practices and purges, see Nam (1974) and Kim (1980).

14. Interestingly, while we have recent real world examples of nations exemplifying antifields, we do not have nations that perfectly or near perfectly exemplify social fields. This is because of the near universal growth of government and its intrusion and control over socioeconomic affairs. The two closest examples of a social field are Hong Kong, which is a colony of Great Britain; and the international social field of nations, with the most minimum of government and maximum of freedom to the social units within the field.

15. Rummel (1994, 1996).

16. See, for example, Conquest (1968, 1990). His 20,000,000 or more killed (calculated in his 1968 work and unrevised in 1990) under Stalin, which has become a much-quoted figure in the literature, takes into account only one period during Stalin's rule. I have taken into account his figures and compared them to those of others. For his period our figures are not much different (Rummel, 1990, pp. 22–24).

17. As for example, the work of Bueno de Mesquita (1981); Bueno de Mesquita and Lalman (1992); and Kilgour (1991).

18. The "in general" is an important qualification, for there are crises during which decision making becomes highly centralized and even reduced to that of the president or prime minister and a few selected subordinates, as in the 1962 Cuban missile crisis. On this crisis, see Rodman (1982).

19. Domke (1988, p. 103).

20. Engelhardt (1992, p. 55).

21. Czempiel (1992, pp. 262–63).

13

Power Kills

> There is . . . no fundamental, but that every su-
> preme power must be arbitrary.
> —George Savile (Marquis of Halifax),
> *Political, Moral, and Miscellaneous Thoughts*
> *and Reflections Of Fundamentals* (1750)

In review we thus have at one end the social field with its democratic regime. The regime is but one pyramid of power among many in
the social field. Behavior among all in the field is patterned by structures of expectations that evolve between individuals and groups, the
sum total of which act to check and balance, to cross-cut and cross-
pressure, interests, and thus to severely limit the intensity of collective
violence, and its spread across society. Moreover, the constant hubbub
of individuals and groups adjusting and readjusting to each other as
they and their environment change, of social trial and error and social
learning, develops an exchange culture, one of negotiation, compromise, and toleration. At the other extreme is the coercive society organized by a regime to achieve some goal. Society is divided into those
who give the orders and those who must obey, and all major issues
become polarized along this axis. Violence becomes a way of insuring
obedience, or achieving the organizational goals, and of restructuring
expectations were they to break down. This is an antifield. It is ruled
by raw coercion and force; pervasive fear assures obedience.

The most fundamental explanation of the democratic peace, then, is
that Freedom promotes nonviolence and Power kills. This conclusion
leaves two questions to answer. One of these concerns how this idea
fits into the political triangle.

Recall that democratic regimes in an exchange society are at one corner of the political triangle while totalitarian regimes with the coercive society they have constructed are at another. They therefore are at opposing ends of one side of the triangle, which is a continuum ranging from Freedom to Power. But there is also the third corner of the triangle, that of authoritative regimes, where absolute monarchies would lie at the very tip. How do authoritative societies and their authoritarian regimes relate to the social field, antifield dimension?

First, true authoritarian regimes should not be confused with military dictatorships or rule by some leader who has taken over power by a coup d'état or that has assumed dictatorial power once elected. A true authoritarian regime is one that rules according to the traditions and customs of the nation and has assumed power according to these traditions, such as a King's oldest son, upon the King's death, ascending the throne with all the traditional pomp to be crowned the new King. The regime rules largely through its authoritative power. The people largely believe that this rule is right and proper, and indeed, would fight to maintain it. Says Lord Acton of the monarchies that developed after the Middle Ages, they "exerted a charm over the imagination . . . that, on learning of the execution of Charles I, men died of the shock; and the same thing occurred at the death of Louis XVI and the Duke of Enghien."[1]

Were the monarch's rule to greatly depart from what the people or powerful elites believe it should be, rebellion may occur, the monarch deposed, and even their head cut off. However, there is much room for variation among monarchies from one culture to another. The tradition according to which they are crowned with the right to rule may also grant them the use of considerable arbitrary and coercive power, particularly if the monarch is adept at playing off possible enemies against each other and appealing to his legitimacy. One of the worst examples of this was King Louis XIV of France, of whom wrote Lord Acton wrote,

> With half the present population, he maintained an army of 450,000 men; nearly twice as large as that which the later Emperor Napoleon assembled to attack Germany. Meanwhile the people starved on grass. France, said Fénelon, is one enormous hospital. French historians believe that in a single generation six millions of people died of want. It would be easy to find tyrants more violent, more malignant, more odious than Louis XIV., but there was not one who ever used his power to inflict greater suffering or greater wrong; and the admiration with which

he inspired the most illustrious men of his time denotes the lowest depth to which the turpitude of absolutism has ever degraded the conscious of Europe.[2]

Another such example is Ivan Grozny—Ivan the Terrible—of Russia, perhaps the worst of its monarchs, who in the 1560s and 1570s went on killing sprees and with his own private group of killers, the *Oprichniki,* massacred tens and possibly hundreds of thousands of possible opponents, detractors, the old nobility, and others.[3]

Especially in the arena of foreign affairs Monarchs have traditionally been given much leeway to decide issues of war and peace, to unilaterally define the national interest, and to play at war.

Regarding the domestic affairs of an authoritative society, many individuals and groups are largely left alone to pursue their own interests as long as they do not interfere with those of the regime or its favored institutions, such as a church. There are therefore areas in which a social field exists, such a relatively free market, friendship groups, and within the family and clans. Moreover, where traditional culture is followed, where people do things because this is the way they believe they ought to behave, they are still operating within a social field. That is, they are acting freely, they choose to be guided by customs and norms handed down to them, or they follow these customs and norms unconsciously, as one speaks a language they learned as a child. However, those areas of society that are ruled over by the regime more through force and coercion than through its legitimacy and authority, such as in the maintenance of a state religion or forced service in the military, are not matters of free choice but the power of the regime. As authoritarian rule has recourse to coercion and force it creates a partial antifield; as this becomes the major *modus operandi* it turns part of society into an antifield. No authoritarian regime in modern times has completely relied on the strength of tradition and its authority to rule. All for one reason or another have resorted to extensive coercion, whether to meet the challenge of modernization, to develop and strengthen their nation, to handle the great wealth of its resources, such as oil, to make war, or simply to assure their rule. But also no authoritarian ruler has assumed or resorted to the autocratic power of contemporary totalitarian regimes. Consequently we can place authoritarian regimes between totalitarian and democratic ones on the Freedom to Power dimension.[4]

Then there are a host of other regimes that are neither strictly authoritarian (in relying on authoritative power) nor totalitarian. They are those nations ruled by the likes of an Idi Amin of Uganda, Augusto Pinochet of Chile, Muammar al-Qaddafi[5] of Libya, or Park Chung Hee of South Korea.

In a military coup in 1971, Idi Amin Dada seized power and ruled dictatorially until his abortive invasion of Tanzania in 1978 and the defeat of his army. His rule was completely arbitrary. He murdered his opponents, including high members of his own regime who criticized him. He slaughtered members of competing tribes and instilled fear throughout the country. He also ejected from the country tens of thousands of Asians, many of whom had lived in the country for generations. But although his rule was by absolute power, he did not try to totally control all of Ugandan society. To a great extent, custom—particularly tribal custom—regulated much behavior and whole segments of the society were free from government management and control, especially in economic matters within a mainly preindustrial economy. Private enterprise and exchange or barter were allowed, as long as businessmen kept out of politics or did not interfere with the prevalent government graft and corruption, and paid the appropriate bribes. This was a society partly exchange, partly authoritative, and to a large extent, coercive. If democracy is at the top corner of the political triangle, totalitarian regimes at the lower left corner, and authoritarian regimes—absolute monarchies—at the lower right, then I would place this regime somewhere in the lower middle of the political triangle. On the Freedom to Power dimension, the left side of the triangle, it would be closer to the totalitarian end than the democratic.[6]

Then there is Chile. In 1973, with covert American assistance, the military under General Pinochet overthrew the elected government of Salvador Allende that was based on a coalition of socialists, communists, and leftists. The military instituted a state of siege, including censorship of the press, and proceeded to purge the government and other institutions of communists and leftists, summarily executing thousands of them. More tens of thousands were imprisoned without trial and torture was widespread. Many simply disappeared. However, in subsequent years the regime returned to private owners much of the property, such as banks, land, and businesses that had been taken over by the Allende regime. The Pinochet regime also tried to free the economy of most of the controls and regulations that had limited exchange, and to promote economic growth through a free market.

Then in the late 1980s Pinochet ended many of the political restrictions he had imposed and began the return the country to democracy. He was defeated in a plebiscite he held in 1988, but kept control over the government until a new president was elected in 1989.[7]

The Pinochet regime clearly used coercion and force to purge the country of what it saw as undesirables and to maintain its rule against any possible opposition until it was ready to return democracy to the country. But outside of this, the nation as a whole was a social field. Indeed, outside of politics and political expression, it was more spontaneous than it had been under the Allende government, which had nationalized whole industries and expropriated huge tracks of land. The economy was freer, intervention in the affairs of the Catholic church was less, and people could go about their private business. Tradition and custom, bargaining and exchange, prevailed where they were independent of the regime's interests in maintaining its power and protecting the nation against communism, socialism, and radical leftists.

This regime has been especially condemned by the international community for its abysmal human rights record and military rule, and I should be especially clear as to what I mean. None of the allegations of human rights violations, mass murder, and undemocratic rule are being denied. What I am saying is that aside from this there were large regions of Chilean society in which behavior was spontaneous, a social field. I would place Pinochet's regime during this period toward the middle right of the political triangle. Pinochet's rule was absolute but he allowed much exchange, and also tradition and custom played a large role in Chilean society, as for example, in the social dominance of the Catholic church. On the Freedom to Power dimension the regime would be closer to the Freedom end than Idi Amin's, since while neither was totalitarian, and Amin tended more in his use of power to coercively intervene in society than did Pinochet.

As to Qaddafi, he is a radical Arab nationalist and socialist who with his Revolutionary Command Council took power after deposing King Idris in 1969. He has ruled dictatorially, and has followed the socialist one-party model in trying to mobilize and organize the population to achieve his five-year plans and for other state purposes. Nonetheless, significant self-management has been allowed and there is meaningful independence for many social groups and businesses. Qaddafi also has been an adventurer in foreign policy, helping rebellious groups in other counties and radical terrorist organizations, and using his army to support radical movements in neighboring countries. In 1990, he aided in the overthrow of the regime in Chad, and his agents have been accused of bombing Pan Am flight 103 out of the air over Scotland. Moreover, Qaddafi has done his share of arrests, torture, and extrajudicial executions (especially after each of the three attempted coups against him), even of Libyans who have fled the country and criticized him abroad. In the political triangle, with the regime's use of coercion and force to effect a partial socialist transformation of Libya, I would place it toward the lower left of the political triangle, recognizing that Islam and associated tradition is still an essential aspect of Libyan society. On the Freedom to Power dimension, Qaddafi's regime would be closer to the totalitarian end and further away from the democratic than would be Amin's regime.[8]

Finally, there was the South Korean regime of General Park Chung Hee. In 1961 the Korean military overthrew President Chang Myun and General Park assumed power. He was elected to the presidency in 1963, but ruled with a strong hand. As a result of increasing protests against this he imposed strict military control over the country in 1972 and in 1975 forbid any political opposition against him. He was assassinated in 1979. The aim of his rule was to maintain a strong South Korea against the subversion, infiltration, and military provocation by North Korea and the increasing threat of an outright North Korean invasion; and to manage the fast paced modernization of Korean society and its rapid economic development.[9]

Human rights abuses were common, but neither as blatant nor extreme as for many similar dictatorships. While internal economic matters were largely free, there was much government regulation, and especially in matters of foreign trade and investment, strong government controls. Korean society, like most Asian societies at this time, was inherently authoritarian. Tradition and cultural norms and rules dominated much social behavior, within the family and between members of other groups, and between individuals. However, with the increasing modernization of Korean society and its economic and technological development, these traditions were being eroded in favor of more social and cultural freedom. Still, I would place the Park regime toward the lower right in the political triangle and on the Freedom versus Power dimension I think it should be closer to the democratic end (but of course not democratic) than for any of the other regimes considered above.

So much for how the explanation that Power kills fits into the political triangle. A second question has to do with how the three levels of explanation—popular will; democratic culture, cross-pressures, and in-group perception; and Freedom versus Power—relate to each other? That based on popular will stands off by itself and gives a partial explanation. It accounts for the inability of President Roosevelt to come to the military aid of Great Britain during her crisis of survival under the rain of German bombs and threat of a cross-channel invasion in the dark days of 1940 and 1941. It helps explain the inability of the Johnson and much harder line Nixon administrations to pursue victory in Vietnam after the North Vietnam-Vietcong Tet Offensive of 1968. It explains the inability of the Eisenhower administration to pursue a clear victory in Korea, or at least to employ large scale offensive operations to force the North Koreans to negotiate a peace earlier than they did. But then there were wars like the Spanish-American war which popular will appeared to demand. That is, the people's will can occasionally work for war. Moreover, a problem is that this explanation depends on the existence of electoral machinery that systematically gauges and reflects and empowers the will of the people, and thus it involves a continuum from fully democratic electoral systems to those without any elections and representational systems, such as the most authoritarian regimes like Saudi Arabia and Kuwait. But those totalitarian regimes with their noncompetitive but existing electoral systems and legislatures would stand in the middle of such an electoral scale. Finally, this explanation is not meant to nor does it relate to the disposition of democracies to be more internally nonviolence than other type of regimes.

For the second-level explanation the crucial variables are two: cross pressures resulting from the diversity and plethora of interests created by an exchange society, and associated exchange culture. The latter not only helps minimize violence within the society but also encourages democratic and oligarchic republican regimes to treat other regimes they perceive to be like themselves in an accommodating manner. Both cross-pressures and culture provide a proper understanding of the democratic peace, in my view, as long as it is understood that they sit along a continuum from the most democratic to least democratic—totalitarian—regimes.

The third-level explanation integrates and extends these two variables within a more basic conceptualization of social fields and antifields, and Freedom versus Power. Moreover, it treats the simple idea of cross-pressures as one of a complex of checks, balances, and inhibitions that result from the interlacing and interwoven expectations and interests created within a spontaneous society. Exchange culture at this level also emerges from the freedom of individuals and groups to establish their own social equilibrium—structure of expectations—with each other. Finally, at this level the explanation makes clearer why the opposite of democracies, totalitarian regimes, should have the most severe violence, why Power kills. This is through the concept of an antifield, an organization with a well-defined hierarchy, command structure, and resulting polarization of interests and expectation.[10]

We thus have at the most fundamental and general level an explanation of why the less democracy the more nations make violence on each other, and the more their internal collective violence and democide. That is, why nondemocracy is an engine of violence. This is because these societies are turned into antifields. They are ruled by coercion and force. And thus, Power kills.

Notes

1. Acton (1967, p. 288).
2. Ibid. Suffice to say that this is from an address he gave in 1877, well before the totalitarian evils of our century.
3. Medvedev (1971, p. 269); Backer (1950, pp. 69–71).
4. If we collapse the two-dimensional space of the political triangle into one dimension along the Freedom to Power (democracy to totalitarian) dimension, then this is where authoritarian regimes would end up.
5. Also spelled Kaddafi, Khadafy, or Gaddafi.
6. On Idi Amin and Uganda, see Avirgan and Honey (1982); Harrison (1976); Kannyo (1987); and Martin (1974).
7. On Pinochet and Chile, see Falcoff (1989); Sigmund (1977); and Politzer (1989).
8. On Qaddafi's Libya, see Anderson (1986); Blundy (1987); Deeb (1982); and Cooley (1982).
9. On South Korea during this period, see Savada and Shaw (1992); Yoon (1990); and Sohn (1989).
10. There are, of course, alternative explanations of the democratic peace that argue that it is not democracy that causes the peace, but something causing the lack of violence that is only accidentally related to democracy. See for example, the overview of some of these in Russett and Antholis (1992, p. 416). Such explanations include those in terms of lack of common borders between democracies, and thus less or no war; the existence of only a relatively few democracies, and thus the lack of violence is only a chance event; the existence of common ties, as in the common market; a common enemy as during the cold war; economic develop-

ment and wealth, which make war between such nations too costly with too little gain; or an accidental concurrence of policies on most issues that helps democracies avoid major disputes, violence, and war. All these and other explanations of which I am aware are too narrow to simultaneously encompass peace between democracies, the greater peace between nations the more democratic they are, the peace within democracies, and their lack of democide. That is, none explain why democracy is a method of nonviolence. In addition, they have been found empirically insignificant, as that concerning borders in my own research and those of others cited in part I (such as Gleditsch, 1995). There is much reason to discount this common explanation. Moreover, the possibility that the interdemocratic peace is a chance finding has been shown by significance test after significance test to be very unlikely (see chapter 2). Consider also that we now have had for decades several dozen democracies, around one-fifth to one-fourth of all nation-states, without war between them.

References

Ackerman, Peter and Christopher Kruegler. *Strategic Nonviolent Conflict: The Dynamics of People Power in the Twentieth Century.* Westport, Conn.: Praeger, 1994.

Acton, Lord. *Essays in the Liberal Interpretation of History: Selected Papers,* edited by William H. McNeill. Chicago: The University of Chicago Press, 1967.

Adelman, Irma and Cynthia Taft Morris. *Economic Growth and Social Equity in Developing Countries.* Stanford, Calif.: Stanford University Press, 1973.

Adelman, Irma, Cynthia Taft, and Jairus M. Hihn. "Politics in Latin America: A Catastrophe Theory Model." *Journal of Conflict Resolution* 26 (December 1982): 592–620.

Alcock, Norman Z. "Freedom and equality among nations." *Peace Research* 5 (July 1974): 53–67.

———. "The political dimensions of compassion." *Peace Research* 7 (January 1975): 1–24.

Alcock, Norman Z. and William Eckhardt. "Comparisons between the attitudes and behaviors of individuals and nations." *Peace Research* (April 1974): 33–44.

Anderson, Lisa, *The State and Social Transformation in Tunisia and Libya, 1830–1980.* Princeton, N.J.: Princeton University Press, 1986.

Arat, Zehra F. *Democracy and Human Rights in Developing Countries.* Boulder, Colo.: Lynne Rienner Publishers, 1991.

Archer, Margaret Scotford. *Culture and Agency: the Place of Culture in Social Theory.* New York: Cambridge University Press, 1988.

Arendt, Hannah. *The Origins of Totalitarianism* (new edition). New York: Harcourt, Brace & World, 1966.

Avirgan, Tony and Martha Honey. *War in Uganda: The Legacy of Idi Amin.* Westport, Conn.: Lawrence Hill, 1982.

Axelrod, Robert M. *Conflict of Interest; A Theory of Divergent Goals with Applications to Politics.* Chicago: Markham, 1970.

Babst, Dean V. "Elective governments—a force for peace." *The Wisconsin Sociologist* 3 (1, 1964): 9–14.

———. "A force for peace." *Industrial Research* (April 1972): 55–58.

Babst, Dean V. and William Eckhardt. "How peaceful are democracies compared with other countries." *Peace Research* 24 (August 1992): 51–57.

Backer, George. *The Deadly Parallel: Stalin and Ivan the Terrible*. New York: Random House, 1950.

Baldwin, David A. *Paradoxes of Power*. New York: Basil Blackwell, 1989.

Banks, Arthur S. *Cross-Polity Time Series Data*. Cambridge: The MIT Press, 1971.

———. "Correlates of democratic performance." *Comparative Politics* 4 (January 1972): 217–30.

Barringer, Richard E. *War: Patterns of Conflict*. Cambridge: MIT Press, 1972.

Barry, Brian M. *Democracy, Power, and Justice: Essays in Political Theory*. New York: Oxford University Press, 1989.

Bebler, Anton and Jim Seroka, eds. *Contemporary Political Systems: Classifications and Typologies*. Boulder, Colo.: Lynne Rienner Publishers, 1990.

Becker, Elizabeth. *When the War Was Over: Cambodia's Revolution and the Voices of Its People*. New York: Simon & Shuster (A Touchstone Book), 1986.

Benjamin, Roger and Stephen L. Elkin, eds. *The Democratic State*. Lawrence: University Press of Kansas, 1985.

Berelson, Bernard and Gary A. Steiner. *Human Behavior*. New York: Harcourt Brace Jovanovich, 1964.

Bernard, Thomas J. *The Consensus-Conflict Debate: Form and Content in Social Theories*. New York: Columbia University Press, 1983.

Bierstedt, R. "An analysis of social power." *American Sociological Review* 15 (1950).

Blanck, Peter David, ed. *Interpersonal Expectations: Theory, Research, and Applications*. New York: Cambridge University Press, 1993.

Blundy, David. *Qaddafi and the Libyan Revolution*. London: Weidenfeld and Nicolson, 1987.

Bollen, Kenneth A. "Issues in the Comparative Measurement of political democracy." *American Sociological Review* 45 (June 1980): 370–90.

———. "Political democracy: conceptual and measurement traps." In *On Measuring Democracy: Its Consequences and Concomitants,* edited by Alex Inkeles. New Brunswick, N.J.: Transaction Publishers, 1991, 3–20.

Bolles, Robert C. *Theory of Motivation* (2nd edition). New York: Harper & Row, 1975.

Bothe, Michael, Karl Josef Partsch, and Waldemar A. Solf. *New Rules for Victims of Armed Conflicts: Commentary on the Two 1977 Protocols Additional to the Geneva Conventions of 1949*. Boston: Martinus Nijhoff Publishers, 1982.

Bremer, Stuart A. "Dangerous Dyads: Conditions Affecting the Likelihood of Interstate War, 1816–1965." *Journal of Conflict Resolution* 36 (2, 1989): 309–41.

———. "Are democracies less likely to join wars?" Paper presented at the annual meeting of the American Political Science Association, Chicago: September, 1992.

———. "Democracy and Militarized Interstate Conflict, 1816–1965." *International Interactions* 18, no. 3 (1993): 231–49.

Brown, B. F. *Psychology and the Social Order*. New York: McGraw-Hill, 1936.

Browning, Christopher R. *Ordinary Men: Reserve Police Battalion 101 and the Final Solution in Poland*. New York: HarperCollins Publishers, 1992.

Bueno de Mesquita, Bruce. *The War Trap*. New Haven, Conn.: Yale University Press, 1981.

———. "The costs of war: a rational expectations approach." *The American Political Science Review* 77 (June 1983): 347–67.

————. "The War Trap revisited: a revised expected utility model." *American Political Science Review* 79 (1985): 156–77.

————. "Toward a scientific understanding of international conflict: a personal view." *International Studies Quarterly* 29 (1985a): 121–36.

————. "The game of conflict interactions: a research program." In *Theoretical Research Programs: Studies in the Growth of Theory,* edited by Joseph Berger and Morris Zelditch, Jr. Stanford: Stanford University Press, 1993, 139–71.

Bueno de Mesquita, Bruce and David Lalman. "The road to war is strewn with peaceful intentions." In *Models of Strategic Choice in Politics,* edited by Peter Ordeshook. Ann Arbor: University of Michigan Press, 1989.

————. *War and Reason: Domestic and International Imperatives.* New Haven, Conn: Yale University Press, 1992.

Burgess, E. and P. Wallin. "Homogamy in social characteristics." *American Journal of Sociology* 49 (1943): 109–24.

Burns, Edward McNall and Philip Lee Ralph. *World Civilizations from Ancient to Contemporary* 1–2 (2nd edition). New York: W. W. Norton & Co., 1955.

Butterworth, Robert Lyle. *Managing Interstate Conflict, 1945–1974: Data With Synopsis.* Pittsburgh, Pa.: University Center for International Studies, University of Pittsburgh, 1976.

Bwy, Douglas P. "Political instability in Latin America: the cross-cultural test of a causal model." *Anger, Violence, and Politics: Theories and Insights,* edited by Ivo K. Feierabend, Rosalind L. Feierabend, and Ted Robert Gurr. Englewood Cliffs, N.J.: Prentice-Hall, 1972, 223–41.

Calvert, Peter. *The Concept of Class: An Historical Introduction.* Calvert. New York: St. Martin's Press, 1982.

Campbell, Angus, Philip E. Converse, Warren E. Miller, and Donald E. Stokes. *The American Voter.* New York: Wiley, 1960.

Carrithers, Michael. *Why Humans Have Cultures: Explaining Anthropology and Social Diversity.* New York: Oxford University Press, 1992.

Cartwright, Dorwin. "A field theoretical conception of power." *Studies in Social Power,* edited by Dorwin Cartwright. Ann Arbor: University of Michigan Press, 1959.

Cattell, Raymond B. "The principal culture patterns discoverable in the syntal dimensions of existing nations." *Journal of Social Psychology* 32 (November 1950): 215–53.

————, ed. *Handbook of Multivariate Experimental Psychology.* Chicago: Rand McNally, 1966.

Chalk, Frank and Kurt Jonassohn. *The History and Sociology of Genocide: Analysis and Case Studies.* New Haven: Yale University Press, 1990.

Chan, Steve. "Mirror, mirror on the war . . . are democratic states more pacific?" *Journal of Conflict Resolution* 28 (1984): 617–48.

————. "Democracy and war: some thoughts on future research agenda." *International Interactions* 18, 3 (1993): 205–13.

Chira, Susan. "Report: North Korea marred by regimentation, rights abuse." *The New York Times* (1989).

Clegg, Stewart R., ed. *Organization Theory and Class Analysis: New Approaches.* New York: W. de Gruyter, 1990.

Cole, Timothy Michael. *United States Leadership and the Liberal Community of States.* Ph.D. dissertation, University of Washington, 1987.

————. "Politics and meaning: explaining the democratic peace." Delivered at the Annual Meeting of the American Political Science Association, 30 August–2 September 1990.

Coleman, James S. "Conclusions: the political systems of the developing areas." In *The Politics of the Developing Areas,* edited by Gabriel A. Almond and James S. Coleman. Princeton, N.J.: Princeton University Press, 1960, 532–76.

————. *Introduction to Mathematical Sociology.* New York: Free Press, 1964.

Conquest, Robert. *The Great Terror: Stalin's Purge of the Thirties.* New York: Macmillan, 1968.

————. *The Great Terror: A Reassessment.* New York: Oxford University Press, 1990.

Cook, Karen S., ed. *Social Exchange Theory.* Beverly Hills, Calif.: Sage Publications, 1987.

Cooley, John K. *Libyan Sandstorm.* New York: Holt, Rinehart, and Winston, 1982.

Coppedge, Michael and Wolfgang H. Reinicke. Measuring polyarchy." In *On Measuring Democracy: Its Consequences and Concomitants,* edited by Alex Inkeles. New Brunswick, N.J.: Transaction Publishers, 1991, 47–68.

Coser, Lewis A. *The Functions of Social Conflict.* Glencoe, Ill.: Free Press, 1956.

Coulter, Phillip. "Framework for analysis: theory and research design." *Social Mobilization and Liberal Democracy: A Macroquantitative Analysis of Global and Regional Models,* edited by Phillip Coulter. Lexington, Mass.: D.C. Heath, 1975.

Cox, Taylor. *Cultural Diversity in Organizations: Theory, Research, and Practice.* San Francisco, Calif.: Berrett-Koehler, 1993.

Cutright, Phillips and James A. Wiley. "Modernization and political representation: 1927-1966." *Studies in Comparative International Development* 5 (1969): 23–44.

Czander, William M. *The Psychodynamics of Work and Organizations: Theory and Application.* New York: The Guilford Press, 1993.

Czempiel, Ernst-Otto. "Governance and democratization." In *Government without Government: Order and Change in World Politics,* edited by Ernst-Otto Czempiel and James N. Rosenau. Cambridge: Cambridge University Press, 1992, 250–71.

Dahl, Robert. "The concept of power." *Behavioral Science* 2 (1957).

————. *Political Oppositions in Western Democracies.* New York: Yale University Press, 1966.

————. *Polyarchy.* New Haven, Yale University Press, 1971.

Dahrendorf, Ralf. *Class and Class Conflict in Industrial Society.* Stanford: Stanford University Press, 1959.

Dalton, Russell J. *Citizen Politics in Western Democracies: Public Opinion and Political Parties in the United States, Great Britain, West Germany, and France.* Chatham, N.J.: Chatham House Publishers, 1988.

Davies, James C. "Aggression, violence, revolution, and war." In *Handbook of Political Psychology,* edited by Jeanne N. Knutson. San Francisco: Jossey-Bass, 1973, 234–60.

Davis, James A. "Structural balance, mechanical solidarity, and interpersonal relations." In *Sociological Theories in Progress,* by Joseph Gerger et al. Boston: Houghton Mifflin, 1966.

Davis, Morris. "Man-made calamities and changes of regime." *The PAPERS of the Peace Science Society (International)* 29 (1979): 79–86.

Deeb, Marius. *Libya Since the Revolution: Aspects of Social and Political Development.* New York: Praeger, 1982.

Dessler, David. "Beyond correlations: toward a causal theory of war." *International Studies Quarterly* 35, 3 (1991): 327–55.

Diener, Paul. "Quantum adjustment, macroevolution, and the social field: some comments on evolution and culture." *Current Anthropology* 21 (August 1980): 423–43.

Dixon, William J. "Democracy and the management of international conflict." *Journal of Conflict Resolution* 37 (March 1993): 42–68.

————. "Democracy and the peaceful settlement of international conflict." *American Political Science Review* 88 (March 1994): 1–17.

Djilas, Milovan. *Tito: The Story from Inside.* Translated by Vasilije Kojic and Richard Hayes. New York: Harcourt Brace Jovanovich, 1980.

Domke, William. *War and Changing Global System.* New Haven: Yale University Press, 1988.

Doyle, Michael. "Kant, Liberal Legacies, and Foreign Affairs, Part I." *Philosophy and Public Affairs* 12 (Summer 1983): 205–35. Part II, Ibid.: 323–53.

————. "Liberalism and World Politics." *American Political Science Review* (December, 1986): 1151–69.

————. "Michael Doyle on the democratic peace." *International Security* 19 (Spring 1995): 180–84.

Ebenstein, William. *Totalitarianism: New Perspectives.* New York: Holt, Rinehart and Winston, 1962.

Ebenstein, William and Edwin Fogelman. *Today's Isms: Communism, Fascism, Capitalism, Socialism* (9th edition). Englewood Cliffs, N.J.: Prentice-Hall, 1985.

Ember, Carol, Melvin Ember, and Bruce Russett. "Peace Between Participatory Polities: A Cross-Cultural Test of the 'Democracies Rarely Fight Each Other' Hypothesis." *World Politics* 44, 4 (1992).

Engelhardt, Michael. "Democracies, Dictatorships and Counterinsurgency: Regime Type Really Matter?" *Conflict Quarterly* 12, 3 (1992): 52–63.

Falcoff, Mark. *Modern Chile, 1970-1989: A Critical History.* New Brunswick, N.J.: Transaction Publishers, 1989.

Falk, Richard A. *A Study of Future Worlds.* New York: Free Press, 1975.

Falk, Richard A. and Saul H. Mendlovitz, eds. *The Strategy for World Order, Vol. IV: Disarmament and Economic Development.* New York: World Law Fund, 1966.

Featherstone, Mike, ed. *Cultural Theory and Cultural Change.* Newbury Park: Sage Publications, 1992.

Fehrenbach, T. R. *Fire and Blood: A History of Mexico.* New York: Macmillan, 1973.

Feierabend, Ivo K. and Rosalind L. Feierabend. "The relationship of systematic frustration, political coercion, and political instability: a cross-national analysis." In John V. Gillespie and Betty A. Nesvold, eds. *Macro-Quantitative Analysis: Conflict, Development, and Democratization.* Beverly Hills, Calif.: Sage, 1971, 417–40.

————. "Appendix: invitation to further research—designs, data, and methods." In *Anger, Violence, and Politics: Theories and Insights,* edited by Ivo K. Feierabend, Rosalind L. Feierabend, and Ted Robert Gurr. Englewood Cliffs, N.J.: Prentice-Hall, 1972, 369–416.

————. "Violent consequences of violence." In *Violence as Politics: A Series of Original Essays,* edited by Herbert Hirsch and David C. Perry. New York: Harper and Row, 1973, 187–219.

Feierabend, Ivo K., Rosalind L. Feierabend, and Betty A. Nesvold. "Social change and political violence: cross-national patterns." In *Violence in America: Historical and Comparative Perspectives: A Report Submitted to the National Commission on the Causes and Prevention of Violence,* edited by Hugh Davis Graham and Ted Robert Gurr. New York: Bantam Books, 1969, 632–87.

Fein, Helen. *Accounting for Genocide: National Responses and Jewish Victimization During the Holocaust.* New York: The Free Press, 1979.

————. "Scenarios of Genocide: Models of Genocide and Critical Responses." In *Toward the Understanding and Prevention of Genocide: Proceedings of the International Conference on the Holocaust and Genocide,* edited by Israel W. Charny. Boulder: Westview Press, 1984, 3–31.

Ferris, Wayne H. *The Power Capabilities of Nation-States: International Conflict and War.* Lexington, Mass.: Lexington Books, 1973.

Finer, S. E. *Comparative Government.* New York: Basic Books, 1971.

Fisher, Ronald J. *The Social Psychology of Intergroup and International Conflict Resolution.* New York: Springer-Verlag, 1990.

Flanigan, William and Edwin Fogelman. "Patterns of political violence in comparative perspective." *Comparative Politics* 3 (October, 1970): 1–20.

Friedman, Milton. *Capitalism and Freedom.* Chicago: University of Chicago, 1962.

Friedrich, Carl J. and Zbigniew K. Brzezinski. *Totalitarian, Dictatorship and Autocracy* (2nd edition). Cambridge: Harvard University Press, 1965.

Fukuyama, Francis. "The end of history." *The National Interest* (Summer 1989): 3–18.

Gaubatz, Kurt Taylor. "Election cycles and war." *Journal of Conflict Resolution* 35 (June 1991): 212–44.

Gaddis, J. L. "The long peace: elements of stability in the postwar international system." *International Security* 10 (1986): 92–142.

Galtung, Johan. "A Structural Theory of Aggression." *Journal of Peace Research,* no. 2 (1964): 95–119.

————. "International relations and international conflicts: a sociological approach." Transactions of the Sixth World Congress of Sociology. Britain Evian (September 1966): 121–61.

————. "Violence, peace, and peace research." *Journal of Peace Research,* no. 3 (1969): 167–91.

Garnham, David. "War-proneness, war-weariness, and regime type: 1816–1980." *Journal of Peace Research* 23 (1986): 279–89.

Gastil, Raymond Duncan. "The comparative survey of freedom: experiences and suggestions." In *On Measuring Democracy: Its Consequences and Concomitants,* edited by Alex Inkeles. New Brunswick, N.J.: Transaction Publishers, 1991, 21–46.

Gergen, Kenneth J., Martin S. Greenberg, and Richard H. Willis, eds. *Social Exchange: Advances in Theory and Research.* New York: Plenum Press, 1980.

Germani, Gino. *Authoritarianism, Fascism, and National Populism.* New Brunswick, N.J.: Transaction Publishers, 1978.

Geva, Nehemia, Karl DeRouen, and Alex Mintz. "The political incentive explanation of the 'democratic peace': evidence from experimental research." *International Interactions* 18, 3 (1993): 215–29.

Ginsberg, Benjamin. *The Captive Public: How Mass Opinion Promotes State Power.* New York: Basic Books, 1986.

Gleditsch, Nils Petter. "Democracy and peace." *Journal of Peace Research* 29, 4 (1992): 369–76.

———. "Geography, Democracy, and Peace." *International Interactions* (1995).

Global Data Manager. Macintosh Version 2.3 Computer Application. Philadelphia, Pa.: World Game Institute, 1990.

Gochman, Charles and Zeev Maoz. "Militarized disputes 1816-1975." *Journal of Conflict Resolution* 29, 4 (1984): 585–615.

Goldstein, E. Bruce. *Sensation and Perception* (3rd edition). Belmont, Calif.: Wadsworth, 1989.

Greer, Donald. *The Incidence of the Terror during the French Revolution: A Statistical Interpretation.* Cambridge: Harvard University Press, 1935.

Gregg, P. and A. S. Banks. "Dimensions of political systems: factor analysis of a cross-polity survey." *The American Political Science Review* 59 (September 1965): 602–13.

Gulick, Edward Vose. Europe's Classical Balance of Power: A Case History of the Theory and Practice of One of the Great Concepts of European Statecraft. Westport, Conn.: Greenwood Press, 1982.

Gurr, Ted Robert. "A comparative study of civil strife." In *Violence in America: Historical and Comparative Perspectives: A Report Submitted to the National Commission on the Causes and Prevention of Violence,* edited by Hugh Davis Graham and Ted Robert Gurr. New York: Bantam Books, 1969, 572–632.

———. *Why Men Rebel.* Princeton, N.J.: Princeton University Press, 1970.

———. "Persistence and change in political systems, 1800-1971. *The American Political Science Review* LXVIII (December 1974): 1482–1504.

———. *Polity Data Handbook.* Ann Arbor: ICPSR, 1978.

———. "Political protest and rebellion in the 1960s: the United States in World Perspective." In *Violence in America: Historical & Comparative Perspectives.* Revised edition edited by Hugh Davis Grahams and Ted Robert Gurr. Beverly Hills: Sage Publications, 1979a, 49–76.

———. "Some characteristics of political terrorism in the 1960s." In The Politics of Terror: A Reader in Theory and Practice, edited by M. Stohl. New York: Dekker, 1979b, 23–49.

———. *Polity II: Political Structures and Regime Change, 1800-1986.* Ann Arbor, Michigan: Inter-university Consortium for Political and Social Research, 1990. [Polity II data code book].

———. and M. I. Lichbach. "Forecasting domestic political conflict." In *To Augur Well: Early Warning Indicators in World Politics,* edited by J. D. Singer and M. Wallace. Beverly Hills, Calif.: Sage, 1979, 153–93.

———. Keith Jaggers and Will H. Moore. "The Transformation of the Western State: The Growth of Democracy, Autocracy, and State Power since 1800." *Studies in Comparative International Development* 25 (Spring 1990): 73–108.

Hamouda, O. F. and Robin Rowley. *Expectations, Equilibrium, and Dynamics: A History of Recent Economic Ideas and Practices.* New York: St. Martin's Press, 1988.

Haney, Craig, Curtis Banks, and Philip Zimbardo. "Interpersonal dynamics in a simulated prison." *International Journal of Criminology and Penology* 1 (1983): 69–97.

Harrison, Charles. "Uganda: The expulsion of the Asians." In *Case Studies on Human rights and Fundamental Freedoms: A World Survey* Vol. 4 (editor-in-chief) Willem A. Veenhoven. The Hague: Martinus Nijhoff, 1976, 287–315.

Hart, Lois Borland. *Learning From Conflict: A Handbook for Trainers and Group Leaders*. Reading, Mass.: Addison-Wesley, 1981.

Hassard, John. *Sociology and Organization Theory: Positivism, Paradigms, and Postmodernity*. N.Y.: Cambridge University Press, 1993.

Hawk, David. "Pol Pot's Cambodia: Was it Genocide?" In *Toward the Understanding and Prevention of Genocide: Proceedings of the International Conference on the Holocaust and Genocide,* edited by Israel W. Charny. Boulder: Westview Press, 1984, 51–59.

Hayek, F. A. *Law, Legislation and Liberty: A New Statement of the Liberal principles of Justice and Political Economy. Volume 1: Rules and Order*. Chicago: The University of Chicago Press, 1973.

———. *Law, Legislation and Liberty: A New Statement of the Liberal principles of Justice and Political Economy. Volume 2: The Mirage of Social Justice*. Chicago: The University of Chicago Press, 1976.

———. *Law, Legislation and Liberty: A New Statement of the Liberal principles of Justice and Political Economy. Volume 3: The Political Order of a Free People*. Chicago: The University of Chicago Press, 1979.

Heider, Fritz. *The Psychology of Interpersonal Relations*. New York: Wiley, 1958.

Hermann, Charles F. "Comparing the foreign policy events of nations." In *International Events and the Comparative Analysis of Foreign Policy,* edited by Charles Kegley, Jr., Gregary A. Raymond, Robert M. Rood, and Richard Skinner. Columbia, S.C.: University of South Carolina Press, 1975, 145–58.

Herz, John H. *Political Realism and Political Idealism: A Study in Theories and Realities*. Chicago: The University of Chicago Press, 1959.

Hewitt, John P. *Social Stratification and Deviant Behavior*. New York: Random House, 1970.

Hibbs, Douglas A., Jr. *Mass Political Violence*. New York: John Wiley & Sons, 1973.

Hodgetts, Richard M. *Organizational Behavior: Theory and Practice*. New York: Maxwell Macmillan International Pub. Group, 1991.

Hoffman, Stanley. *The State of War*. New York: Praeger, 1965.

Holsti, Kalevi J. *Peace and War: Armed Conflict and International Order 1648-1989*. Cambridge: Cambridge University Press, 1991.

Hoole, Francis W. and Dina A. Zinnes, eds. *Quantitative International Politics: An Appraisal*. New York: Praeger Publishers, 1976.

Hospers, John. *Libertarianism*. Santa Barbara, Calif.: Reason Press, 1971.

Howard, Michael. *War and the Liberal Conscience*. New Brunswick, N.J.. Rutgers University Press, 1978.

Jackson, Karl D. "Introduction, The Khmer Rouge in Context." In *Cambodia 1975-1978: Rendezvous with Death,* edited by Karl D. Jackson. Princeton, N.J.: Princeton University Press, 1989, 3–11.

Johnson, Chalmers. *Revolutionary Change*. Boston: Little Brown, 1966.

Jongman, A. J. "The Most Unfortunate Nations in the World: A Brief Survey of Various Databases." PIOOM Newsletter, Vol. 2 (Autumn 1990): 14–17.

Jouvenel, Bertrand de. *On Power: Its Nature and the History of Its Growth*. Translated by J. F. Huntington. Boston: Beacon Press, 1962.

Kampuchea: Political Imprisonment and Torture. London: Amnesty International (June, 1987).

Kannyo, Edward. "Uganda." In *International Handbook of Human Rights,* edited by Jack Donnelly and Rhoda E. Howard. New York: Greenwood Press, 1987, 385–408.

Kant, Immanuel. *Perpetual Peace.* Translated by Lewis White Beck. New York: The Library of Liberal Arts, Bobbs-Merrill, 1957.

Kegley, Charles W. Jr. "The neoidealist moment in international studies? Realist myths and the new international realities." *International Studies Quarterly* 37 (1993): 131–46.

Kende, István. "Dynamics of wars, or arms trade and of military expenditure in the 'third world', 1945-1976." *Instant Research on Peace and War* 2, 2 (1979): 59–67.

Kiernan, Ben. "Pol Pot and the Kampuchean Communist Movement." In Ben Kiernan and Chanthou Boua, *Peasants and Politics in Kampuchea, 1942-1981.* London: Zed Press, 1982, 227–317.

————. "The Genocide in Cambodia, 1975-79." *Bulletin of Concerned Asian Scholars* 22, 2 (1990): 35–40.

Kiernan, Ben and Chanthou Boua. *Peasants and Politics in Kampuchea, 1942-1981.* London: Zed Press, 1982.

Kilgour, D. Marc. "Domestic political structure and war behavior: a game-theoretic approach." *Journal of Conflict Resolution* 35 (June 1991): 266–84.

Kim Myong-sik. *Liquidation in North Korea.* Seoul, Korea: The Institute for North Korea Studies, 1980.

Kiser, Edgar. "A principal-agent analysis of the initiation of war in absolutist states." In *War in the World-System,* edited by Robert K. Shaeffer. New York: Greenwood Press, 1989.

Kissinger, Henry. *Years of Upheaval.* Boston: Little, Brown and Company, 1982.

Koffka, K. *Gestalt Psychology: An Introduction to New Concepts in Modern Psychology.* New York: Liverright, 1947.

Köhler, W. *Dynamics in Psychology.* New York: Liverright, 1942.

Kollintzas, Tryphon. *The Rational Expectations Equilibrium Inventory Model: Theory and Applications.* New York: Springer-Verlag, 1989.

Korb, Margaret P., Jeffrey Gorrell, and Vernon van de Riet. *Gestalt Therapy : Practice and Theory* (2nd edition). New York: Pergamon Press, 1989.

Kuhn, Alfred. *The Study of Society.* Homewood, Ill.: Richard D. Irwin and Dorsey Press, 1963.

Ladouce, Laurent. "Was France the Fatherland of Genocide?" *The World & I* (January 1988), 685–90.

Lake, David A. "Powerful pacifists: democratic states and war." *American Political Science Review* 86 (March 1992): 24–37.

Lasswell, Harold. *Politics: Who Gets What, When, How.* New York: Meridian Books, 1958.

Lasswell, Harold and Abraham Kaplan. *Power and Society.* New Haven: Yale University Press, 1950.

Layne, Christopher. "Kant or cant: the myth of the democratic peace." *International Security* 19 (Fall 1994): 5–49.

Levy, Jack. "Domestic politics and war." *Journal of Interdisciplinary History* 18 (Spring 1988).

————. "The causes of war: a review of theories and evidence." In Philip E. Tetlock et al., eds. *Behavior, Society, and Nuclear War*. Vol. 1. New York: Oxford University Press, 1989.

Lewin, Kurt. *Field Theory in Social Science*. New York: Harper and Row, 1951.

Lipset, Seymour Martin. *Political Man*. Garden City, N.Y.: Anchor Books, Doubleday, 1963.

Majthay, Antal. *Foundations of Catastrophe Theory*. Boston : Pitman, 1985.

Malewski, Andrzej. "The degree of status incongruence and its effects." In *Class, Status, and Power*, edited by Reinhard Bendix and Seymour Martin Lipset (2nd edition). New York: Free Press, 1966, 303–08.

Mannheim, Karl. *Man and Society in an Age of Reconstruction*. New York: Harcourt, Brace & Co., 1940.

Mansfield, Edward D. "The distribution of wars over time." *World Politics* 41 (October 1988): 21–45

Mansfield, Edward D. and Jack Snyder. "Democratization and the danger of war." *International Security* 20 (Summer 1995): 5–38.

————. "Democratization and war." *Foreign Affairs* 74 (May/June 1995b): 79–97.

Maoz, Zeev and Nasrin Abdolali. "Regime Types and International Conflict, 1816-1976." *Journal of Conflict Resolution* (March 1989): 3–35.

Maoz, Zeev, Nasrin Abdolali, and Bruce Russett. "Alliance, contiguity, distance, wealth, and political stability: is the lack of conflict among democracies a statistical artifact?" *International Interactions* 17, 3 (1992): 245–68.

————. "Normative and structural causes of democratic peace, 1946-1986." *American Political Science Review* 87 (September 1993): 624–38.

Marcus-Newhall, Amy, Norman Miller, and Rolf Holtz. "Cross-cutting category membership with role assignment: A means of reducing intergroup bias." *The British Journal of Social Psychology* 32 (June 1993).

Martin, David. *General Amin*. London: Faber and Faber, 1974.

May, Rollo. *Power and Innocence*. New York: W. W. Norton, 1972.

McClelland, Charles A. and Gary Hoggard. "Conflict patterns in the interactions among nations." In *International Politics and Foreign Policy* (revised edition), edited by James N. Rosenau. New York: The Free Press, 1969, 711–24.

McGowan, Patrick J. "Dimensions of African foreign policy behavior: in search of dependence." Paper presented to the annual meeting of the Canadian Association of Africa Studies, Ottawa, 16–18 February 1973.

McWhirter, Norris and Ross McWhirter. *Guinness Book of World Records* (1977 edition). New York: Bantam Books, 1977.

Medvedev, Roy. *Let History Judge: The Origins and Consequences of Stalinism*. Translated by Colleen Taylor. New York: Knopf, 1971.

Melko, Mathew. "The remission of violence in the west." *International Journal on World Peace* II (April–June 1985): 48–55.

Merritt, Richard L. and Dina A. Zinnes. "Democracies and war." In *On Measuring Democracy: Its Consequences and Concomitants*, edited by Alex Inkeles. New Brunswick, N.J.: Transaction Publishers, 1991, 207–34.

Mey, Harold. *Field Theory: A Study of Its Application in the Social Sciences*. Translated by Douglas Scott. New York: St. Martin's Press, 1972.

Michels, Robert. *Political Parties*. Glencoe: Free Press, 1949.

Midlarsky, M. I., ed. *Handbook of War Studies*. Boston: Unwin Hyman, 1989.

Milgram, Stanley. *Obedience to Authority: An Experimental View.* New York, Harper & Row, 1974.

Minogue, Kenneth R. *Alien Powers: the Pure Theory of Ideology.* New York: St. Martin's Press, 1985.

Mintz, Alex and Nehemia Geva. "Why don't democracies fight each other? An experimental study." *Journal of Conflict Resolution* 37, 3 (1993): 484–503.

Mintzberg, Henry. *Power in and Around Organizations.* Englewood Cliffs, N.J.: Prentice-Hall, 1983.

Modelski, G. "Is world politics evolutionary learning?" *International Organization* 44 (1990): 1–24.

Modelski, G. and Gardner Perry III. "Democratization in long perspective." *Technological Forecasting and Social Change,* 1990.

Morgan, T. Clifton and Sally Howard Campbell. "Domestic structure, decisional constraints, and war—so why Kant democracies fight?" *Journal of Conflict Resolution* 35 (June 1991): 187–211.

Morgan, T. Clifton, Sally Howard Campbell, and Valerie L. Schwebach. "Take two democracies and call me in the morning: a prescription for peace?" *International Interactions* 17 (1992): 305–20.

Morgenthau, Hans J. *Politics Among Nations: the Struggle for Power and Peace* (6th edition). Revised by Kenneth W. Thompson. New York: Alfred A. Knopf, 1985.

Morrison, Donald G. and Hugh Michael Stevenson. "Political instability in independent Black Africa." *Journal of Conflict Resolution* XV (September 1971): 356–64.

Mosca, Gaetano. *The Ruling Class.* Revised and edited by Arthur Levingston, translated by Hannah D. Kahn. New York: McGraw-Hill, 1939.

Most, Benjamine and Harvey Starr. *Inquiry, Logic, and International Politics.* Columbia: University of South Carolina Press, 1989.

Mueller, John. *Retreat from Doomsday: The Obsolescence of Major War.* New York: Basic Books, 1989.

———. "Is war still becoming obsolete?" Paper. Presented to the 1991 Annual Meeting of the American Political Science Association, 29 August to 1 September 1991.

Muller, E. N. "Income inequality, regime repressiveness, and political violence." *American Sociological Review* 50 (1985): 47–61.

Nam Koon Woo. *The North Korean Communist Leadership 1945-1965: A Study of Factionalism and Political Consolidation.* University, Alabama: The University of Alabama press, 1974.

Nee, Victor. *Social Exchange and Political Process in Maoist China.* New York: Garland, 1991.

Nesvold, Betty A. "Scalogram Analysis of Political Violence," In *Macro-Quantitative Analysis: Conflict, Development, and Democratization.* Beverly Hills, Calif.: Sage Publications, 1971, 167–86.

Ngor, Haing. *A Cambodian Odyssey.* New York: Macmillan, 1987.

Northedge, F. S. and M. D. Donelan. *International disputes: The Political Aspects.* New York: St. Martin's Press, 1971.

Orbell, John M. and Brent M. Rutherford. "Can leviathan make the life of man less solitary, poor, nasty, brutish and short?" *British Journal of Political Science* 3 (1973): 383–407.

Organski, A. F. K. *World Politics.* New York: Alfred A. Knopf, 1958.

Organski, A. F. K. and Jacek Kugler. *The War Ledger*. Chicago: The University of Chicago Press, 1980.

O'Sullivan, Noel, ed. *The Structure of Modern Ideology: Critical Perspectives on Social and Political Theory*. Brookfield, Vt.: Gower Pub., 1989.

Owen, John M. *Testing the Democratic Peace: American Diplomatic Crises, 1794-1917*. Ph.D. dissertation, Harvard University, 1993.

———. "How liberalism produces democratic peace." *International Security* 19 (Fall 1994): 87–125.

Pareto, Vilfredo. *The Mind and Society*, Vols. 1-2. New York: Dover, 1963.

Parkin, Frank. *Class Inequality and Political Order; Social Stratification in Capitalist and Communist Societies*. New York, Praeger, 1971.

Perlmutter, Amos. *Modern Authoritarianism: A Comparative Institutional Analysis*. New Haven: Yale University Press, 1981.

Petri, Herbert L. *Motivation: Theory and Research* (2nd edition). Belmont, Calif.: Wadsworth, 1986.

Phillips, W. and D. R. Hall. "The importance of governmental structure as a taxonomic scheme for nations." *Comparative Political Studies* 3 (April 1970): 63–89.

Politzer, Patricia. *Fear in Chile: Lives Under Pinochet*. New York: Pantheon Books, 1989.

Poston, Tim and Ian Stewart. *Catastrophe Theory and Its Applications*. Boston: Pitman, 1978.

Powell, G. Bingham Jr. "Political cleavage structure, cross-pressure processes, and partisanship: an empirical test of the theory." *American Journal of Political Science* XX (February 1976): 1–23.

———. "Party systems and political system performance: voting participation, government stability and mass violence in contemporary democracies." *American Political Science Review* 75 (1981): 861–79.

———. *Contemporary Democracies: Participation, Stability, and Violence*. Cambridge: Harvard University Press, 1982.

Pride, Richard A. *Origins of Democracy: A Cross-National Study of Mobilization, Party Systems, and Democratic Stability*. Sage Professional Papers on Comparative Politics, Vol. 1, Series 01-012. Beverly Hills: Sage Publications, 1970.

Prior, Elizabeth. *Dispositions*. Aberdeen: Aberdeen University Press, 1985.

Pruitt, Dean G. and Peter J. Carnevale. *Negotiation in Social Conflict*. Buckingham: Open University Press, 1993.

Puddington, Arch. "The Khmer Rouge File," *The American Spectator* (July 1987): 18–20.

Ray, James Lee. "The abolition of slavery and the end of international war." *International Organization* 43 (1989): 405–39.

———. "The future of international war." Paper. Presented to the 1991 Annual Meeting of the American Political Science Association, 29 August to 1 September 1991.

———. "Wars between democracies: rare, or nonexistent?" *International Interactions* 18, 3 (1993): 251–76.

———. *Democracy and International Politics: An Evaluation of the Democratic Peace Proposition*. Columbia: University of South Carolina Press, 1995.

Reagan, Ronald [President]. Speech before the British Parliament, London, 8 June 1982. [Current Policy No. 399, United States Department of State, Bureau of Public Affairs, Washington, D.C., June 8, 1992.]

Richardson, Lewis F. *Arms and Insecurity*. Pittsburgh: The Boxwood Press, 1960.

Rittberger, Volker. "On the peace capacity of democracies. Reflections on the political theory of peace." *Law and State* 39 (1989): 40–57.

Roberts, Blaine and Bob R. Holdren. *Theory of Social Process: An Economic Analysis*. Ames: Iowa State University Press, 1972.

Rock, Irvin. *The Logic of Perception*. Cambridge, Mass.: MIT Press, 1983.

Rodman, Peter W. "The Missiles of October: Twenty Years Later." *Commentary* (October 1982): 39–45.

Rogers, Carl. *On becoming a Person: A Therapist's View of Psychotherapy*. Boston: Houghton-Mifflin, 1961.

Rothbard, Murray. *Man, Economy, and the State*, Volumes 1-2. Princeton, N.J.: D. Van Nostrand, 1962.

Rothstein, Robert L. "Weak Democracy and the Prospects for Peace and Prosperity in the Third World." Prepared for Delivery at the United States Institute of Peace Conference on "Conflict Resolution in the Post-Cold War Third World," October 3-5, 1990.

Rummel, R. J. "Domestic attributes and foreign conflict." In *Quantitative International Politics*, edited by J. David Singer. New York: Free Press, 1968.

———. *The Dimensions of Nations*. Beverly Hills: Sage Publications, 1972.

———. *Understanding Conflict and War, Volume 1: The Dynamic Psychological Field*. Beverly Hills: Sage Publications, 1975.

———. *Understanding Conflict and War: Vol. 2: The Conflict Helix*. Beverly Hills, Calif.: Sage Publications, 1976.

———. *Field Theory Evolving*. Beverly Hills: Sage Publications, 1977.

———. *Understanding Conflict and War: Volume 3: Conflict in Perspective*. Beverly Hills: Sage Publications, 1977b.

———. *Understanding Conflict and War: Vol. 4: War, Power, Peace*. Beverly Hills, Calif.: Sage Publications, 1979.

———. *National Attributes and Behavior*. Beverly Hills, Calif.: Sage Publications, 1979b.

———. *Understanding Conflict and War: Vol. 5: The Just Peace*. Beverly Hills, Calif.: Sage Publications, 1981.

———. "Libertarianism and International Violence." *The Journal of Conflict Resolution* 27 (March 1983): 27–71.

———. "Current strategic realities." In *Defending a Free Society*, edited by Robert W. Poole, Jr. Lexington, Mass.: Lexington Books, 1984, 57–97.

———. "Libertarianism, Violence within States, and the Polarity Principle." *Comparative Politics* 16 (July 1984b): 443–62.

———. "Libertarian Propositions on Violence Within and Between Nations: A Test Against Published Research Results." *The Journal of Conflict Resolution* 29 (September 1985): 419–55.

———. "A catastrophe theory model of the conflict helix, with tests." *Behavioral Science* 32 (October 1987): 241–66.

———. "On Vincent's view of freedom and international conflict." *International Studies Quarterly* 31 (1987b): 113–17.

———. "Triadic struggle and accommodation in perspective." In *The Strategic Triangle: China, the United States and the Soviet Union*, edited by Ilpyong J. Kim. New York: Paragon House, 1987c, 253–78.

————. *Lethal Politics: Soviet Genocide and Mass Murder*. New Brunswick, N.J.: Transaction Publishers, 1990.

————. *China's Bloody Century: Genocide and Mass Murder since 1900*. New Brunswick, N.J.: Transaction Publishers, 1991.

————. *The Conflict Helix: Principles and Practices of Interpersonal, Social, and International Conflict and Cooperation*. New Brunswick, N.J.: Transaction Publishers, 1991b.

————. "Political Perception, Latent Functions, and Social Fields: A Quantum Theory Approach to Politics." In *Quantum Politics: Applying Quantum theory to Political Phenomena,* edited by Theodore L. Becker. New York: Praeger, 1991c, 101–25.

————. *Democide: Nazi Genocide and Mass Murder*. New Brunswick, N.J.: Transaction Publishers, 1992.

————. *Death by Government: Genocide and Mass Murder Since 1900*. New Brunswick, N.J.: Transaction Publishers, 1994.

————. *Statistics of Democide: Estimates, Sources, and Calculations on 20th Century Genocide and Mass Murder*. Charlottesville: Center for National Security Law, University of Virginia, 1996.

Runciman, W. G. Relative Deprivation and Social Justice. Berkeley: University of California Press, 1966.

Russell, Bertrand. *Power*. London: George Allen & Unwin, 1938.

Russett, Bruce M. *International Regions and the International System*. Chicago: Rand McNally, 1967.

————. *Controlling the Sword: The Democratic Governance of National Security*. Cambridge: Harvard University Press, 1990.

————. "Toward a more democratic and therefore more peaceful world." In Burns Weston, ed. *Alternative Security: Living without Nuclear Deterrence*. Boulder: Westview, 1990b.

————. *Grasping the Democratic Peace: Principles for a Post-Cold War World*. Princeton, N.J.: Princeton University Press, 1993.

————. "The democratic peace: 'And yet it moves.'" *International Security* 19 (Spring 1995): 164–77.

Russett, Bruce M. and William Antholis. "Democracies rarely fight each other? Evidence from the Peloponnesian War." New Haven, Conn.: Yale University, International Security Programs, 1991.

————. "Do Democracies Fight Each Other? Evidence from the Peloponnesian War." *Journal of Peace Research* 29, 4 (1992): 415–34.

Russett, Bruce M. and William Antholis with Carol R. Ember, and Melvin Ember. "The Democratic Peace in Nonindustrial Societies." In *Grasping the Democratic Peace: Principles for a Post-Cold War World,* by Bruce Russett. Princeton, N.J.: Princeton University Press, 1993, 99–118.

Russett, Bruce M. with William Antholis. "The imperfect democratic peace of ancient Greece." In *Grasping the Democratic Peace: Principles for a Post-Cold War World,* by Bruce Russett. Princeton, N.J.: Princeton University Press, 1993, 43–71.

Russett, Bruce M. and William Antholis with Zeev Maoz. "The democratic peace since World War II." In *Grasping the Democratic Peace: Principles for a Post-Cold War World,* by Bruce Russett. Princeton, N.J.: Princeton University Press, 1993, 72–98.

Sampson, Edward E. "Status congruence and cognitive consistency." *Sociometry* 26 (June 1963): 146–62.

Savada, Andrea Matles and William Shaw, eds. *South Korea, a Country Study* (4th edition). Washington, D.C.: Federal Research Division, Library of Congress, 1992.

Schattschneider, Elmer Eric. *The Semisovereign People; A Realist's View of Democracy in America.* New York, Holt, Rinehart and Winston, 1960.

Schermerhorn, Richard A. *Society and Power.* New York: Random House, 1961.

Schumpeter, Joseph A. *Capitalism, Socialism and Democracy.* Third Edition. New York: Harper Torchbooks, 1962.

Schweller, Randall. "Domestic structure and preventative war: are democracies more pacific?" *World Politics* 44 (January 1992): 235–69.

Sharp, Gene. *The Politics of Nonviolent Action.* Boston: Porter Sargent, 1973.

Sherif, Muzafer. *In Common Predicament: Social Psychology of Intergroup Conflict and Cooperation.* Boston: Houghton Mifflin, 1966.

Sherif, Muzafer and Carolyn W. Sherif. *Groups in Harmony and Tension: An Integration of Studies on Intergroup Relations.* New York: Harper, 1953.

Shub, Norman, ed. *Gestalt Therapy: Perspectives and Applications.* New York: Gardner Press, 1992.

Sigmund, Paul E. *The Overthrow of Allende and the Politics of Chile, 1964-1976.* Pittsburgh: University of Pittsburgh Press, 1977.

Simmel, Georg. *Conflict and the Web of Group-Affiliations.* Translated by Reinhard Bendix. Glencoe, Ill.: Free Press, 1955.

Simon, Herbert. *Models of Man.* New York: John Wiley, 1957.

Simowitz, Roslyn L. *The Logical Consistency and Soundness of the Balance of Power Theory.* Denver, Colo.: Graduate School of International Studies, University of Denver, 1982.

Sin Sam-Soon. "The repressions of Kim Il-sung." *Korea and World Affairs* [Seoul, Korea] (Summer 1991): 279–301.

Singer, J. David. "Accounting for international war: the state of the discipline." *Journal of Peace Research* XVIII, 1 (1981): 1–18.

———. "Reconstructing the Correlates of War data set on material capabilities of states, 1816-1985." *International Interactions* 14 (1988): 115–32.

———. "Peace in the global system: displacement, interregnum, or transformation?" In Charles W. Kegley, Jr., ed. *The Long Postwar Peace.* New York: HarperCollins, 1991.

Singer, J. David and Melvin Small. *The Wages of War 1816-1965: A Statistical Handbook.* New York: John Wiley & Sons, 1972.

Singer, Max and Aaron Wildavsky. *The Real World Order: Zones of Peace/Zones of Turmoil.* Chatham, N.J.: Chatham House Publishers, 1993.

Siverson, Randolph M., and Juliann Emmons. "Birds of a feather: democratic political systems and alliances choices in the twentieth century." *Journal of Conflict Resolution* 35 (1991): 285–306.

Small, Melvin. and J. David Singer. "The War Proneness of Democratic Regimes, 1816-1965." *The Jerusalem Journal of International Relations* 1 (Summer 1976): 50–69.

———. *Resort to Arms: International and Civil Wars 1816-1980.* Beverly Hills, Calif.: Sage Publications, 1982.

Smirnov, Alexander D. and Emil B. Ershov. "A catastrophe change of economic reform policy." *Journal of Conflict Resolution* 36 (September 1992): 415–53.

Smith, Arthur K., Jr. "Socio-economic development and political democracy: a causal analysis." *Midwest Journal of Political Science* 13 (February 1969): 95–125.

Snyder, Glenn H. "'Prisoner's dilemma' and 'chicken' models in international politics." *International Studies Quarterly* 15 (March 1971): 66–103.

Sohn, Hak-Kyu. *Authoritarianism and Opposition in South Korea*. New York: Routledge, 1989.

Solzhenitsyn, Aleksandr I. *The Gulag Archipelago 1918-1956: An Experiment in Literary Investigation I-II*. Translated by Thomas P. Whitney. New York: Harper & Row, 1973.

Sorokin, Pitirim A. *Social and Cultural Dynamics* Volumes 1-4. New York: American Book Co., 1937-1941.

———. *Social and Cultural Dynamics* (revised and abridged edition). Boston: Porter Sargent, 1957.

———. *Society, Culture and Personality*. New York: Cooper Square, 1969.

Sperlich, Peter W. *Conflict and Harmony in Human Affairs: A Study of Cross-Pressures and Political Behavior*. Chicago: Rand McNally, 1971.

Spiro, David E. "The insignificance of the liberal peace." *International Security* 19 (Fall 1994): 50–86.

———. "And yet it squirms." *International Security* 19 (Spring 1995): 177–80.

Stankiewicz, W. J. *Approaches to Democracy: Philosophy of Government at the Close of the Twentieth Century*. New York: St. Martin's Press, 1981.

Starr, Harvey. "Democratic Dominoes: diffusion approaches to the spread of democracy." *Journal of Conflict Resolution* 35, 2 (1991): 356–81.

———. "Democracy and war: choice, learning, and security communities." *Journal of Peace Research* 29 (1992b): 207–13.

———. "Why don't democracies fight each other? Evaluating the theory-findings feedback loop." *Jerusalem Journal of International Relations* 14, 4 (1992c): 41–59.

Stivers, Eugene and Susan Wheelan, eds. *The Lewin Legacy: Field Theory in Current Practice*. New York: Springer-Verlag, 1986.

Stroebe, Wolfgang et al. *The Social Psychology of Intergroup Conflict: Theory, Research, and Applications*. New York: Springer-Verlag, 1988.

Stuart-Fox, Martin with Bunheang Ung. *The Murderous Revolution: Life and Death in Pol Pot's Kampuchea*. Chippendale, N.S.W. Australia: Alternative Publishing Cooperative Ltd., 1985.

Sydenham, M. J. *The French Revolution*. New York: Putnam, 1965.

Svalastoga, Kaare. *Prestige, Class, and Mobility*. Copenhagen: Gyldendal, 1959.

Taylor, Jay. *The Rise and Fall of Totalitarianism in the Twentieth Century*. New York: Paragon, 1993.

Thompson, William R. *On Global War: Structural-Historical Analysis in World Politics*. Columbia: University of South Carolina Press, 1988.

Tilly, Charles. "War making and state making as organized crime." In P. Evans, D. Rueschemeyer and T. Skocpol, *Bring the State Back In*. Cambridge: Cambridge University Press, 1985.

Tilly, Charles, L. Tilly, and R. Tilly. *The Rebellious Century 1830-1930*. Cambridge: Harvard University Press, 1975.

Tolman, Edward C. "A psychological model." In *Toward a General Theory of Action,* edited by Talcott Parsons and Edward A. Shils. New York: Harper Torchbooks, 1951, 279–361.

Torr, Christopher. *Equilibrium, Expectations and Information: A Study of the General Theory and Modern Classical Economics.* Cambridge: Polity Press in association with Basil Blackwell, 1988.

Turner, John Kenneth. *Barbarous Mexico.* Austin: University of Texas Press, 1969.

Ushenko, Andrew Paul. *The Philosophy of Relativity.* London: George Allen and Union, 1937.

———. *Power and Events: An Essay on Dynamics in Philosophy.* Princeton, N.J.: Princeton University Press, 1946.

———. *Dynamics of Art.* Bloomington: Indiana University Press, 1953.

———. *The Field Theory of Meaning.* Ann Arbor: University of Michigan Press, 1958.

Valenzuela, J. Samuel and Arturo Valenzuela, eds. *Military Rule in Chile: Dictatorship and Oppositions.* Baltimore, Md.: Johns Hopkins University Press, 1986.

Vickery, Michael. *Cambodia: 1975–1982.* Boston, Mass.: South End Press, 1984.

Vincent, Jack. "Freedom and international conflict: Another look." *International Studies Quarterly* 31 (1987): 103–12.

———. "On Rummel's omnipresent theory." *International Studies Quarterly* 31 (1987b): 119–26.

Von Mises, Ludwig. *Human Action* (3rd edition). Chicago: Henry Regnery, 1963.

Wain, Barry. "Cambodia: What Remains of the Killing Grounds." *The Wall Street Journal* (29 January 1981).

Waltz, K. N. *Man, the State and War: A Theoretical Analysis.* New York: Columbia University Press, 1954.

———. "Reductionist and systemic theories." In R. O. Keohane, ed. *Neorealism and Its Critics.* New York: Columbia University Press, 1986.

———. "The origins of war in neorealist theory." In R. I. Rotberg and T. K. Rabb, eds. *The Origin and Prevention of Major Wars.* Cambridge: Cambridge University Press, 1989.

Wang, Kevin, Noh Soon Chang, and James Lee Ray. "Democracy and the use of force in militarized disputes: a subdyadic level analysis." Paper prepared for the annual meeting of the American Political Science Association. 3–6 September 1992, Chicago, Illinois.

Wartenberg, Thomas E., ed. *Rethinking Power.* Albany: State University of New York Press, 1992.

Weart, Spencer. "Peace among democratic and oligarchic republics." *Journal of Peace Research* (preprint 1994).

———. *Never at War: Why Democracies Will Not Fight One Another* (draft manuscript) 1995.

Weede, Erich. "The impact of democracy on economic growth: Some evidence from cross-national analysis." *KVKLOS* 36 (1983): 21–39.

———. "Democracy and War Involvement." *Journal of Conflict Resolution* 28 (1984): 649–64.

———. "Political democracy, state strength and economic growth in LDCs: A cross-national analysis." *Review of International Studies* 10 (1984a): 297–312.

————. "Some new evidence on correlates of political violence: Income inequality, regime repressiveness, and economic development." *European Sociological Review* 3 (September 1987): 97–108.

————. "Some simple calculations on democracy and war involvement." *Journal of Peace Research* 29, 4 (1992): 377–83.

Wheelan, Susan A., Emmy Pepitone, and Vicki Abt, eds. *Advances in Field Theory.* Newbury Park, Calif.: Sage Publications, 1990.

Wildavsky, Aaron. "No War Without Dictatorship, No Peace Without Democracy: Foreign Policy as Domestic Politics." *Social Philosophy & Policy* 3, 1 (Autumn 1985): 176–91.

Wilkenfeld, Jonathan. "Some further findings regarding the domestic and foreign conflict behavior of nations." *Journal of Peace Research* 2 (1969): 147–56.

Wilkenfeld, Jonathan, Michael Brecher, and Sheila Moser. *Crises in the Twentieth Century Volume II: Handbook of International Crises.* New York: Pergamon, 1988.

Worchel, Stephen and Jeffry A. Simpson, eds. *Conflict Between People and Groups: Causes, Processes, and Resolutions.* Chicago: Nelson-Hall, 1993.

Wright, Quincy. *A Study of War Vol. I-II.* Chicago: The University of Chicago Press, 1942.

————. *The Study of International Relations.* New York: Appleton-Century-Crofts, 1955.

————. *A Study of War.* Second Edition, with a Commentary on War since 1945. Chicago: The University of Chicago Press, 1965.

————. "The escalation of international conflict." *The Journal of Conflict Resolution* 9 (December 1965b): 434–49.

"Why they don't fight: democracies, oligarchies, and peace." *In Brief* (No. 48). Washington, D.C.: United States Institute of Peace, November 1993.

Yathay, Pin. *Stay Alive, My Son.* New York: The Free Press, 1987.

Yinger, Milton. *Toward a Field Theory of Behavior.* New York: McGraw-Hill, 1965.

Yoon, Dae Kyu. *Law and Political Authority in South Korea.* Boulder: Westview Press, 1990.

Yough, Syng Nam. "Modernization, institutionalization, and political violence." *The Journal of East Asian Affairs* 1 (January 1981): 1–48.

Zinnes, Dina A. and J. Wilkenfeld. "An analysis of foreign conflict behavior of nations." In *Comparative Foreign Policy: Theoretical Essays,* edited by W. F. Hanrieder. New York: David McKay, 1971, 167–213.

Name Index

Subject Index